Alan Hardis

6. VIII. 2005

THE RECORD SOCIETY OF LANCASHIRE AND CHESHIRE

FOUNDED TO TRANSCRIBE AND PUBLISH
ORIGINAL DOCUMENTS RELATING TO THE TWO COUNTIES

VOLUME CXLI

The Society wishes to acknowledge with gratitude the support given towards publication by

Lancashire County Council

© The Record Society of Lancashire and Cheshire
E.M.E. Ramsay
A.J. Maddock

ISBN 0 902593 68 4

Printed in Great Britain by Arrowsmith, Bristol

THE CHURCHWARDENS' ACCOUNTS OF WALTON-ON-THE-HILL, LANCASHIRE 1627–1667

Transcribed and edited by
Esther M.E. Ramsay
and
Alison J. Maddock

PRINTED FOR THE SOCIETY
2005

CONTENTS

ACKNOWLEDGEMENTS

During the transcription process we initially received help from the Merseyside Record Office and subsequently access and assistance were made available by the Liverpool Record Office, where the book of accounts is now kept. We are very grateful to past and present staff of both institutions for their help.

The work was begun as a result of our studies in the Diploma in Local History at the Department of Continuing Education, Liverpool University, and would never have been completed without the support and encouragement of Paul Booth, Senior Lecturer in History, who is warmly thanked.

Specialist advice was generously provided by R.J. Griffiths, the Curator of Horology at Prescot Museum, and the Vernacular Architecture Group.

Thanks are also due to the Rev. Trevor Latham, Rector of Walton, who read the relevant parts of the Introduction and updated us on aspects of the Church at the present day.

Alison Maddock
Betty Ramsay

ABBREVIATIONS USED IN THE INTRODUCTION

BIHR	Borthwick Institute of Historical Research (York).
CRO	Cheshire Record Office.
LaRO	Lancashire Record Office.
LRO	Liverpool Record Office.
RSLC	Record Society of Lancashire and Cheshire.
THSLC	Transactions of the Historic Society of Lancashire and Cheshire.
LPRS	Lancashire Parish Register Society
VCH Ches	B.E. Harris, ed., *The Victoria History of the County of Chester*, iii (London, 1980).
VCH Lancs	W. Farrer & J. Brownbill, eds, *The Victoria History of the County of Lancaster*, ii (London, 1908), and iii (London, 1907).

In the interests of brevity, accounting years are referred to in the Introduction by the start year only, e.g. '1633' refers to an entry in the 1633–34 account.

INTRODUCTION

1. The parish background

The purpose of this volume is to make accessible a further example of the relatively small stock of churchwardens' accounts that survive from before the late seventeenth century in north-west England. Walton's extant parish registers start in 1586, after which these accounts are the earliest parish records known, though unfortunately they lack the years 1642 to 1648, as is often the case with such accounts during the Civil War period.

At the date of these accounts, the extensive parish of Walton-on-the-Hill still numbered Liverpool among its subsidiary townships, a source of irritation and frustration to the inhabitants of that burgeoning town whose centre was some four miles away. Also owing allegiance to the mother church of St Mary (situated in what is now called County Road) were the townships of Walton-cum-Fazakerley, West Derby, Everton, Bootle-cum-Linacre, Kirkdale, Kirkby and Formby (detached). Tudor legislation notwithstanding, and in contrast to Manchester with its eight churchwardens, this large area was served by only a single churchwarden, acting with one sidesman. Liverpool, West Derby, Kirkby and Formby, however, had chapels of ease with their own chapelwardens. Simonswood and Toxteth Park were extra-parochial.

The Commonwealth church survey of the county valued the church with its parsonage and lands at £4 2s 4d *per annum* and the vicarage and grounds at 30s; details for the chapelries and figures for the tithe revenue from the townships may also be found in this source.[1]

Located in the south-west Lancashire stronghold of Roman Catholicism, many of Walton's parishioners were Catholics; the *Notitia* records 20 of 102 families as such in the early eighteenth century.[2] Prominent among these were Fazakerley, Chorley and Breres (Briars), together with leading members of the Molyneux family. Despite their faith, covertly or overtly practised, members of these families often appear to be playing a prominent role in the parish. At the other end of the religious spectrum of the day, the influential Moore family of Bank Hall and Old Hall were leading puritans, contributing a military governor to the town of Liverpool during the Civil War, and the chapel at Toxteth Park was always associated with dissenting worship.

In common with most other churchwardens' accounts, those of Walton can be tapped for a range of information from changes in ecclesiastical practice and aspects of social history, including reflection of national events at local level, to specifics

1 H. Fishwick, ed., *Lancashire and Cheshire Church Surveys 1649–1655: Part I, Lancashire*, RSLC, i (1879), p. 81.
2 F.R. Raines, ed., *Notitia Cestriensis: or Historical Notes of the Diocese of Chester*, Chetham Society, Old Series, 21 (Manchester, 1850), p. 221.

such as the operation of the poor law, building crafts, wages and prices, family history and dialect. Perhaps of particular interest here is the contribution they make to the history of Liverpool, including its struggle for independent parish status (not finally achieved until 1699), which manifested itself in litigation and recrimination over payment of leys. The unusual dual incumbency of rector and vicar is also of note, and there is information about lost architectural features of the building itself, as well as further light on the notoriously variable parish government practices of north-west England. Though mute during the bulk of the crucial Civil War period, the accounts do have something to contribute to our knowledge of mid-century events at local and national level, and usefully add to the sources for studying how far and fast local practice followed the religious turmoil of the day.

Publication of this transcript will not only make available this information, but will enable the Walton-on-the-Hill churchwardens' accounts to be used alongside the contemporary ones of nearby Prescot (already published by the Record Society) and Childwall, of which an unpublished transcript for the years 1571–1674 is available at the Liverpool Record Office.[3]

2. Incumbents

The Church of St Mary was granted in 1093 to Shrewsbury Abbey and the vicarage established in 1326.[4] The Molyneux family of Sefton held the advowson from the time of its purchase by Thomas Molyneux in 1470 until 1747.[5] The family remained Roman Catholic throughout, and from time to time sold the right of presentation. The rectory was never appropriated, so that right down to 1890 (when the vicarage was suppressed) Walton was served by both a rector and a vicar in holy orders, with curates under them at the chapelries. Little indication of how the duties at the mother church were shared in this unusual situation comes through in the accounts, unfortunately. We see entries for buying and washing surplices and hoods for both men (e.g. f.148r), and both rector and vicar often add their signatures at the audit. There is an impression that much of the work fell to the vicar, and at least one of the rectors was a pluralist with duties elsewhere (see Table 1). Among early rectors were some of the Molyneux family itself, including Alexander Molyneux, apparently presented as a child in 1565 and still serving when these accounts begin.

Normal practice seems to have been followed (except during the interregnum) whereby the patron nominated the rector and the rector nominated the vicar. Records of incumbencies are incomplete, however, and Tables 1 and 2 indicate discrepancies between compilations such as that in VCH and 'on the ground' evidence from the accounts themselves.

3 Thomas Steel, ed., *Prescot Churchwardens' Accounts, 1635–1663*, RSLC, cxxxvii (2002); Eveline B. Saxton, trans., *Childwall Parish Church: Churchwardens' Accounts, vol.I pt.2, 1625–1674*, unpublished typescript at LRO, ref. H.283.1 ALL.
4 *VCH Lancs*, iii, p. 6.
5 *VCH Lancs*, iii, p. 6; LaRO, DDM 51/58.

Poor survival of relevant diocesan records means that little can be gleaned from such sources about Walton and its incumbents during the early years of these accounts, before the abolition of the bishopric, beyond a mention of Nevill Kay being implicated in solemnising an irregular marriage.[6] From 1661 the consistory court papers (EDC 5) at Cheshire Record Office have much useful background.

During the interregnum, appointments, sequestrations and measures to support preaching ministers were handled by parliamentary committees, whose records provide much of the detail for changes in personnel at Walton. It was a time when non-resident clergymen and those loyal to the king or otherwise regarded as leaning too far to the 'popish' lost their livings. Walton's vicar was one of those who succeeded in keeping on the right side of prevailing opinion and retained his living until his death in 1654. This fact is in accordance with Morrill's finding that as many as two-thirds of ministers held on to their parishes in the 1640s despite the upheaval.[7] The incumbents of the rectory had a much more turbulent time, as summarised in Table 1.

The Committee for Plundered Ministers was one of the parliamentary committees that had evolved through a number of incarnations and dealt with a miscellany of responsibilities, most of which impinged on Walton parish. These included the ejection of clergy not of the puritan persuasion and their replacement by ministers who had suffered from royalist depredations. By administering the livings sequestered from royalist sympathisers, and fuelled by income from tithes and the estates of the now-abolished bishops, the Committee paid the ministers' stipends, funded repairs and in due course carried out parish-by-parish valuations of parsonages and made recommendations concerning parish boundaries and the elevation of chapelries to parish status.[8] In 1645 the Committee heard that the royalist rector of Walton, Andrew Clare, 'hath wholy deserted his cure and betaken himself to the forces raised against Parliament', while the authorities in Liverpool subsequently complained to them about Dr Clare 'shewing the violence he used against this Towne and how hee preached heere'.[9] William Ward was the Committee's choice to replace him, but in a humanitarian move it ordered the sequestrators of the tithes and profits of the rectory to pay an allowance to Dr Clare's wife, who apparently remained in England after her husband had fled abroad. This was one of a series of financial provisions that caused friction among the chapelries. The tithes, rents and other dues of the sequestered rectory were to be allocated in stipulated proportions: those arising from Liverpool, Toxteth Park, Kirkby and Formby to pass in full to the ministers appointed to those cures, and a third of those from West Derby to go to the incumbent there, the remaining income and tithes to be for Ward's use but with an obligation on him to pay a further £10

6   CRO, EDC 5/1627/35.
7   John Morrill, 'The Church in England 1642–1649', in John Morrill, ed., *Reactions to the English Civil War 1642–1649* (London, 1982), p. 100.
8   H. Fishwick, ed., *Lancashire and Cheshire Church Surveys*, op.cit., pp. 81–5.
9   W.A. Shaw, ed., *Minutes of the Committee for the Relief of Plundered Ministers, and of the Trustees for the Maintenance of Ministers: Relating to Lancashire and Cheshire 1643–1660*, RSLC, xxviii (Part 1, 1643–1654) (1893), pp. 1–2; George Chandler, *Liverpool under Charles I* (Liverpool, 1965), p. 376.

Table 1: Rectors of Walton during the period of these accounts

Dates of office	Name	Details
Presented 15 October 1565; died in office 1631	Alexander Molyneux	Younger son of Sir Richard Molyneux, who presented him. Criticised as unlearned in 1591. Vicar's memo in Walton burial register 1 February 1631 records his bequest of £40 to the parish poor, £20 towards running the school, and his theology books for the use of the current vicar and subsequent rectors. Signs the accounts 1629.[10]
Instituted 1 February 1631;[11] died in office 1639	Thomas Legh DD	A member of the Legh of Lyme family. Concurrently rector of Sefton from 1633. Buried at Walton 29 May 1639. Signs the accounts 1633–38.
Instituted 29 June/ 1 July 1639; stated in March 1645 to have joined the Royalist forces[12]	Andrew Clare DD	Presented by the patron, Viscount Molyneux (a minor, necessitating a second institution). Had been rector of Ickenham. Staunch royalist, went abroad and rectory sequestered by Parliament. Chaplain to Charles I.[13] No examples of his signature in the accounts.
Replaced Dr Clare about March 1645; died in office 1655	William Ward MA	Previously rector of Warrington. Recommended to the sequestered rectory of Walton 18 March 1645 by the Plundered Ministers Committee, who found him a 'godly and orthodox divine'.[14] Signed the Harmonious Consent 1648. Buried at Walton 1 March 1655. Signs the accounts as pastor 1653 and 1654.
?[15]	John Heywood DD	Not officially recorded until 1660, but signs as pastor at the election in April 1655.
Nominated 13 October 1655 though apparently not immediately admitted; replaced 1660	Robert Eaton	Nominated to the sequestered rectory by the Plundered Ministers Committee;[16] tried but failed to have his office confirmed at the Restoration. Died in 1701. Signs the accounts 1657–60. In list of Liverpool freemen 19 October 1655.[17]
Instituted 1660 (5 September at York, 20 December at Chester);[18] died in office 1671	John Heywood DD	Grant by the Crown confirming him in office treated Ward and Eaton as intruders and held the vacancy to be caused by Dr Clare's death. Presented by the patron, the Countess of Southampton, widow of Richard Lord Molyneux. Signs the accounts 1661–66. In list of Liverpool freemen 22 August 1662.[19]

Main sources: *The Victoria History of the County of Lancaster*, iii, pp. 7–9 (based on diocesan records etc); *The Registers of the Parish Church of Walton-on-the-Hill*, LPRS, 5 (1586–1663) and 91 (1663–1746); and the accounts themselves. Other references as shown in the footnotes (see p. xi).

Table 2: Vicars of Walton during the period of these accounts

Dates of office	Name	Details[20]
Instituted 9 May 1624 (VCH), though note in parish register gives induction 24 May 1621; died in office 1654	Nevill Kay BA	Apparently a puritan sympathiser; selected by the Common Council of Liverpool as preacher 1629; signed the Harmonious Consent of the Ministers of Lancashire in 1648 and deemed 'godly and able' by Parliament but accused by Bishop Gastrell's editor of putting survival in office before principle.[21] Buried at Walton 15 June 1654. Signs the accounts 1629, 1632, 1633, 1636–40, 1650–53.
Succeeded Kay 30 July 1654; expelled for nonconformity 1662	Henry Finch	Born at Standish 1633.[22] Efforts to have him officially admitted to the living did not bear fruit until 25 November 1657.[23] Signs the accounts 1655–59, 1661–62 (as 'pastor' in 1656). In list of Liverpool freemen (as 'William Fynch, vicar of Walton') 19 December 1654.[24]
Instituted 29 January 1663	John Walton MA	Signs the accounts 1663–64.[25]
Instituted 7 Sept. 1665; served until his death in 1720	Thomas Marsden BD	Signs the accounts 1666–67. Lived to be 84 according to graveyard inscription.[26]

Main sources: *The Victoria History of the County of Lancaster*, iii, pp. 7–9 (based on diocesan records etc); *The Registers of the Parish Church of Walton-on-the-Hill*, LPRS, 5 (1586–1663) and 91 (1663–1746); and the accounts themselves. Other references as shown in the footnotes.

10 Note that apparent absence of his signature in some years may be due to the audit being missing.
11 Inductions of Legh and Clare by the vicar Nevill Kay are recorded in the parish register shortly after institution.
12 W.A. Shaw, ed., *Plundered Ministers Accounts Part I*, op.cit., p. 1.
13 *Notitia Cestriensis*, op.cit., p. 223.
14 W.A. Shaw, ed., *Plundered Ministers Accounts Part I*, op.cit., pp. 2 and 143.
15 Not in the VCH tabulation.
16 W.A. Shaw, ed., *Plundered Ministers Accounts*, RSLC, xxxiv (Part II, 1655–1660) (1897), pp. 93 and 103–4.
17 Michael Power, ed., *Liverpool Town Books 1649–1671*, RSLC, cxxxvi (1999), p. 84 (minutes p. 625).
18 CRO, EDC 5/1662/82.
19 Michael Power, ed., *Liverpool Town Books*, op.cit., p. 143 (minutes p. 730).
20 Presented by the rector in all instances.
21 George Chandler, *Liverpool under Charles I*, op.cit., p. 158; H. Fishwick, ed., *Lancashire and Cheshire Church Surveys*, op.cit., p. 81; *Notitia Cestriensis*, op.cit., p. 223.
22 From memo in parish register also containing family details at the time of his succession to Walton, signed by churchwarden William Ryding.
23 W.A. Shaw, ed., *Plundered Ministers Accounts Part II*, op.cit., p. 208.
24 Michael Power, ed., *Liverpool Town Books*, op.cit., p. 72 (minutes p. 608).
25 *VCH Lancs* has a John Walton incumbent respectively at Farnworth 1647, Formby 1650 and Altcar 1657 but does not connect these as one individual.
26 David Ensign Gardner, *Liverpool and District Epitaphs I* (1936), unpublished typescript at LRO, ref. Hq 929.5 GAR, pp. 107 and 109.

per year to Liverpool and Toxteth Park. The arrangements for this £10 were a source of dispute and added to the strains as Liverpool and Kirkby aspired to parish status (pp. xxxiv–v). In 1658 the value of the tithes of Walton township was given as £65 12s 4d whereas those of Liverpool chapelry were worth £75, the rest of the profits of the rectory (including the other chapelries) being valued at £312.[27]

Beyond the occasional oblique reference, changes of rector or vicar, through death or otherwise, almost never give rise to any specific entries in the accounts other than a change of signature at audit. Even the end of the immensely long rectorial incumbency of Alexander Molyneux is not marked at the time. The exception occurs in the case of Henry Finch in 1654. Evidently the churchwarden (William Ryding) supported his succession to the vicarage after Neville Kay's death. We see him 'laboringe to get Master finch establised our vicaer' (f.100r), and from this date Finch appears in the records as vicar, despite the fact that he was not admitted until 1657. In 1656 he signs in the presbyterian form 'pastor', use of which term seems to be somewhat confused at Walton, since it is used by the putative rector John Heywood in April 1655 when Finch is shown as vicar. The hold of these two individuals on their office at this time seems to have been of dubious legality. As Table 1 shows, Heywood does not otherwise appear in official records until 1660, so his appearance in 1655 is a mystery, while Finch – who presumably held doctrinally opposing views – was eventually declared in these words never to have been ordained at all: 'you ... are no Clarke nor are you Capable to undergoe or have Care of Soules ... yet you have lately taken upon you to Officiate at the Church of Walton as vicar there.'[28]

After the Restoration, bitter words were exchanged between Finch, Heywood and their supporters. It was a time of religious disharmony in the parish, manifesting itself particularly in tithe disputes, as the chickens of Commonwealth arrangements came home to roost and set incumbents of the puritan era in conflict with incoming traditionalists. At hearings held at Chester in 1662, previous churchwarden John Bennett and his successor in the post spent three days testifying (f.146r). Bennett averred that he was not sure that Henry Finch had ever administered the sacrament, that he never read or used the *Book of Common Prayer* obtained for him, and that he carried out baptism not according to the prayer book.[29] The new rector John Heywood was at odds with Finch over tithes of corn, hay etc, as he was with Thomas Crompton (incumbent of Toxteth Park chapel), Peter Aspinwall (Formby) and John Fogg (Liverpool), among others. Commonwealth-appointed rector Robert Eaton had granted them tithes and they were misappropriating some of them to their own barns instead of to Heywood's use; indeed Eaton, it was now asserted, did not have legal right to the tithes so could not grant them.[30] No doubt this is what is behind the mention of 'demanding possession of the Barnes' (f.132v) and the accounting for legal costs of tithe orders

27 W.A. Shaw, ed., *Plundered Ministers Accounts Part I*, op.cit., p. 14; *Part II*, op.cit., pp. 215–16.
28 CRO, EDC 5/1661/14, EDC 5/1661/56.
29 CRO, EDC 5/1662/4.
30 CRO, EDC 5/1663/57, EDC 5/1663/72 and others.

to Fogg and Crompton (f.133r). Insults were exchanged and old slanders dredged up. Against Heywood, Walton schoolmaster Peter Hurdis described how he had become drunk after six hours at an alehouse and fallen off his horse (1662). Finch alleged that Heywood's sermons were plagiarised from a book; (his preaching credentials were also called into question in 1665 when he was called a dumb dog by an opponent, who said Heywood 'could preach no more than a tub' and was 'more fitter to drive the plough than preach'.) In order to assert his right to the tithes, Heywood had to present proof of his lawful induction, while Finch was unable to do so, and was expelled for unconformity in the purge of 1662, the unlicensed schoolmaster Hurdis also losing his job.[31]

3. Churchwardens in office

The single churchwarden or 'guardian' and his sidesman were elected annually by the incumbent and leading parishioners according to custom at the 'Easter' meeting (traditionally held the week after, but sometimes later here), and held office for a year. There appears to have been little attempt to draw the churchwarden from each township in turn, and those with their own chapelwardens seem to have been under-represented except for West Derby. Table 3 shows the names of the churchwardens and their years of office as far as they can be derived from the accounts; uncertainty exists in some years where the election is not recorded, when a substitution had to be made part way through the year or when pages of the accounts are disordered, and this is indicated by notes within the transcript.

The electors are never referred to here by the term vestry, nor can we necessarily infer the number present from the list of signatures surviving in the accounts. There does seem to be a trend to larger meetings after the Civil War, however, perhaps indicating increased interest in the running of the parish during the church's presbyterian phase, or maybe due to various disputes that surfaced in the 1650s. The 1649 account records 'more in Number then formerly use to bee' at the Easter meeting (f.76v), and in 1656 the churchwarden had to lay out 4s on the election, 'beinge a great Company there' (f.107r), with 21 people signing or marking in addition to the vicar, instead of the half dozen or so earlier in the accounts. A peak of 30 was reached in 1660 (f.137).

The office of churchwarden is known to have continued unbroken through the interregnum – it played too important a role in parish government to be abolished. Directives from Parliament and Quarter Sessions addressed to churchwardens issued during the period of Walton's missing years, particularly concerning maintenance of the fabric of churches, confirm this.[32] There are also some slight indications in the surviving Walton accounts. In 1649 John Whitfield is concerned about money 'in the old Churchwardens handes' (f.74v), referring to his predecessor John Ellison, recently dead and subject of a ley stall payment. Ellison may have been the 1648 office-holder; alternatively he should have served in 1649 but died, Whitfield being co-opted to take over. The latter had also been

31 CRO, EDC 5/1661/14, EDC 5/1662/16, EDC 5/1662/82, EDC 5/1665/42.
32 E.g. LaRO, QSP/11/32.

Table 3: Churchwardens and sidesmen during the period of these accounts

Year	Churchwarden	Sidesman
1627–28	Nicholas Goore	
1628–29	William Wainwright	
1629–30	Humphrey Walley	William Johnson (*see note 1*)
1630–31	Thomas Hey	John Robinson (*see note 2*)
1631–32	Lawrence Bridge	
1632–33	Robert Boulton of Clubmoor	Roger Richardson
1633–34	Richard Johnson of Everton	William Aspinwall
1634–35	Nicholas Cooper of Kirkdale	
1635–36	James Rycroft of West Derby	William Boulton of Walton
1636–37	Thomas Mercer of Walton	
1637–38	John Mercer of West Derby	
1638–39	Richard Greaves of Everton	
1639–40	Nicholas Goore	
1640–41	Thomas Ryding of West Derby	
1641–42	John Whitfield of Fazakerley	
1642–48	Name or names unknown; may include John Ellison (*see discussion*)	
1649–50	John Whitfield of Fazakerley	
1650–51	John Whitfield of Fazakerley	
1651–52	Edward Henshaw of West Derby	John Bankes (John Wigan of Kirkdale struck through)
1652–53	Thomas Martin of Fazakerley	Richard Boulton of Walton cum Fazakerley
1653–54	Thomas Boulton	Thomas Henshaw
1654–55	William Ryding	John Swift
1655–56	Henry Halsall of Bootle	Thomas Knowles of Walton
1656–57	John Boulton of Newsham	Robert Pemberton of Walton
1657–58	James Standish of West Derby	Thomas Hughson
1658–59	James Standish of West Derby (*see note 3*)	Lawrence Turner of Fazakerley
1659–60	Thomas Boulton of Kirkdale	John Hey of Everton
1660–61	Thomas Knowles of Walton	Nicholas Mercer of Walton
1661–62	John Bennett of Tuebrook	Matthew Gleave of Low Hill
1662–63	William Syre of Kirkdale	Lawrence Wetherby
1663–64	Richard Fazakerley of Fazakerley	John Eaton of Fazakerley
1664–65	Richard Henshaw of Green Lane	Thomas Whitfield of West Derby
1665–66	William Halsall (of Bootle?)	Thomas Hollis of Bootle
1666–67	Robert Hitchin of Toxteth Park, replaced mid-term by Nicholas Mercer (*see note 4*)	John Bridge of Walton
1667–68	Nicholas Mercer of Walton	Edward Turner of Fazakerley

Notes for Table 3:
Names are derived from elections and headings to annual accounts unless stated.
1. Referred to as 'sworne man'.
2. Name derived from mention on f.9v.
3. Thomas Boulton of Kirkdale was elected but Standish prepared the accounts, apparently serving a second consecutive year, Boulton deferring his year of office for some reason.
4. Hitchin had been excommunicated in 1664 so his election was a surprising mistake, necessitating an order from the consistory court the following November, replacing him by Mercer.

churchwarden for the last extant account, 1641, but the circumstances do not suggest that he had been in office continuously, though an additional term during the missing years is indicated by his being owed 3s 6d on a previous account, a sum not matching his deficit at the end of 1641 (10s 2d). Most probably he served in 1648 and also stepped in for the rest of 1649 after Ellison's death.

Although men of some standing in the community, the churchwardens did not necessarily have any particular ability in accounting, or even writing. Judging by handwriting, which sometimes remains the same over more than one year, the accounts were often written by another person acting as scribe (see pp. xix–xx for discussion on the office of clerk). Payment for writing up the accounts is always claimed, but this could equally be to pay a scribe or to reimburse the churchwarden himself. His Anglican credentials might also be less than perfect: even members of Roman Catholic families were sometimes required to serve, and the opposite extreme is exemplified by the case of Robert Hitchin. Two years before his election he was found guilty of keeping a conventicle at the house of Thomas Crompton (Toxteth Park), and of failing to attend church and receive the sacrament, resulting in his excommunication.[33]

4. Finances, duties and colleagues

In keeping with universal practice, each churchwarden's account details his income (receipts) and expenditure (disbursements) and strikes a balance between them at the end of his year of office, his successor receiving any surplus or reimbursing the outgoing churchwarden for any overpayment claimed. The accounts were presented to the Easter meeting for audit, at which time a ley for the following year was often agreed as well as the election of the new churchwarden and sidesman. Not all the audits or records of election survive in these accounts, however.

There is no means of knowing what sources of income the churchwarden had at his disposal other than those shown in the accounts. It is always possible that some collections for a specific purpose were applied directly to that purpose and did not pass through the books. Unlike many other town parishes, Walton gives no hint of any substantial income from endowments of land or property owned by the church. Early references to the receipt of small payments due for Ackers End are ambiguous and may not come into this category.[34] The chief source of income here as elsewhere

33 CRO, EDC 5/1664/71.
34 They appear to be ley payments for a farm between Old Swan and Broad Green (*VCH Lancs*, iii, p. 11), the reason for their separate listing being uncertain.

was the church rate or ley, supplemented by charges for ley stalls or burial within the church at the rate of 2s 4d for an adult (in contrast to the fairly widespread rate of 6s 8d found in contemporary accounts from other English parishes including Prescot), and the occasional sale of surplus materials. Of other possible sources of income – such as pew rents, church stock, charges for hire of the hearse or tolling the passing bell, or collections to pay for communion wine – there is no mention.

Church leys were levied by consent of the parishioners on those above a certain income, but there is no local information to confirm the traditional figure of 12d in the pound of 'ancient rent'.[35] Leys were divided between the townships in set proportions. Not every churchwarden serving at Walton itemised his receipts by township, but when he did these proportions can be clearly seen, except in the rather confused 1631 totals. They were: 1 unit from Everton, 1½ units each from Kirkdale and Bootle, 4 units each from Formby, Kirkby and Walton-cum-Fazakerley, 8 units from Liverpool, and 12 units from West Derby.[36] Based on a unit of 6s 8d one ley brought in £12. This could itself be levied more than once per year and in varying proportions, from one half (£6) upwards. Leys totalling £18 or £24 over the year were common in the 1630s, except for 1633 and 1634: years dominated by fulfilling directives from above for repairs and improvements, when the leys totalled respectively £36 and £54 (ignoring underpayments). In the 1650s £12 was commonly the figure, even in 1659, when a massive £240 was deemed to be necessary to remedy years of decay and a ley of £120 was agreed but somehow never collected. However, there was plenty of variation in this decade too, e.g. £30 in 1651 (2½ times the basic ley) and £6 in 1654, and variations upwards from £12 occur in the 1660s. The annual budget that the churchwarden found himself handling was thus of extremely variable magnitude: broadly speaking more than at Childwall but markedly less than at Prescot.

In some years the ratepaying inhabitants took a considerable 'hit' from an extra-large demand, and what to our own budget-minded society seem almost capricious year-to-year variations must surely have caused hardship, yet the townships usually paid up in full or nearly so. West Derby seems always to have been a conscientious payer and was assessed as the wealthiest township at that period, while Liverpool became increasingly reluctant to pay (see pp. xxxiv–v) and for some reason many townships were partially defaulting in 1658. Precepts or orders to pay were sent out as early as possible in the churchwarden's term of office, normally to the petty constables of each township, who were responsible for collecting the money. Liverpool paid through its bailiffs, Kirkby and Formby sometimes through their chapelwardens. Walton and Fazakerley, together forming a single township, evidently each had a constable whose payments are sometimes itemised separately. Whether the townships were paying up promptly or not, the accounts show a deficit

---

35 Ernest Broxap, ed., 'Extracts from the Manchester Churchwardens' Accounts 1664–1710' in *Chetham Miscellanies IV*, Chetham Society, New Series, 80 (Manchester, 1921), p. iii.

36 This tallies well with the division of the county rate into three equal parts as given in *VCH Lancs*, iii, p. 5: Walton-cum-Fazakerley+Kirkby+Formby; West Derby; Liverpool+Kirkdale+Bootle-cum-Linacre+Everton.

more often than a surplus at the end of the year. Errors of arithmetic are common and are indicated in footnotes to the transcript.

Forming as they do the core of the value of such accounts to historians, the churchwarden's multifarious outgoing payments are the basis for almost all sections of this introductory analysis, where details will be found in their appropriate place.[37] The burdensome list of ecclesiastical and secular duties that fell to a seventeenth-century churchwarden's lot must have been an onerous workload for one man. Not surprisingly, the Walton churchwarden relied much on his sidesman – often referred to as 'my partener' – to accompany or deputise for him on official business.

The churchwarden's post-election oath and his regular presentments, technically due to the archdeacon of Chester, were in fact normally made to the rural dean of Warrington (often at Prescot or Upholland), since at that period there was no archdeacon as such. Citations to appear at the usually twice-yearly local visitations were delivered by the apparitor, who took payment for the article books with their long lists of questions for the churchwarden concerning the state of the church building, the conduct of the minister and the moral well-being of the parish at large including the attendance record of its parishioners. Bishop Bridgeman of Chester (in office 1619–45) had an audience court at Wigan, which may be the reason for some of the recorded journeys there by the Walton churchwarden. There were major visitations by the Archbishops of York in 1633 and 1662 and Canterbury in 1629, not of course in person but in the form of Commissioners, that of Neile in 1633 being well reflected at Walton in a flurry of resultant activity (see p. xxii).[38]

The diocesan administration disintegrated after 1643 and church courts were abolished. The effect of this upheaval on the survival of diocesan sources which might shed light on the churchwardens' activities from 'the other side' is to render them disappointingly lacking. No presentments survive before 1667, though a few relevant items for the period crop up in consistory court papers, which also contain much on the tithe disputes of the 1660s (see p. xii).[39] Some visitation court books held at the Borthwick Institute include occasional references to Walton.

Under his remit for religious policing, the churchwarden lists Easter communicants in the years up to 1641. Previously, parishioners contributing to the rushbearing are also recorded (up to 1634): the activity seems to have had similar significance as a check on churchgoing. Most of the churchwarden's parochial duties continued during the suspension of diocesan authority due to the Civil War, under a parliamentary ordinance of February 1648. In the absence of church courts, presenting for disciplinary offences was made to JPs, but numerous items in the accounts make it clear that the Walton churchwarden had always had the task of making presentments of another kind – to the High Constable, for the assizes. Such

---

37 Useful summaries in: J.S. Purvis, *Dictionary of Ecclesiastical Terms* (London, 1962); W. Bennett, ed., *The Churchwardens' Accounts of the Parish of Burnley* (Burnley Historical Society, 1969); Charles Drew, ed., *Lambeth Churchwardens' Accounts 1504–1645 and Vestry Book 1610*, Surrey Record Society, 18, vol.1 (1941).

38 *VCH Ches*, iii, pp. 33–4.

39 CRO, EDC 5.

reports feature in most years up to 1639 and again from 1657, and also occur at Childwall and Prescot. If they concerned recusants rather than perpetrators of other 'crimes', there is some confusion, because in 1640 the churchwarden presents recusants to the justices while also separately itemising unspecified presentments to the assizes. Mention of the 'inquisition' in 1635 probably equates to the listing of recusants' property by the churchwarden and constables (see also pp. xxxi–ii). In a more concerted operation of this kind in 1637 (f.49v), the townships provide appraisers to report to the JPs.[40]

A churchwarden's day-to-day ecclesiastical duties are well known and date in large part from Archbishop Grindal's instructions of 1571. The uses to which he was required to apply the parish funds in his hands are well reflected in the Walton accounts by purchases of a diversity of items such as prayer books, books of canons, communion bread and wine, provision and care of surplices, repairs to the communion chalice or flagon, remuneration of the parish clerk, payments to visiting preachers (first noted in 1638), and provision of a desk and chain for Bishop Jewel's *Apology of the Church of England*. Sometimes these activities contain a hint of developments on the wider, national stage, as discussed in section 8.

As always, the maintenance of the fabric of the church was a perennial concern: deductions that can be made from the accounts about the building and its furnishings are discussed in section 5. Whenever structural work was required or repairs were needed, the entries furnish many glimpses into the network of craftsmen and labourers in the area. The church was clearly a well-tapped source of income for cohorts of builders, roofers and masons. Some indication of relative costs and rates of pay can be extracted, and the churchwarden himself always claimed his attendance allowance of 8d per day. Contracts did not always run smoothly, a 'sute against some werke men' being contemplated in the litigious 1650s (f.102r).

Craftsmen were often recruited from further afield if they had special skills, such as Prescot clock expert Thomas Rothwell, the artist/decorator Webster from Ormskirk and carpenters from Tarbock and Knowsley. William Blackey of Childwall was among several other names called in regularly to repair the clock, as later was Jonathan Gleave, a locksmith who also worked on the church clocks of Childwall and St Nicholas, Liverpool.[41] Names encountered at Walton often crop up in the Childwall churchwardens' accounts; other examples are James Boates, a carpenter who worked on the bell wheels, and John Chantrell, a joiner who made items of furniture. The passing of craft and trade skills from one generation to the next is often apparent, as with the Corkers (glaziers as well as plumbers in the sense of attending to the leads), and the Stranges, who were blacksmiths and able to turn their hand to forging numerous pieces of customised ironwork for repairs. Corker's services were particularly in demand at both Walton and Childwall after the church windows sustained damage in the not infrequent high winds. The accounts preserve the names of many such ordinary working people from oblivion, not least

---

40 See also Prescot f.10v (1637) in Steel, ed., *Prescot Churchwardens' Accounts*, op.cit., p. 28.

41 Pers. comm. from R. J. Griffiths, Prescot Museum, who also supplied technical information on the clock construction.

'Johnson's wife and daughter' who carried rubbish out of the church on so many occasions.

Certain aspects of the relief and management of the poor were among the churchwarden's secular duties, and their exemplification in these accounts is covered in section 6. As elsewhere, payments to the bellringers for special peals appear regularly – the going rate here was 5s per session. Refreshments at election time and when meeting workmen or officials are routine expenses, and all receipts (quittances) and other paperwork incur a cost to be itemised. Much of the concern about recusants and their holding of arms, mentioned above, reflects the churchwarden's civil function, as does the listing of able-bodied men, presumably for the muster (f.55v, 1638). He was also school reeve (see p. xxvii). Litigation of various sorts often fell to his lot. That other eccentric imposition on the churchwarden's time, payment of bounties on vermin, though a recognised duty since the 1530s, does not put in an appearance until 1654. Apart from an unfortunate owl and its young captured during roof work in 1663, no bird pests feature at Walton; the only vermin payments are for fox heads at one shilling each (a widely encountered fixed rate). The mid-century date for their rise to prominence is encountered in many churchwardens' accounts: an increasing acknowledgement of whole-parish responsibility over and above that of landowners has been suggested to explain this.[42]

It was normal though not universal practice for churchwardens to pay the parish clerk, and indeed such payments do appear at Walton, but the person referred to as clerk sounds more like a sexton, the latter term not being used in these accounts. Such blurring of the roles is also apparent in other contemporary churchwardens' accounts. Christopher Shurliker seems to have the role at the start of the Walton accounts, but his payments are not described as clerk's wages, rather as payments to him for looking after the clock and bells, for which he received 13s 4d per year at first. He also performs odd jobs such as walling, but it is a John Shurliker who is paid for some writing of the register. The 'Clark' is mentioned in connection with duties at the rushbearing in 1631, and a seat for the clerk in 1633. At the annual meeting in May 1636 some formalisation of the situation occurs, with the laying down of a standard 6s 8d payment to Christopher Shurliker for bell ropes etc and 20s to the clerk for the clock, ringing curfew and sweeping the church (f.41r). This seems to make a clear distinction between the two, and thereafter we have the named clerk (Nicholas Boulton) receiving £1 a year and his wife washing the surplices, an additional source of income widely characteristic of the spouses of parish clerks. The salary of £1, on the other hand, was commonly the figure paid to a sexton. Boulton's tenure and the above duties continue until 1655 and the parish register describes him as clerk at his burial on 7 May 1656. Thereafter Thomas Rose steps into the role. Whether these men were performing 'normal' clerical duties – keeping the register, leading responses in church, reading out notices – seems questionable. The vicar, 'pastor' and schoolmaster occasionally receive payments for writing, e.g. special presentments, petitions and lists, and the accounts

---

42 Charles Drew, ed., *Lambeth Churchwardens' Accounts*, op.cit., p. xlix.

often record payment to someone unspecified (implying the churchwarden himself) for writing the register.

Although some references point in conflicting directions, therefore, it appears that the parish clerk of Walton addressed the duties of attending to the clock, ringing curfew and sweeping the church, but others were called upon when writing was required. Practice may of course have varied according to the abilities of the available personnel, and the post-holder might also be pocketing direct payments from parishioners for duties at funerals, etc which do not appear in the accounts. The Liverpool Town Books record a similar apparent overlap of the roles of sexton and clerk.[43] At Childwall, clerk and sexton are mentioned separately in 1635.[44]

5. The church building and its furnishings

Thanks to nineteenth-century rebuilding followed by partial devastation during the Second World War, the church today shows nothing of its seventeenth-century appearance. The accounts are therefore a valuable source of information from an otherwise largely undocumented period. An old print reproduced in VCH gives some indication of its external architecture, with squat tower and a two-gabled east end.[45] This latter feature agrees with references in the accounts to the 'two chancels', the door between them and the valley in the roof (f.71r, f.152r and f.159r), and may represent the survival of a chantry chapel, perhaps the St Paul's Chapel referred to on f.78r, though the *Notitia* mentions only chantry chapels of St John and St Trinity, dissolved in 1548. According to VCH, however, there are thirteenth- and fourteenth-century references to a chapel of St Paulinus.[46]

Although the accounts speak of a steeple, e.g. being re-pointed in 1663, this term was used generally for any kind of church tower, and there is nothing to suggest that a spire once existed. A similarly ambiguous term used in the accounts is the bellhouse, which to the modern reader sounds like, but probably was not, a detached adjunct to the church. It appears to refer to the area below the tower and belfry, separated from the main church by a partition (f.17r and f.39r). Several references to dormer windows (e.g. f.129r, f.147v) add to the scant indications of the church's external architecture. The stone perimeter wall, at least part of which had some sort of 'battlements' (f.148r), and its two gates or stiles facing respectively towards Liverpool and Bootle, receive frequent attention, as does the schoolhouse, whose upkeep was clearly among the churchwarden's responsibilities. Remarkably, this early seventeenth-century building within the churchyard has survived to the present day, despite vandalism including arson attacks. Its masonry walls and stone-flagged roof give some indication of the building materials of that date.

---

43 Michael Power, ed., *Liverpool Town Books*, op.cit., p. 93 (minutes p. 644).
44 Eveline B. Saxton, trans., *Childwall Churchwardens' Accounts*, op.cit., p. 169, – also has details of salary and duties of bellringers.
45 *VCH Lancs*, iii, p. 6, from a watercolour drawing by E. Beattie.
46 *Notitia Cestriensis*, op.cit., p. 222; *VCH Lancs*, iii, p. 10. The reference in the accounts cannot be to one of the chapels of ease as none were dedicated to St Paul.

Numerous entries concerned with work on the church roof, windows and walls indicate a roof of slates and at least some walls constructed of lath and daub (clamstave). Probably all or most of the external walls were of sandstone but required much less maintenance and so feature less in the accounts. Toxteth Park quarry supplied sandstone slates for the roof, which had lead flashings and was weatherproofed with moss. Indeed copious quantities of this material were required for 'mossing' both roof and wall joints. When packed between stones or under the leads, dry moss swells in the rain and makes a passably watertight seal. Use of the term 'thacktable' (thatch table) on f.76r might suggest that some part of the roof was thatched, but it is more likely a dialect survival that has lost that precise connotation. The windows must have comprised many small leaded lights, the panes being referred to as quarrells – a recurrent item in the accounts. An interesting detail of local building practice is the inclusion of horsehair, of which quantities were always being purchased, not only as an aid to adherence in the daub filling for the clamstave walls but also specifically in mortar for repointing of, for example, the windows (f.76r). When a leaded light panel has been repaired, reinstatement into the stone or wooden frame requires careful pointing inside and out with a specially soft mortar.

Lime for building purposes (e.g. plaster, mortar, limewashing the walls) was made on a suitable site (presumably nearby) by the lime-burning process, the accounts referring on numerous occasions to payments in connection with this. Even the fire is itemised. In 1631 (f.12v), for example, there is a full account for building the kiln, buying and carting two tons of limestone and the requisite coal, burning the crushed stone, and then slaking the resulting lime with water. This produced a creamy liquid which was sieved and left for a few weeks – 'laid in steep' – to ensure all lumps or particles of unslaked lime were fully slaked before use. The Walton accounts are typical in furnishing many dialect terms for building processes and materials such as nails, and notes on these will be found in the Glossary (Appendix 1). When timber is purchased its purpose is not always clear: the timber support erected in 1649 (f.76) appears to be emergency buttressing, while the exact nature of the eve poles acquired for the porch (f.81v and f.159v) is uncertain, as noted in the Glossary. Two trees from Simonswood were purchased and purpose-felled for the churchwarden in 1665, and the timber apparently used for several purposes including forms and partitioning.

Since the nave itself is never referred to as such, no clear information is forthcoming as to whether the traditional allocation of responsibility of chancel to vicar and nave to parishioners was followed. The churchwarden certainly arranges payment for work on the chancel roof as part of his general duty to organise and pay workmen, but does not record any incoming payment from the incumbent to offset this, though there is one reference to Rector Ward contributing to the cleansing of the chancel under the exceptional circumstances of 1651 (f.85r and see p. xxxiii).

At the Metropolitan visitation of 1633, Archbishop Neile of York laid down particular instructions to all churches in the diocese regarding internal improvements, particularly paving and the provision of uniform seating in accordance with Laudian principles.[47] In 1633 and 1634 particularly, the Walton accounts share with others across the north of England a multitude of expenditure items concerned with these requirements. Churchwardens were also given their own specific lists of defects to remedy (f.19v), and we see the churchwarden of the day working through this in his accounts. The orders, including in Walton's case the provision of a new pewter pot for communion and flagging the church floor, are contained in the Visitation Court Books for Chester, which also report on an inspection of progress in December 1634, at which date still 'a little of the floor of the church is not flagged'.[48] The bellhouse and porch were evidently not flagged until 1635. A number of bones from earlier burials (the ley stalls which brought income to the church) were disturbed during the work and had to be reburied in the churchyard (f.18v). Very probably the floor had previously never been more than beaten earth; indeed until then the church must still have been largely in its medieval state. Since the annual rushbearing ceases to be mentioned at the time the floor was flagged, the custom would appear to have become a purely practical exercise by then, for the purpose of strewing over the dirt floor and sweetening the atmosphere.

The list of improvements ordered by Neile was expensive and called for the levy of a special ley of £18 (f.27v, 25 April 1634) so that 'therby the orders given out by the deputed Commissioners ... of the Lord ArchBishopp of Yorke may be observed and performed.' Limewashing and the erection of partitions between the body of the church and the chancel and bellhouse were among the other works at this date. The chancel partition was painted in colours (f.29r) and sounds like a rood screen.

The interior was of course furnished with a pulpit and a font: in fact the roughly-carved circular sandstone font of Norman date is the only internal feature to survive from before the Reformation, albeit in a restored version following wartime damage.[49] At several dates, and in response to various directives, their presence and state are attested by such expenditure as painting, purchase of serge and silk for the pulpit cover (which was apparently suspended with tenterhooks), removal and repositioning of the pulpit when the floor was flagged, fitting and later rehanging a pulpit door, and the provision of a lock for the font cover and a line for its lifting mechanism. Possibly the cover was removed during the puritan years – there is an entry regarding its erection in 1657 but it might simply have been taken down for repair.

At the date of the start of these accounts it would not have been unusual for a church to have no seats for the general congregation, though references to repairing forms in 1628 and 1629 indicate that there was seating for some. This term is overwhelmingly used instead of 'pew' in the accounts, so that it is difficult to be certain of the nature of seating provision. The three mentions of pews are on f.68r (referring to the churchwarden's seat), f.80v (Col. Moore's pew) and f.85r (glazing Edward Moore's pew), suggesting perhaps a single substantial family pew for the

47   *VCH Ches*, iii, pp. 33–4.
48   BIHR, V.1633 CB 2B, f.360r.
49   John W. Ellis, 'The Mediaeval Fonts of the Hundreds of West Derby and Wirral', *THSLC*, 53 (New Series, 17) (Liverpool, 1902), p. 60.

influential Moore family of Bank Hall, in addition to the special seating for the church officers, and probably simple benches for the rest, at least after Neile's visitation in 1633.

Archbishop Laud's doctrinal regime also called for communion tables (altars) to be moved to the east end, surrounded by rails and furnished with a 'carpet of silk' or similar. (Subsequent removal of the rails became a symbol of incoming Puritanism; see p. xxix). Walton duly attended to these requirements, buying and adjusting a table in 1633 (f.19v and f.20r), and setting up the railing in 1634 – taking Standish parish church as its model (f.31r). Thirty years later it was the parish church at Huyton that provided a model for a new reading desk (f.162r), during another period of energetic structural repair and refurbishment of the interior, this time in the years following the Restoration.[50] Expenditure on 'beautifying' in 1664 included £4 4s for work by James Webster (f.158r) and the services of a 'pensall man' (brush artist?), while in 1665 the churchwarden laid out for a new kersey carpet and silk fringe for the communion table.

Of monuments inside the church at this period we have no information, except for the Berry brass (see p. xxvii) and, unlike Prescot, Walton church did not boast an organ, to judge by the total absence of any mention. The bells, however, come in for frequent mention as in all churchwardens' accounts, being in perennial need of attention. The presence of at least three can be deduced; see for example the references on f.10v in 1630 and f.76v in 1649. They are probably the three bells hung in 1581, when Liverpool is recorded as contributing to the cost.[51] Two are often referred to as the great bell and the little bell. Purchase of new bell ropes is a frequent entry, and repair or replacement of a clapper, wooden wheel or headstock is itemised from time to time. Bells are occasionally rehung, most notably when a new one was cast from the old at a Wigan bell foundry in 1657. After weighing the old bell it was found necessary to add extra metal. In 1651 we first hear of strewing rushes on the bellhouse floor, more specifically replaced by starr grass from local sandhills in 1655 and thereafter. This was almost certainly to save wear on the parts of the rope that came into contact with the floor (f.105v).

Demanding much attention, too, was the tower clock. A new one was bought in 1634 for £5 plus as much again in consequent expenses, to replace a predecessor that may have been of Tudor date. The purchase of the new clock was a serious business and required at least one visit to Thomas Rothwell, a Prescot clock expert, to inspect and take patterns from the church clock there. Rothwell bought '46 poundes of old Iron being all the old clocke' for 7s 8d (f.28r). Without face or pendulum, the type of clock installed at Walton would have been regulated by a verge escapement and foliot, with a wire that lifted a hammer to strike one of the bells, marking the hours only. The movement was housed in a lockable wooden

---

50 A carved reading desk 'dated 1639' is mentioned in *VCH Lancs*, iii, p. 5, but presumably did not survive the Blitz. Curiously, it was in 1639 that the Childwall churchwardens went to Huyton to copy the reading seat there (*Childwall Churchwardens' Accounts*, op.cit., p. 178). Could it be the same desk?

51 J.A. Twemlow, ed., *Town Books of Liverpool: II 1572–1603* (Liverpool, 1935), pp. 416–17.

case or 'clockhouse' to keep out dust, and the clock was also equipped with a weight chute (referred to as the tunnel) containing the large weights or clock stones, one on the time or going side and one on the striking. Small lead weights also feature in the maintenance schedule and were probably used on the balance. Clocks such as the one at Walton were regulated from sundials, and indeed a new dial was set up on a post in the churchyard in 1633. Expenditure on cleaning the clock, spare parts and repairs is a constant theme throughout the accounts, and indicates that it was a costly piece of equipment for the parish to maintain. The copious amounts of wire were for the clock hammer, while the cord was for weight lines. The Glossary further explains the purpose of many of the other clock-related entries.

6. Poor relief and charities

Under the Tudor laws, the churchwarden would *ex officio* act as one of the overseers, but it has not proved easy to establish from the accounts exactly how parochial responsibilities for the operation of the poor laws were financed and shared out. The low number of references to payments to the poor in the earlier accounts suggests that separate collection and accounting of a poor rate must have been going on, as might be expected, but it was evidently thought appropriate for certain payments to come out of the church rate. That there was also a collecting box for the poor is confirmed by an entry relating to its repair (f.64r), but income from this does not appear in the accounts. There are many references to business that concerned the churchwarden and the overseers together (e.g. f.87v), and one would expect Walton to be following the system, already pursued in Lancashire in advance of the 1662 Act of Settlement and Removal, whereby townships operated separately with their own overseers. Under this system the Walton churchwarden would be overseer of the poor for Walton township only. Indeed there are references to meetings and sometimes disagreements with the overseers of the other townships. But in 1660 the churchwarden makes account for the spending of £1 10s received from a *parish* poor rate, recipients from the townships of Derby and Kirkby being included (f.132r and f.133v).

The period preceding this seems to have been one during which attempts were made to lay down just where local responsibility for the poor lay. A number of meetings were held in 1650, with the overseers of West Derby, Kirkby and Liverpool among others (f.78v and f.79r). In 1652, in conjunction with instructions from the justices concerning overseers' duties, the churchwarden and overseers made a joint list of the able-bodied and impotent poor and the pauper apprentices of the parish (f.91v). Disagreement as to whether or not the parish as a whole was responsible for keeping the poor of Walton, Liverpool and Kirkby in particular seems to have rumbled on through the decade: JPs ordered the churchwarden to pay the Kirkby overseers for the upkeep of a child in 1656, for example (f.110v), and there is further allusion to the tension between parish and these townships in 1660 with an attempt to establish precedent by certifying 'how long every quarter have kept theire poore' (f.135v). The novel parish poor rate entry in the 1660 accounts appears to be related to these events. Separate whole-parish accounts for other years may have been kept and lost, or this insertion may indicate a response to the order from JPs referred to in Liverpool's petition of 1661 (see below).

Undoubtedly some of these strains bear relation to the aspirations of the townships of Kirkby and Liverpool for parish status, which was indeed promised them during the Commonwealth though not implemented. But while Kirkby 'denyed to keepe theire poore' (f.136r), the Liverpool Town Books reveal a determination to support the town's own poor and keep others out, levying their own rate and confirming the custom that the old churchwardens (strictly chapelwardens) become overseers in the year following their term of office.[52] By this date it was already a longstanding practice and indeed a matter of pride for corporate towns to take responsibility for their own poor. Kirkby's winning of an order at Quarter Sessions committing the parish to support the townships' poor left this attitude in disarray. Rightly claiming that they had more poor than any other township, in 1661 the mayor and bailiffs of Liverpool felt compelled themselves to petition for parish support towards the maintenance of a named group of individuals.[53]

As noted at the start of this section, the relatively low number of outgoing payments made directly to the poor implies separate accounting for most types of these, both before and after the 1660–61 ruling. The churchwarden seems to have become involved and responsible in particular when payment of relief was accorded to strangers with passes or warrants to travel and solicit alms, and also to a large extent when cases had to be resolved at Quarter Sessions, where he would frequently appear to contest liability with regard to providing for a destitute person or family. These observations agree with examples from elsewhere, where it appears that the settled poor were relieved by the overseers while vagrants, strangers and special funds fell to the churchwarden's remit, at least from the later seventeenth century.[54] Parochial practice in this field varied widely, however.

Several individual cases can be followed in the accounts, telling stories of personal tragedy as well as illustrating the prevailing spirit and operation of the poor laws, under which parishes strove unremittingly to avoid or divert financial responsibility. The first mention of any payment under the system comes in 1632 (f.13v) and is to a nurse caring for 'the bastard', probably the same unwanted child to feature in subsequent visits to Quarter Sessions for which expenses were claimed by the churchwarden. In another typical case, when the two young children of William and Katherine Blinston(e) lost first their mother and then their father in quick succession in 1634–35,[55] their maintenance by quarterly payments of £1 to Ralph Burgess and then to James Higginson and Jane Rose becomes a regular

52 Michael Power, ed., *Liverpool Town Books*, op.cit., p. 92 (minutes p. 642).
53 LaRO, QSP/207/61.
54 Henry R. Plomer, trans., *The Churchwardens' Accounts of St. Nicholas, Strood, Part II: 1603–1662*, Kent Records 5 (Kent Archaeological Society, 1928); W.E. Tate, *The Parish Chest: a Study of the Records of Parochial Administration in England*, 3rd edn (Cambridge, 1969), p. 86.
55 The *Registers of the Parish Church of Walton-on-the-Hill*, LPRS, 5 (1586–1663) (Wigan, 1900) and 91 (1663–1746) (Preston, 1950).

feature (f.38v *et seq.*). The parish had originally intended to pay 12d per week (£2 12s per year), but this was increased to £4 by Lord Molyneux, and in 1638 the churchwarden then in office, Richard Greaves, refused to pay this. Folio 54r records his attendance at Quarter Sessions in connection with this dispute.[56]

The Strange family of blacksmiths track their way through the accounts not only for services rendered but also in the support, by order of the Sessions, of Ellen, widow of William Strange, and her two small children, from 1639 until the break in the accounts after 1641.[57] Again the rate is £1 per quarter. In the case of Mary Adamson and her children, payments of 10s per quarter (f.48v *et seq.*) came to an end when the obligation was discharged by a once-for-all payment of £2 10s in 1639 by order of the justices (f.60r). Such final payments occur elsewhere (e.g. f.100r to replace quarterly payments of 15s to Sarah Govett for keeping a child), and this was clearly an arrangement to be aspired to. 'Quarterage' is also paid to Mary Gorsuch, perhaps an elderly pauper. Mary Higginson of Kirkdale and her child were laid on the parish in 1651 after Robert Higginson was executed for desertion from the army at Preston.[58] Colonel Birch, Governor of Liverpool, set a figure for regular payment, but in 1652 agreement with the father-in-law to keep the child discharged the parish (f.91v).

Removal to another parish was always a desirable route to avoid liability. In a 1651 example, concerning removal of a bastard child, we see Liverpool being treated as 'out of the parish' for this purpose, well before the 1658 Commonwealth order for it to achieve parish status.

From the 1650s, perhaps reflecting the social changes of the Commonwealth period, there are many references to payments to poor travellers bearing passes or orders for collection from the justices. Briefs, however, are not often mentioned: these special collections did not pass through the churchwarden's books, though some are recorded in the parish register.[59] Briefs such as those for the 'poore protestantes in Savoy' in 1655 (victims of a religious massacre) and for Ripon in 1661 appear in the accounts only because of costs incurred in collecting or passing on the money or obtaining a receipt (f.103v and f.141r). A collection for the Irish poor early in 1642 (f.72v), though ostensibly voluntary, was in fact a form of taxation (see p. xxxii).

The churchwarden also paid out to the High Constable of the hundred the parish's share of two rates levied by the county, namely those for the support of the 'maimed soldiers' and the poor prisoners in Lancaster Gaol. Generally the sum was 17s 4d plus 2d for the receipt or quittance, though accounting for the rates is sometimes haphazard, and no payments are noted in the years after the lacuna. It was common practice for such rates to be paid out of general resources, hence their frequent appearance in churchwardens' accounts, often as a combined sum.

---

56 LaRO, QSB1/146/48, QSB1/218/53.
57 LaRO, QSB1/214/82.
58 LaRO, QSP/51/21, QSP/63/20.
59 *Registers of Walton*, op.cit.

As a parish, Walton seems to have lacked significant endowments by wealthy inhabitants to supplement its resources, but a charity established in 1601 under the will of Elizabethan merchant Thomas Berry puts in regular appearances in the form of payments made for obtaining and certifying the 'bread money' from London. (Sometimes the vicar himself journeyed to the capital about this business.) Berry, said to have been a fishmonger, had family connections with the parish. He left his Red Cross tenement in Edward Street, Southwark to the parish of St Mary Magdalen, Old Fish Street, with the instruction that out of the rents 54s per year should be paid to the Walton churchwarden, for the weekly supply of penny loaves to twelve poor persons every Sunday with recompense of 2s for his pains. A further 50s went to two 'honest and sufficient men' of Bootle, to provide a dinner every St Thomas day in his brother James's house at Bootle for all the householders and married people of the town, and supper for the young people.[60] A brass dated 1586 (apparently before Berry's death), recording the benefaction and removed from St Mary Magdalen after the Fire of London, can still be seen on the north wall of the city church of St Martin Ludgate.[61] A near-identical one at Walton church was partially destroyed in the the Liverpool blitz in May 1941 but has been recreated. The brass depicts the elderly Berry in ruff, tunic and cloak and bears ten anti-papist verses beginning with the letters of his name (spelled Thomas Beri) in reverse order.[62] References to the bread money appear intermittently in the accounts from 1631, and in 1656 some related enquiry seems to have necessitated obtaining a copy of James Berry's will about a twice-yearly dole, perhaps the dinner and supper referred to above (f.112v).

7. The school

A number of items in the accounts show that the churchwarden's remit encompassed the repair and maintenance of the school building, situated as it was within the churchyard, but his responsibility extended beyond this. Folio 41r records a ley-laying meeting in May 1636 at which it was also ruled that the churchwarden for the current year would become school reeve the next. By the 1650s both offices were apparently held simultaneously and it is in his capacity as school reeve that the churchwarden of 1664 accounts for an expenditure item in connection with the hearth tax (f.163r). There was of course also a schoolmaster, whose writing skills were called upon by the churchwarden from time to time; according to the *Notitia* he was nominated by both rector and vicar. The school probably owes its origin to the will of Thomas Harrison of Walton ('of New Inn'

---

60 *VCH Lancs*, iii, p. 10; *Notitia Cestriensis*, op.cit., p. 225. There seems to be uncertainty as to the exact date of the charity's foundation, and perhaps also as to the amount of the total bequest: Thornely, see note 62, states that the will was proved in 1608; the *Notitia* gives a figure of 108s per annum.

61 Simon Bradley & Nikolaus Pevsner, *The Buildings of England. London 1: the City of London* (London, 1997), p. 238.

62 James L. Thornely, *The Monumental Brasses of Lancashire and Cheshire With Some Account of the Persons Represented* (Hull, 1893), pp. 243–8.

according to the burial register), proved in 1615, though it is possible that a school existed before this date. Harrison left £120 for the maintenance of a free school – his executors, the churchwarden and two members of the Moore family of Bank Hall being enjoined to see it established. Beyond these known facts, an unsubstantiated story is given in the *Notitia* and repeated elsewhere later that the school owed its foundation to £300 given by an old aleseller and his wife.[63]

The £120 was evidently lent out as school stock, and lists of the bonds and odd money survive with most of the accounts dated from 1654 to 1662, as one churchwarden/school reeve delivered up and accounted for them to the next. This handover is also mentioned (though without a surviving list) in 1638, and a memo in the parish register dated 1643 records bonds deposited in the parish chest by Thomas Riding, who was churchwarden in 1640 and probably school reeve the next year: it includes mention of a bill of Mr Alexander and Mr Thomas Molyneux for £4.[64] At the 1662 handover the interest taken is shown, and can be seen to be 3% per half year. The lists show a large additional item of £42 as a 'desperatt bill of Master Alexander Mollineux', apparently the former rector, though how it relates to his bequests of £40 to the poor and £20 to the school (see Table 1) is unclear. In fact confusion reigns in published sources over whose the debt was and for how much. From the churchwardens' accounts we know that in 1655 action was instituted against the executors of Viscount Molyneux's father and grandfather and Sir Vivian Molyneux to try to recoup the loss represented by unpaid interest (f.102), though the loan comes to be referred to as £40 rather than £42. The second viscount had just died without issue, and been succeeded by his brother, perhaps prompting the action: the executors mentioned appear to be those of the first viscount (d. 1636) and his father Sir Richard (d. 1623), the latter being Alexander's nephew and father of both Sir Vivian Molyneux and the first viscount. Sir Vivian was still living at the date of the churchwardens' action, and it is he to whom the debt is attributed by the *Notitia* and subsequent sources, which record that *£50* lent to him was lost when he died insolvent.[65]

Under the auspices of the Commissioners for Pious Uses, witnesses – former churchwardens among them – were summoned to testify their knowledge of the financial arrangements that led to this debacle (f.102r). The following year the churchwarden obtained an order at Preston 'either to give bond or pay forty Pound to the Reeve' and served it on Viscount Molyneux at Croxteth (f.111). The issue appears to have remained a live one in later years, with the bond continuing to be itemised up to 1663, and the accounts themselves do not reveal whether the debt was paid.

---

63 LaRO, WCW Supra, Thomas Harrison 1615; *Registers of Walton*, op.cit. (1615 and 1631); *Notitia Cestriensis*, op.cit., p. 225. A memo of 1624 in the parish register seems to be the source of an incorrect date of 1613 for Harrison's bequest, repeated in many sources incl. *VCH Lancs*, ii, p. 615.
64 *Registers of Walton*, op.cit. (22 July 1643).
65 *Endowed Charities (Lancashire) Returns*, III (London, 1908) (quoting 1828 details), pp. 412–13; *Notitia Cestriensis*, op.cit., p. 225; genealogical details from *VCH Lancs*, iii, pp. 70, 73.

8. Reflections of national events

Examination of the evidence from the accounts is best considered in two chronologies, dealing first with liturgical and other developments in the church and then with more secular aspects.

Churchwardens' accounts have been quarried by historians looking for evidence of the extent to which the general populace followed the roller-coaster of doctrinal change in the seventeenth century. Increasingly under puritan influence, Parliament through the mid-1640s proceeded to order the removal of crucifixes, candles and any images or practices that smacked of idolatry, decreeing reduction in the use of utensils, levelling of chancels, removal of altar rails and relocation of the communion table in a more accessible position. Baptism at the font and use of the surplice were discontinued during the Commonwealth, and the Easter and Christmas festivals banned. Admission to the sacrament was to be by examination. Questions to which answers are sought in churchwardens' accounts include: how rapidly (or conversely how reluctantly) were directives to remove the trappings of Anglicanism carried out, how quickly did the old order return after the Interregnum, to what extent did the frequency of communions change, how far were images cherished, and how deeply ingrained was the observance of the Anglican year enshrined in the *Book of Common Prayer*? Morrill has argued from material in such accounts that the ordinances of the 1640s and 50s were largely ineffective in stifling innate Anglicanism. Apart from removal of altar rails in 1641, they were slow to be implemented and the quick return to old ways around the Restoration suggested a response in terms of beliefs rather than apathy or laziness.[66]

These accounts, with their lacuna from 1642 to 1648, are not well placed to provide evidence, though they are not completely without a contribution to the debate. The Walton churchwardens followed numerous other contemporary examples in the prompt implementation of the most visible manifestation of the Laudian changes in the year that they were ordered, 1634, notably the erection of altar rails at the east end, and took these down also in the year Parliament vetoed them, 1641. Walton also complied with Laudian directives by buying James I's book of instructions to vicars, the *Book of Sports and Pastimes*, reissued by decree in 1633. As elsewhere, too, a feature of the politically turbulent pre-war years is the appearance in the accounts of more frequent payments for 'books' containing the form of service for days of fasting, public humiliation and penance, in response to directives first from the king and Archbishop of Canterbury and then from Parliament.

Beyond this, it is difficult to argue either way from these accounts as to how far the successive rulings aimed at eroding Anglican ways and establishing a new form of worship in the puritan mould were welcomed and implemented. Little hard evidence emerges; we see the making of a bag for the silver bowl and the taking down of glass (perhaps stained glass) in 1641 (f.70v and f.71v), both of which could have been for safe-keeping, or in response to doctrinal directives, or merely

66 John Morrill, ed., *Reactions to the English Civil* War, op.cit., pp. 89–114.

to fulfil some practical necessity. The accounts are silent during the mid-1640s period of changes imposed by the *Directory for the Public Worship of God*, the presbyterian formulary drawn up at the instance of Parliament in 1644 to replace the *Book of Common Prayer*, which was supposed to be collected and destroyed by county committees. Certainly Walton had to buy new Prayer Books after the Restoration. Evidence for actual removal of the altar and the replacement of the font by a basin is not forthcoming, though again there is activity to renovate the font after the Restoration; see below, p. xxxi.

The missing years cover the period when bishops were abolished and ordinances enjoining presbyterianism were in force, advocating the setting up of a classis comprising minister and lay elders to oversee parish affairs, with classes grouped in assemblies. Again there is little in the accounts to refer to this save the use of the term 'pastor' instead of rector in the 1650s. The republic's ideal of religious freedom for all, embodied in the 1650 Toleration Act and including removal of the compulsion to attend parish churches, fell far short of realisation in practice. Extremism flourished, and among the fears was that of the threat from Quakers. A collection towards their suppression was ordered in 1652 and is recorded in the accounts (f.93r). Disaffection with the authority of the parish at this period may account for the increased attendance at elections already noted, and the strains of religious disharmony are evident in the rise in disputes, ejections and litigation.

Before putting forward the evidence from communions – or lack of them – it is necessary to establish the normal number *per annum* in the 1620s and 1630s, before the Civil War. Here church practice already varied enormously, with 10–12 communions in some places (i.e. monthly), and as few as four in others. Easter Day always features whatever the regime, other dates being Palm Sunday, Good Friday, Whitsunday and a date around Christmas. Those following a quarterly pattern might opt for Easter, Whit, Michaelmas and Christmas.[67] At Walton we have mentions of usually four only up to 1633, the year of Archbishop Neile's visitation, thereafter as many as seven in the years up to 1641.

Churchwardens' accounts of course provide this information in the form of entries for purchase of bread and wine, though absence of such entries might in some places be due to direct collections being made to pay for these items. While curtailment or cessation might in theory simply reflect the expense of wine, the widespread disappearance of communion purchases from churchwardens' accounts from the mid 1640s to the 1650s is accepted as a true reflection of the suspension of holy communion. Some ministers feared that the new obligation of admission to the sacrament by examination would exclude too many of their parishioners, and preferred not to celebrate communion rather than let this happen. Parishes are known where communions continue to be celebrated throughout the

---

67 Francis N.A. Garry & A.G. Garry, trans., *The Churchwardens' Accounts of the Parish of St Mary's, Reading, Berks 1550–1662* (Reading, 1893); John Booker, *A History of the Ancient Chapels of Didsbury and Chorlton*, Chetham Society, Old Series, 42 (Manchester, 1857), pp. 86–96; S. Cooper Scott, 'Extracts from the Churchwardens' Accounts and Vestry Minutes of St John's Chester', *Journal of the Chester Archaeological & Historic Society*, New Series, 3 (1890), pp. 48–70.

Commonwealth, but most appear to stop. In many of the latter instances, however, they are reintroduced well before 1660. Morrill identified the year 1657 as the most common date for resumption, as the doctrinal pressures relaxed, and Walton falls exactly into this category.[68] Here, no purchases of bread or wine are recorded after the lacuna until 1657, after which the number of mentions per year varies from one rising to five. Another reflection of the gradual reversion to former custom is the reappearance of the presenting of recusants, also in 1657.

The first indication at Walton of a return to the pre-war machinery of episcopal administration comes in 1661, when the purchase of Articles for the visitation reappears. Keys are bought for the parish chest, perhaps to secure the newly-returned parish register books, custody of which had passed to elected Parish Registers during the Interregnum; (such an election at Walton is recorded in the parish register in 1653). Did Walton's silver bowl emerge from its hiding place (if such is the interpretation of the 1641 entry mentioned above)? In 1662 – the year of the Act of Uniformity – we read of changing the flagon, buying bread plates and paying for surplices and hoods for the vicar and the parson. In 1663 a reference to fitting the font cover suggests its renovation. Many churchwardens' accounts record the painting of the king's arms in church after the Restoration in 1660; while there is no specific reference to this at Walton, a burst of painting and 'beautifying' requires much attention from the churchwarden in 1664, which was the year in which the arms were drawn at Childwall.[69] Money had first to be spent remedying dilapidations to the building, so the relative delay is more likely to have been due to shortage of funds than lack of enthusiasm, though it should be noted by those looking to deduce beliefs from actions (or lack of them) that altar rails were not re-erected at Walton until 1663.

The administration of parish affairs as revealed in the accounts also reflects a number of additional secular demands on the time of the churchwarden stemming from the political and military situation during the period. Responsibility for payment of certain county rates was always his, but he also acquired duties in relation to the collection of the novel taxes and subsidies sought by Charles I in the pre-war phase, as well as to the confiscation of arms held by individuals who might pose a threat. Such issues became entangled with regular duties arising from rate collection, the county militia and the problem of recusants. Mentions in the 1630s of listing recusants and able-bodied men (presumably for the muster) were apparently part of normal duties and it is hard to say how far they relate to the politics of the time. Nothing in the accounts refers to the collection of 'ship money' in 1635, and an apparent interest in the assessments for West Derby hundred in 1636 (f.43v) may simply reflect some query about the county rates. In 1640, after eleven years of personal rule, the king summoned Parliament because of his need to raise money by taxation, and in the 1640 accounts a record suggesting something less routine occurs, about the reporting of recusants to the Justices by parliamentary

68 John Morrill, ed., *Revolution and Restoration: England in the 1650s* (London, 1992), p. 81; John
    Morrill, ed., *Reactions to the English Civil* War, op.cit., pp. 105–6.
69 Eveline B. Saxton, trans., *Childwall Churchwardens' Accounts*, op.cit., p. 245.

order (f.64v). Recusants were seen as a source of revenue and were targeted in the assessment of 1641, as discussed below. On the next folio (f.65v) there is reference to a parliamentary order concerning subsidies and one from the king's privy council ordering the listing and seizing of the arms and armour of recusants: 'payd in expences of the high Constabell and others in goeing thrugh the parish in Disarming and takinge notise of all the Armor weaponns and Furniture belonging to recusantes'. In a document dated 6 April 1641, churchwarden John Ryding reported the results at the Quarter Sessions, itemising 'one Pyke, one Corslet compleate and one headpiece and a gorget' found in the house of George Standish of West Derby.[70]

Written records relating to the listing of recusants at this time, apparently primarily for taxation purposes, survive both in the Walton accounts themselves and in the 'Recusant Roll for West Derby Hundred', which has been published.[71] The latter enumerates all the convicted recusants aged 16 or over, and non-communicants for the last year aged 21 or over, presented at Ormskirk Sessions on 17 June 1641 to the Commissioners charged with the 'rating and assessing of the two latter of the four subsidies' granted by Parliament the previous year 'not being contributory to the rates expressed in the Act made for the said subsidies of 4s in the pound for land or 2s 8d in the pound for goods; all which said persons were charged ... with the payment of 16d the Pole for the said two subsidies.' The poll hit the less well off who escaped payment of the subsidy itself, and recusants were doubly charged. The list in the accounts (the misplaced f.84v) apparently dates from 25 May 1641 and is not dissimilar to the published roll where it relates to Walton itself – both lists include women (wives, widows and unmarried) and feature the prominent Fazakerley and Chorley families – but there are a number of differences, so it may be a separate but related listing, or represent the certificated 'converted recusants' (perhaps the same as church papists who avoided fines by minimal church attendance) noted on f.70v.

Although it is difficult to be certain, references in the accounts to the 'great pole munie' (f.68v and f.69r) appear to refer to the June 1641 presentations, rather than the subsidy voted by Parliament in July 1641 (16 Charles I c.9) to pay for disbandment of the armies and 'settling the peace' of England and Scotland. In many places the collection of this subsidy was made at the same time as the supposedly voluntary 'Collection in Aid of Distressed Protestants in Ireland', ordered following the killing of 'planted' Protestants in the rebellion of autumn 1641 and in part intended to pay for a punitive force. Churchwardens were instructed to collect 'gifts' and list the 'donors'. At Walton, the collection seems to have been treated as a genuine one, with involvement of the overseers (f.72v); relevant entries in the Childwall churchwardens' accounts are fuller on this score, and collection of money from recusants that year is also more fully itemised there.[72]

---

70 LaRO, QSB1/246/61.
71 W.E. Gregson, trans.,'Recusant Roll for West Derby Hundred 1641', *THSLC*, 50 (New Series, 14) (Liverpool, 1900), pp. 237–8.
72 Eveline B. Saxton, trans., *Childwall Churchwardens' Accounts*, op.cit., pp. 187–90.

That same year, 1641, the churchwarden was busy with taking and supervising the local administration of the Protestation oath (f.71v). In its expanded form all adult males were required to make their oath to defend the Protestant religion in a pledge of allegiance ostensibly to the king but in fact to Parliament. If the time devoted to this by the churchwarden can be taken as an indication of the conformity of the local population, it seems that a good percentage of Walton people may have complied: the names of those who did not were, as usual, taken down for possible use in evidence against them.

Nine years later and the other side of events that must have shaken the parish to its foundations, another oath was required of those in public office. By a parliamentary enactment early in 1650 known as the Engagement, all such office-holders, churchwardens included, were required to make their oath before JPs to affirm their allegiance to the government of the Commonwealth. The Walton churchwarden and sidesman were duly summoned to Prescot for the purpose (f.75v).

Thanks mainly to the missing years, we find no echo of the Civil War campaigns of the 1640s culminating in the king's execution, during which period Liverpool was taken by Parliamentary forces, regained by Prince Rupert, and lost again by the Royalists (1643–44). As we have seen, Walton's rector Andrew Clare joined the Royalist camp and fled abroad, the rectory being sequestered and appointments to both rectory and vicarage becoming the responsibility of secular agencies.

The only direct impact of military action on the parish to feature in the accounts comes in 1651. Around 700 unfortunate royalist soldiers had been herded into the church, which was commandeered to serve as a makeshift prison following Cromwell's defeat of Charles II's Scottish army at Worcester on 3 September. After more than a month of their confinement, the conditions there can only be imagined from the churchwarden's recording of payments for subsequent removal of the prisoners, burying of the filthy straw and rubbish left behind, repairing, cleaning and whitewashing of the church, and burning pitch and incense in an attempt to purify the building and banish the smell (f.86r–f.87v). In a petition to Quarter Sessions submitted by the churchwarden and sidesman, over £20-worth of damage to forms and windows and defacement of the interior (no doubt by graffiti) was alleged, but their request for help from a special rate on the hundred was denied.[73]

Churchwardens' accounts around the country record through payments to bellringers the occasions when a special peal was rung. These have sometimes been examined for possible clues to the political sympathies and general mood of the populace at times of significant events but, at Walton at least, it is difficult to tell at which point on the scale from genuine rejoicing to grudgingly following instructions we should rate these entries. Following almost universal practice, Walton rang on 5 November throughout the period, to mark the preservation of Parliament, and there is no reason to suppose that this practice ceased in the missing years.[74] Up to 1638 the occasion receives the designation 'King's Holiday'. No other dates are recorded in the pre-war period until 4 September 1641,

73 LaRO, QSP/55/3.
74 See for example John Booker, *Didsbury and Chorlton*, op.cit., pp. 86–96.

possibly the same 'day of thanksgiving' ordained by the king as was marked around the same time by a peal at Childwall.[75] How often and for what the Walton bells tolled during the Civil Wars we cannot know, though Chester rang for the taking of Liverpool,[76] and the events of 1643–44 are unlikely to have gone unmarked. Walton may well have shared the strong support of Parliament shown in Liverpool. The Cromwellian victory in Ireland was commemorated on 3 November 1649, and 'several victories' on a day of thanksgiving held on 29 January 1651. Later that year the ringers were active on 10 September and 24 October, the former probably to celebrate the decisive victory at Worcester. If Parliamentary sympathies can be discerned in any of the above, the bellringing prompted by the Restoration restores the balance, with peals for the King's proclamation and arrival in England in 1660, coronation day and 29 May (the king's birthday) in 1661 and relevant royal anniversaries thereafter. A naval victory during the second Dutch war was able to unite the country in patriotism in 1666, when the Walton bells rang out for 'victorie over the Hollander' (f.170r).

9. Reflections of Liverpool's history

Given the relative importance of Liverpool and Walton, it is not surprising that the former chafed at being treated as a mere township of the latter. As early as 1636 the accounts show a reluctance by Liverpool to pay its share of the parish ley on time. From 1649 onwards amounts were withheld and recorded as owing, though these were not rolled up year on year: in 1649 the amount owing was £2 13s 4d, in 1651 (a year with higher payments all round) £5 6s 8d, and in 1652 £2 13s 4d, for example. In 1652 the churchwarden sought an order at the Quarter Sessions to enforce payment, church rates by now having received statutory recognition. Repeated fruitless trips to demand the ley and further recourse to the JPs are recorded in subsequent years – in 1655 a quart of wine was required to lubricate the process (f.104v) – but a warrant for payment of £2 13s 4d was rejected by Liverpool and the matter referred to the town's recorder. Liverpool Common Council must have been well aware that Walton functioned with a single churchwarden, but they took the opportunity of belittling the parish authorities by mentioning, as if it implied doubtful legitimacy, that the warrant was signed by only one churchwarden.[77]

The councillors were determined not to pay up unless compelled by law to do so. Their ostensible justification for withholding the money was an objection to contributing to the repair of Walton church when they had a chapel of their own (Our Lady and St Nicholas) to maintain and were struggling with losses incurred during the war, but the long-held determination of Liverpool to become a parish in its own right was at the root of the problem. By the ruling of March 1645 following sequestration of Walton rectory (see p. ix), Liverpool and Toxteth Park could retain the tithes arising directly from them and Rector Ward was to hand over a

75 Eveline B. Saxton, trans., *Childwall Churchwardens' Accounts*, op.cit., p. 188.
76 S. Cooper Scott, 'Churchwardens' Accounts of St John's Chester', op.cit., p. 52.
77 Michael Power, ed., *Liverpool Town Books*, op.cit., p. 73 (minutes p. 610).

supplementary £10 per year. But this was an insufficient degree of independence in Liverpool's view, and by 1654 Ward was in arrears in any case. Liverpool claimed to have all the privileges of a parish, having had 'time out of mind' the nomination of its own minister, clerk and churchwardens, claiming indeed actually to have been a parish formerly, and petitioned Parliament for distinct parish status in 1657.[78] This separation was in fact granted but the victory did not last: the division of Liverpool was confirmed by the Protector in 1658, to take effect after the present rector and vicar of Walton (Eaton and Finch) had gone, but since both were alive at the Restoration, the order lapsed.[79]

In the 1650s the Walton churchwardens had entered a period of much litigation, having to devote time not only to the problem with Liverpool but also to pursuing the Molyneux family for a bad debt (see p. xxviii) and fighting their corner over management of the parish poor. The stakes were raised in the Liverpool dispute after the churchwarden obtained a Crown Office order against the town, and the lawyer acting for the Walton side, Nicholas Valentine, moved to distrain the mayor's goods (f.111v–f.112v). The goods in question were the mayoral silver plate – specifically a silver can was seized and is referred to on f.121r as well as in the Town Books. As Peet put it, 'suit followed suit in rapid succession', and this can be followed in the accounts as the churchwarden itemises the legal and travel costs incurred.[80] They included seeking a writ of certiorare to remove the suit from Liverpool to the High Court. The height of the dispute was during the mayoralties of Gilbert Formby (in office 1656–57) and Thomas Blackmore (1657–58), who were determined to take the fight through the courts as far as the legal process would allow. This included instituting a personal action in their own borough court against the churchwarden James Standish for removing the can, as well as a formal action of replevin. However, Walton's right to the ley was upheld – at exactly what stage of the legal proceedings is not clear – and, as a result of negotiations referred to as the parish's 'treatie with Liverpoole' (f.118r), some payments were gradually made by the bailiffs from 1658 on (e.g. £11 10s, f.120v). The ransomed can was returned. The Town Books also record an agreement with the vicar (wrongly entered as 'Mr Smith') in 1659, whereby arrears and a yearly sum for glebe and church dues were to be paid him from public stock.[81]

Disagreements over keeping the poor surfaced in 1660 and are mentioned in section 6, p. xxiv. The Walton rectors also from time to time exerted what they felt was their right to a say in the choice of curate for Liverpool. In practice this had been in the gift of the mayor and Common Council since at least 1643, when part of the sequestered tithes of Walton were approved for the maintenance of a minister: indeed a 1669 minute asserted that the right derived from a grant dated 7 Elizabeth. The town

78 Ibid., pp. 44 (minutes p. 558), 58 (minutes p. 583), 70 (minutes p. 604), 92 (minutes p. 641) and others.
79 *Plundered Ministers Accounts Part II*, op.cit., pp. 224 and 229–30. Similar provision had been made for Kirkby: *Plundered Ministers Accounts Part II*, op.cit., pp. 178–9 and 211–12.
80 Henry Peet, ed., *Liverpool Vestry Books 1681–1834*, I (Liverpool, 1912), p. xx.
81 Michael Power, ed., *Liverpool Town Books*, op.cit., pp. 104–5, 109–10, 118 (minutes pp. 666–7, 675–6, 689).

chose and where appropriate paid its own minister, preachers, churchwardens, clerk, sexton, etc.[82] Jurisdictional disagreements clearly arose, as evidenced by entries in the Liverpool Council minutes: two concern the keeping of a separate parish register book (and hence securing the fees for entering births, burials and marriages) during the Commonwealth and one contests a claim by the Walton parish clerk to a fee allegedly due to him from Liverpool. The former led to an order from the JPs that Liverpool should elect its own Parish Register (i.e. the officer with that title).[83]

After the Restoration Liverpool paid its leys apparently without demur, and the town's efforts to sever completely all links to the parish of Walton were not successful until 1699. The changing times may well have led to a diminution of official support for Liverpool's independent stand.

10. Physical description

At the time of transcription, the accounts comprised a leather-covered book in which the original folios had been mounted on new paper pages in the nineteenth century. An inscription, 'This book was Bound by Thomas Crook October 31st 1837', gives the date of this action. Fading, bleed through, blots, tears and attack by insects and damp have all taken their toll on the legibility of many of the folios, and some must have been lost altogether, judging by missing details such as the audit and election in certain years. The years 1642–48 are completely lacking. The book is at reference number 283 SMW 11/3 in the keeping of the Liverpool Record Office, which also holds a microfilm copy of the subsequent accounts, 1667–1721, the originals of which are located in the archives of the Borthwick Institute (acc. 3473).

Many folios had come loose and some – both loose and pasted down – were clearly out of order, so for the purposes of this edition an attempt has been made to correct this. With the permission of LRO staff, folio numbers were added in pencil, superseding the partial and erratic page numbering of the nineteenth-century compilation and a further partial numbering system on the folios themselves (see Appendix 2). Where loose folios could be returned to their proper place this was done, but if there was no space or the folio was pasted down then numbering was given in sequence as found, but the material has been transcribed in its most likely true position, as explained in the italic notes inserted in the transcription. In deducing the correct order, handwriting, layout, dates where given, content (e.g. mention of ley stall payments which can be matched to dated burials in the register) and the matching of stains and worm holes have all been used. A few entries appear to have been written out of their proper place in the original, e.g. f.94v. These have not of course been altered.

The folio size is approximately 19cm x 15cm (variable) and there are 173 surviving folios.

82 George Chandler, *Liverpool under Charles I*, op.cit., pp. 92, 322; Michael Power, ed., *Liverpool Town Books*, op.cit., p. 239 (minutes p. 908).
83 Michael Power, ed., *Liverpool Town Books*, op.cit., pp. 58–9 (minutes pp. 583–4), 152 (minutes p. 747).

EDITORIAL METHOD

Headings to indicate the date of each account have been added in bold text at the start of the accounting year. The election of the new churchwarden and the setting of the ley for the following year were usually made at the same parish meeting as the audit of the previous year's account (sometimes held as late as May), so for convenience these events have normally been considered to mark the end rather than the beginning of an accounting year, where a decision has had to be made on the dividing line between accounts. Lists of school bonds delivered by the old churchwarden to his successor, which occur with some of the later accounts and are usually in the handwriting of the previous year's scribe, are thus normally treated as belonging to the old year unless circumstances dictate otherwise.

Illegible, missing, or potentially missing text is indicated by ... regardless of how many letters appear to be lost. Loss is usually due to tears, fading or abrasion at the edges of pages, but sometimes results from illegible handwriting, particularly where matter has been overwritten or struck through.

Text struck through or otherwise deliberately obliterated is indicated by < >. Where a correction by over-writing or striking through concerns only one or two letters, this has not been indicated.

Text inserted with a caret or interlined is indicated by > <, except where written above struck-through text as a correction.

Roman numerals have been converted to arabic except when missing digits make it impossible to convert; in such cases the partial numeral is given, in italic. Numerals that are arabic in the original in an otherwise roman set, and vice versa, are indicated by footnotes.

Pence over 11 and shillings over 19 are left as given, and not converted to shillings or pounds respectively.

Except where internal to a sentence or part of a summary, monetary amounts are given in a single column at the right-hand side of the page without preceding dashes or brackets, regardless of how they appear in the original. Column headings (£ s d) are shown only where used in the original. Dividers between figures (e.g. –, =, :), where they occur, are omitted except from totals, but their nature is indicated in the notes. The number of horizontal lines between totals in sums has also been reduced for simplicity.

In long entries, memoranda, etc, line ends are indicated by / rather than new lines, to save space.

All standard contractions such as ampersand and *Mr*, and all words where a superscript or mark of contraction has been used, have been silently expanded, but *li*, *s* and *d* have been left as £ *s d* (or *li* changed to *lb* according to context). Where there is no obvious sign of contraction, the word has normally been left unexpanded, except that abbreviated first names have always been expanded, as have *pd* and *rec* (for *paid* and *received/receipts*, or as per the scribe's normal spelling), and in cases of uncertainty square brackets have been used (see below). The *-es* abbreviation, use of which for plurals was being relaxed by the later seventeenth century, has for consistency been expanded as *-es* throughout, except for the 1659 and 1660 accounts, where there is evidence that the scribes were using the character loosely for a simple *-s* ending. A colon used in dates (e.g. *15: October*) has been expanded to *st*, *rd* or *th* as appropriate. *Etc* and *&c* have been expanded to *et cetera*, *viz* to *videlicet* and *sc.* to *scilicet*.

Square brackets are used in two ways: within the text to indicate uncertainty, and to enclose descriptive comment added by the editors (including folio numbers but excluding the annual headings in bold type). Examples of the former are where a letter apparently omitted by accident has been restored for clarity, where it is not clear whether or not a scribe intended his spelling as a contraction, where the spelling he would have used in an expanded word is uncertain, and where the reading of a character or characters is difficult to determine. Editorial comment appears in italic.

Some scribes do not distinguish well between capital and lower case letters, or are inconsistent in so distinguishing. This is particularly so for *d*, *m* and *w*, so **all** occurrences of these as the first letter of names of places and people (including titles) have been automatically capitalised, in the interests of clarity and consistency, even in those accounts where there does seem to be a distinction. In the case of other letters such as *k*, *l*, *n* and *s*, a capital has been used for proper names if there is any doubt as to the scribe's intention.

Where appropriate, *i* has been transcribed as *j* according to modern usage.

Dates: *th* after numbers such as 22 has been transcribed as in the original following the way it would have been spoken, e.g. 'two and twentieth'.

Changes in handwriting are noted where appropriate, but not for every single signature or annotation entered at the time of audit: it can be assumed that these are in a different hand from the main body of the account.

Footnotes to unusual words, spellings or usage are kept to a minimum, a glossary being provided in Appendix 1.

THE PARISH OF
WALTON-ON-THE-HILL, LANCASHIRE

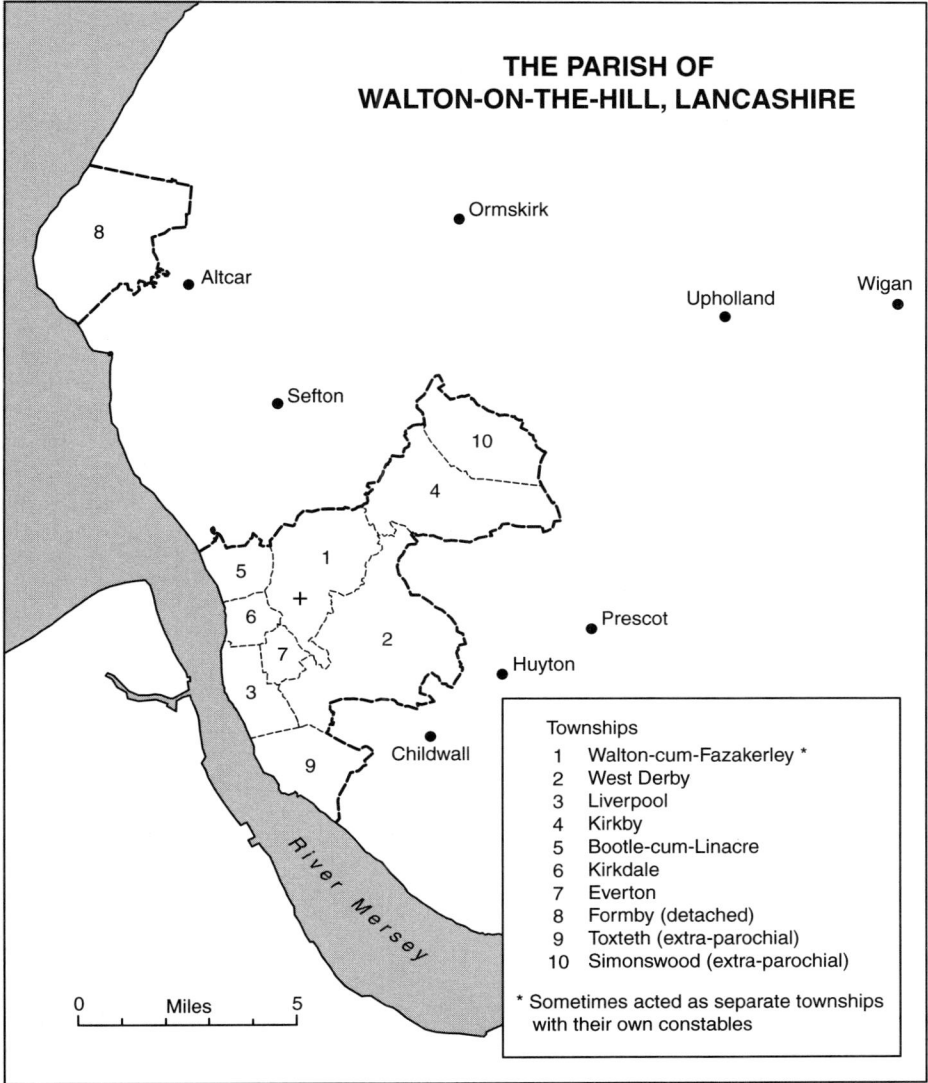

Ormskirk

8

Altcar

Upholland

Wigan

Sefton

10

4

1

5

+

6

2

Prescot

7

Huyton

3

Childwall

9

River Mersey

Townships

1	Walton-cum-Fazakerley *
2	West Derby
3	Liverpool
4	Kirkby
5	Bootle-cum-Linacre
6	Kirkdale
7	Everton
8	Formby (detached)
9	Toxteth (extra-parochial)
10	Simonswood (extra-parochial)

* Sometimes acted as separate townships
with their own constables

0   Miles   5

IN MEMORIAM

As this volume was going to press, we learned with great sadness of the death in April 2005 of Dr E.M.E. (Betty) Ramsay, after years of battling with amazing fortitude against ill-health and near-blindness. It was her groundwork in laboriously making the first transcription of these accounts which laid the foundations for the present publication.

THE CHURCHWARDENS' ACCOUNTS OF WALTON-ON-THE-HILL, LANCASHIRE, 1627–1667

Liverpool Record Office, 283 SMW 11/3

1627–1628

[f.1 is transcribed in its correct place after f.57]

[f.2r]

Accountes of Nicholas Goore Ch... / of Walton Anno domin...

[The dates of this and the following account are confirmed by internal evidence, e.g. burials in the parish register matching the ley stall payments, and the date of Whitsunday. All numerals from here to f.11r (top) are roman in the original except dates, unless stated in the notes.]

Received for one church ley from the parish	...
Received for another church ley for the parish	v...
Received for Jane Dawse widdow ley stall	2s ...
Received for Alice Rose her ley stall	2s ...
Receved in toto	£12 ...

Disbursementes

Spent in goeing to Ormeschurch Aprill 6th to m... / the dean rurall and hee came not upon the... / old churchwardens and new	2s
Aprill 26 spent upon the old churchwardens ... / new churchwardens	2s 4d
paid to the deane for his fees	8d
paid for writeing presentmentes to the dean... according to the booke of Articles	12d
spent on churchwardens and constables at / makeing the same presentmentes	...
paid for bread and wyne the 13th of Maye bein... / whitsondaye for a communion	13d
paid for writeing eight precepts for ...	...

[f.2v]

...	17s 4d
... quittance	2d
... bringing the same to Prescot	8d
... upon two rushbearing dayes to see who did / ... did not	6d
... in makeing t[h]e presentmentes to the high / ...tables for churchwardens and constables for / ... assysses the 18th of July	16d
... for writeing presentmentes to the high / ...nstables <for making prese> the July 20th	12d
...d for bread and wyne for a communion the 16th / ...aye of September	13d
...tem paid for tymber for the church style and / ...kemanshippe	3s
spent in makeing presentmentes to the deane / at severall tymes	12d

3

...ent in bringing presentmentes to the deane / ...irst to Liverpoole and then to Ormeschurch	8d
... to the deane for his fees	8d
...m paid to Henry Rychraft oweing by the / ...for the last yeare	14s 3d
... the workemen when they came to / ...e of the clocke	12d

[f.3r]

paide ...manshippe of ...	...
spent on them while they were doinge the worke	6...
paid to Christopher Shurliker for mending the / clocke and bellropes	13s 4d
paid for bread and wyne for acommunion the / First of January	13d
spent in bying the same	3d
Item paide for three yards of Serge for a / covering for the pulpit	15s
Item spent in goeing to Ormeschurch and Liverpoole / to buye the cloath	8d
paid for writeing for eight precepts for a / church ley	12d
paid to Master vicar for getting Sir Richard... / and Master Alexanders hand to the precepts[1]	4d
spent in delivering the precepts abroad	4d
paid the glazier for worke done at the church / for Fourteen Foote of new glasse at 6d[2] / the foote	7s
Item for Fyve foote of old glasse in new lead / at 3d a foote	15d
Item for two dayes labour in takeing downe ... / and setting up	2s
Item paid for tenne odde quarrell	10d

[f.3v]

... Butler for dressing leads	3d
...ent ...ttending the glazier at takeing down / and setting up	6d
paid for silke fring for the pulpit cloath	20s
...ent in bying in the same	6d
...t in bying silke to sowe it with	12d
Item spent on the taylors and others while hee / was setting it on	6d
... the latter tyme the windowes being broken / with the great wynd for foote of new glasse	2s
... for two foote of olde glasse	6d
... for his dayes labour	8d
...t on the glaziers and others while they / were doeing the glasse	6d
...aid to John Butler for dressing the / windowes with lyme and morter	6d
paid for writeing presentmentes to the high / constable agane the last assyses	12d

1 Sir Richard Molyneux, Patron, and Alexander Molyneux, Rector.
2 Arabic numeral.

...tem spent on the churchwardens and constables / in makeing the
    presentmentes   18d
Spent in bringing them to Prescot   8d
...de to Torner for getting stones and / ...ssing the church wall   8[?][3]

[Possibly part of 1627–28 is missing here. There are no totals and no audit.]

1628–1629

[f.4r]

Accountes of William Wainright... / of the parish of Walt...

Received for achurch ley of £6 the some of   ...
Received for a ley stall for George Wood...   2s 4...
debet Master William Chorley for a ley stall   2s ...
Item received from William Rose for a ley sta... / for his brother Robert   2s 4d
Received for the ley stall of Robert Fletcher   2s 4d
Received in all   £6 7s[4] <8d>

Dis ...[5]

[f.4v]

Disbursed

... the old and new churchwardens and >toth deane< / ...men and fees for
    their oaths   2s 4d
... the Article booke at the Bishops visitation   3s
...r the charges of the old and new churchwardens and / ...ne men going
    to Wigan to the visitation   2s
... for writeing   16d
...nt in delivering them at Wigan   12d
...m spent in charges for writeing presentmentes to / ... the high
    constables   20d
Item for writeing them   12d
Item for going to Prescot to deliver them   6d
For apparance fees and the syde men cyted to bee / at Wigan   4s 7d[6]
Item to Christopher Shirliker for the clocke / and the belles   13s 4d
For makeing presentmentes to the deane and for / deliverye   8d
For writeing   8d

---

3 Appears to be *d* changed to *s*.
4 Corrected from, or possibly to, *4s*. The pence have been scratched out, and the year-end calculation
   shows that this sum was treated as £6 7s 0d.
5 Practice writing or annotation in a different hand.
6 Arabic numerals; may be 2 rather than 7.

...or other appearance before the deane	12d
...tem for charges at making	8d
...tem for writeing	6d

[f.5r]

Item for writeing presentmentes to the head ...	...
Item for writeing eight precepts to the constab...	...
Item for bread and wyne for three communions	...
Item for charges to fetch them	6d
Item paid to the slater for the church	35s
For the mosse	5s 6d
Item spent in reckoning and accounting and looking u... / them and measuring	12d
spent for two dayes going to Liverpoole and Walton / for them	8d
Item to Thomas Banester for mending clock	2...
for bread and wyne for a communion	19d
Item for writeing pre<cepts>sentmentes[7] the second tyme	12d
Item for charges on <charges> churchwardens and / constables and sworne men	18d
Item paid to the glaser	13s <4d> 7d
Item for bell wheeles[8] and mending formes	14d
For the names of the communicantes	2s
For washing the surples and table cloath	2s [?7]d
Item for the maymed soldiours >and acquittance<	17s 6d
spent in going to paye it	6d
Item for lyme and mosse	3s
Item for leading from Liverpoole	12d

[f.5v]

...	2s 6d
... Fetching	2s
...t in going to bye and fetch them	6d
...r a yate and post	9s
...tem spent in going to buye it	4d
...for leading to Walton	20d
... Fill bowes and gudgeuns	18d
...m for labour to buye and fetche them	4d
...or hanging the yate	14d
...m for parchement to the register	6d
... for writeing the Register	12d
...t makeing and casting spent	4d

---

7 Corrected above the deleted matter in a different hand.
8 Or *wheells*.

Item for writeing the accountes	12d
For sending presentmentes to the Bishoppe	8d
<for> Summa totalis[9]	£7 11s 11d

Disbursed more then received <...> / 24s 11d

Aprill the 10th anno domini 1629 / Holmfrey Walley elected gardian / William Johnson Sworne man[10]

[f.6r]

[*The handwriting suggests that this was written at the same time as the election note on f.5v.*]

A Laye of Six pounds out of ... / parishe by equall proportions to be a... / and gathered at or before midsomer / next ensuing

Alexander Molineux
Thomas Molyneux
Nevill Kaye / vicar Walton
Hughe Rose
Robert Boulton
Nicholas Goore

[*f.6v is blank*]

1629–1630

[f.7r]

The accountes of Humfrey Walley / Churchwarden of Walton in anno / 1629

Receaved for a Church ley	6...
Receaved for foure ley stalles	9s 4d

Disbursed as followeth

Inprimis for wrytinge presentmtes to the deane / made accordinge to the booke of articles	12d
Spent then on the new and old Churchwardens	16d
Spent at Prescott on both Churchwardens / and swornemen and for their oathes	3s 6d
Paid for sendinge presentmtes to Holland[11]	6d
Paid for bread and wyne for a Comunion	17d

---

9 Different hand, arabic numerals.
10 Added in a different hand.
11 i.e. Upholland.

Paid to Christofer Shurliker for mendinge formes	18...
Paid for bread and wyne for a communion in July	17d
Paid for wrytinge presentmtes to the high Cunstable	12d
Charges spent on Churchwardens and / Cunstables at that tyme	12d
Spent in deliveringe them to the high Cunstable	7d
Spent in makinge presentmentes to the Inquisicion	12...
Paid for wrytinge those presentmtes	4...
Charges of the vicar Churchwardens and / Cunstables at Wigan	4s
Paid for wrytinge eight preceptes	x...

[f.7v]

... gettinge my lords hand and others to the preceptes	6d
...d for bread and wyne for a Communion	17d
... paid to the old Churchwarden which was / due upon his accountes	27s
Spent in makinge presentmtes to the / deane the second tyme	12d
Paid for wrytinge the same	12d
Charg[e]s at Prescott in meetinge the deane / and for sendinge	
presentmentes to Holland	2s
Paid to Shurliker for Clocke and bells	13s 4d
Paid to the maymed souldiers	17s 4d
Paid for an acquittance	2d
Spent in payinge the same at Prescott	6d
Paid for wyre and oyle	9d
Charg[e]s in makinge presentmtes to the high / Cunstable the second	
tyme	12d
Paid for wrytinge the same	12d
Spent on Churchwardens and Cunstables / in deliveringe the same	12d
Paid for bread and wyne for a Communion	17d
Paid to the glasiour	7s 5d
Spent on him at measuringe	4d
Spent on two smithes at three tymes / cominge about the clocke	12d
Paid to the smith for the watch parte	15s
Paid to the painter for worke	8s

[f.8r]

Paid for fetchinge and bringinge the board	7...
and spent on him	4...
Paid to the joyner for the board	4...
Paid for wrytinge the comunicantes names	2...
Paid for washinge surplesse and table / clothes all the yeare	2s 8d
Paid to Edward Strange for worke	18...
Paid to Shurliker for mendinge the / churchwall and formes	12d
Paid for wrytinge the Register	12d
Paid for parchment	6d

Spent at the Castinge of the / Churchwardens accountes	6d
Paid for wrytinge them by partes all the yeare	12d
Paid for wrytinge them into the booke	12d
paid for Altering the Surplesse	12d
The whole receipt is	£6 9s 4d
The disbursementes are	£7 20d <...>
Disbursed more then receaved	12s 4d

Receiptes £6 9s 4d paid £7 20d: d[isbursed][12] more then receipt 12s 4d[13]

1630–1631

[f.8v]

[*The ley stalls named on this folio relate to burials in June to October 1630, and it appears that the following reconciliation statement for Thomas Hey's year of duty 1630–31 was written in on a blank page before the expenditure accounts. The page is much corrected by a second hand using arabic numerals. At 'Sum receipt', the shillings have been corrected following the deletion in line 1, but the old figure in pence has accidentally been left. The line 'is in toto' is also added in this hand.*]

Received by Thomas Hey	£6[14] <6s 8d>
Item for three ley stalles of John Rose / Mistress Boore and Robert Bouton	7s
Sum receipt	£6 <...> 7s 8d
the Constable of Fazakerley oweth / for the Church ley	3s 4d
Disburst in all	£8 4s 9d
...isburst more then received	<...>
is in toto	<...> 37s 9d

[f.9r]

The accountes of Thomas Heye / Churchwarden of Walton / in Anno 1630

Imprimis in three pyntes of wyne for acommunion	12...
Item in bread	1d
Item spent in meeting my lord at the Church	8d
Item spent for sixe men and six horses in going to my lord / Bishops visitation[15]	6s
Item for their oathes and articles bookes	5s

12 Actual abbreviation unclear, perhaps *dus.*
13 Added at foot of page in note form, different hand, arabic numerals.
14 Possibly corrected from *iv* to *vi.*
15 Entry followed by pen-testing doodles.

Item to Master Kaye for writeing presentmentes to the deane / at our first comming in	18d
Item payd to the deane for putting to his hand	13d
Item for the precepts	12d
Item spent in getting Master Alexanderes >hand< to the presentmentes	4...
Item for two quartes of wyne and one bread for the / Communion	13d
Item spent upon the bayliffes at the receiving of the / Church leye for Liverpoole	4d
Item spent at the making of the presentmentes	12d
Item for writeing the presentmentes	12d
Item payd to the maymed souldiers	17s 4d
Item for an acquittance	2d
Item spent at the paying of the monye to the high / Constable	6d
28s 1d[16]	

[f.9v]

...pent at the receiving <for> of the Church leye for / ...bye	6d
...m spent at the parting of the old Church wardens / when they had made their presentmentes	1s 6d
...tem for oyle to the clocke	1d
Item for nayles to the Clocke	1d
Item payd by John Robinson Sodman at Chester / to him that received the presentmentes for the / Archbishops visitation	2s 6d
Item for his charges	3s 4d
Item spent upon the Constables, and other honest men of / the severall towne ships at three severall meetinges / about recusantes	3s 10d
Item payd to Christopher Shirliker for the clocke / belles and bell ropes	13s 4d
Item spent by Master Kaye and the sydeman themselves / and their horses at Preston	5s
Item spent by Master Kaye and the sidman at Wigan / staying out two nights they and <h> their horses	8s
Item payd to Master Kaye for getting the presentmentes / written at Wigan to the Commissioners	18d
...tem payd to the visitors at Chester to spayer <the for> the / appearance >of the churchwarden<	2s 6d
...tem spent by Master Kaye and sidman going to / Chester to returne the correction and order bookes / ...e <6s 9s>	[blank]

[f.10r]

Item in Coardes for the Clocke	1...
Item to Robert Gorsuch for mending the Church	...

---

16 Added in a different hand in mixed roman and arabic numerals; not a total of the items on this page.

Item for >bread and< wyne <and bread> for acommunion 13d
Item for the ringers upon the kinges holydaye 12d
Item for washing the surples 12d
Item for nayles 8d
Item for boardes for frames 20d
Item to Edward Strange for his workemanshipp... / and iron 10s
Item to Boates for seaven dayes worke his man / and himselfe 15s
Item spent upon the workeman[17] 16d
Item for the Churchwardens labour and expences 4s
Item in bread and wyne for acommunion 18d
Item payd for the Communion table cloath 10s
Item payd to the deane at my appearance <and> at / Holland 8d
Item for my charges 6d
Item spent upon the constables and swornemen at the / makeing of the
  presentmentes >and foure neighbours< 2s
Item payd for wrieing the presentmentes <2s ...> 18d

[f.10v]

... payd to Shurliker for mending the formes and / ...e to the clocke 4d
...tem spent at the meeting of the high Constables at / the daye
  appointed 4d
Item payd to Izabell Pilkinton for washing the / Surples and communion
  Cloath 20d
Item payd to Edward Strang for making the / third bell Clapper 5s
Item payd to the old Churchwarden for what / hee had formerly layd out
  of his owne monye / the last yeare 12s 4d
Item spent at the same tyme 4d
Item payd to the old Schoolemaister[18] for writeing / the names of the
  communicantes 2s
Item for parchement 4d
Item to Christopher Shurliker for makeing / a payre of pulleyes 4d
Item for writeing the accountes 18d
Item for the Churchwardens expences with / others 8d
Item for the repaire of the church wall 18s

[f.11r]

[*This page comprises the end of 1630–31 plus an out-of-sequence entry from
the end of 1631–32 apparently written here in error or to use up a blank half
page. All numerals from the memorandum until f.13r inclusive are arabic in the
original.*]

---

17 Or *workemen*.
18 Annotated by an X-shaped mark within, but larger than, the text and probably added later by
   someone interested in references to the school. See the notes on annotations, p. 176.

Item for writeing the presentmentes to the high cons... / at the last Assyzes　　18d
Item spent in deliverye　　2d
Item for writing the presentemente to the high[19]

Memorandum that the 18th daye of aprill / the accompts of Lawrence Bridge gardian anno 1631 / were befor my Lord Molineux Master Moore Master Fazakerly / Master Dwarihouse Robert Mercer Robert Worral Nich... / Goore Master Kaye viccar and divers others of the / parish read and a laye £12 allowed for the future / expences of >the< next yeare and payment of such due / as were owing to the late gardian which lay / by equall portions is to be gathered at the feast / of pentecost next and the first >day< of august next by / <...> the ordinary courses of the custome / of the parishe and paid to Robert Boulton of / Clubmore gardian elect for this yeare 1632 to who... / Roger Richardson is elect Sidman [?et] Jur[atus] Ita testor / Nevill Ka... / vicarius W...

1631–1632

[f.11v]

1631
Memorandum that I Lawrence Bridge / did disburse money for the Bread / which was delt to the poore for / Thomas Berries Dowlle[20] uppon / Soonday the first of May

Received of the Churchwarden / of Formby >13s 4d and<	13s 4d
Received of the Balive of / Liverpoolle >26s 8d and 26s 8d and<	26s 8d
received of the Cunstables of / Everton >3s 4d and 3s 4d and<	3s 4d
received of the Cunstables / of Bootle	<...>s
received of the Cunstable of / Fazakerley >5s 2d<	6s 8d
Hugh Rosse is to pay	7d
received of the Cunstables / of Kirkdalle >5s 5s and<	5s
received of the Cunstable of Walton	6s 8d
received of the Cunstable of Darby	4[?9]s
received of the Churchwarden / of Kirkby >13s 4d and 13s 4d and<	13s 4d

[f.12r]

1631
The accoumptes of Lawrence Brid...

Inprimis 8 preceptes for 2 Church / leyes	12d
Item spent in procuringe my / Lord Molyneux his hand to / them Master Leighs and >Master< Mores[21]	6d

---

19　Incomplete entry in a different hand.
20　See Introduction, p. xxvii for Thomas Berry's charity.
21　New Rector Thomas Le(i)gh, and John Moore of Bank Hall.

Item spent in sendinge them / abrode into the Parrishe	4d
Item spent uppon the Sydeman / and my selfe and my horsse att /	
Ormskirke the 19 of May / beinge Cyted before the Dean	14d
Item payd to the Dean	8d
Item payd for Bread and Wyne / for a Communion uppon /	
Whittsoonday	2s 7d
Item payd to the high Cunstable / for the maymed Souldiers	17s 4d
Item for an acquittance	2d
Item spent in bringinge it to prescott	...

24s 3d

[f.12v]

Item payd for 2 tunnes of / lymestones	4s 8d
Item for leadinge them beinge / foure lodes	4s
Item spent att buyinge and fetchinge them	4d
Item for 2 loades and a halfe / of Colles	5s 5d
Item for more <...> Colles 4 bushells	8d
Item for stones and leadinge / 3 loades for the lyme kilne	12d
Item for woodd for the same	8d
Item for buildinge the kilne breakinge / the lymestones and burninge	
them	2s 6d
Item spent uppon the workmen and my / selfe whyle they were in	
burninge	6d
Item spent att my Lord Bushops / visitation the 16th of June uppon /	
the ould Churchwardens and new	6s 3d
Item payd for the book of artickles	3s 6d
Item payd for drawinge the lyme Carying / it into the Church >caryinge	
water< and slekkinge it	12d
Item payd to Chrstopher Shorlikers / for keepinge the Bell Ropes in	
repayre	6s 8d

37s 2d

[f.13r]

Item for 5 bushells of hayre	...
Item for fetchinge it att Liverpoolle	...
Item for layinge the lyme in steepe	[*blank*]
Item spent uppon Master Vykar the Clark / and my selfe att the	
Rushbearinge to / fynde out who brought and who not	3d
Item payd to Master Kay for wrytinge / presentmentes accordinge to	
the book / of artickles to my Lord Busshop his / visitation <uppon the	
ould Churchwardens / and new>	16d
Item spent att that tyme / uppon the ould Churchwardens / and new	2s 2d
Item payd to Edward Strange for / a springe for the Clock	6d

Item payde[22]

[*The second half of f.11r, above, should be read here.*]

1632–1633

[f.13v]

[*All numerals except dates from here to f.73v inclusive are roman in the original unless stated.*]

Accountes of Robert Boulton Churchwarden 1632

Paid for writeing eight precepts for a church ley	12d
...pent in delivering forth the same	4d
paid to the deane at Upholland for his fees	16d
paid to the apparitor the same tyme	4d
Spent upon the old and new churchwardens and sydemen in / <makeing> going to Upholland and upon their horses in all	5s 6d
Spent at two severall tymes on the old and new churchwardens / and sydmen in making presentmentes to the deane according / to the booke of Articles	2s 8d
paid for writeing the same	12d
paide for repaireing the church style	8d
paide for bread and wyne for a communion on trinitye / sundaye	2s 1d
spent at two severall tymes in taking notice who brought / rushes upon the sydeman and my selfe	12d
paid to the maymed souldiers	17s 4d
paide for an acquittance	2d
Spent in bringing the same to Childwall to the high / Constable	4d
Spent in making presentmentes to the high Constable / on the church warden sydeman and all the Constables	2s 8d
paide for writeing the same presentmentes	12d
Spent in going to Ormeskirke to the quarter sessions on both / ...ld and new churchwardens, and their horses being there two Dayes / ...cerning the bastard	6s

[f.14r]

Spent on the churchwarden and sydeman in going to Childwall ... / high Constable concerning presentmentes	12...
paide to Christopher Shurliker for setting the clocke and / repaireing the bell roapes	13s 4d
paide for oyle to the clocke	1d

---

22 Incomplete entry in a different hand.

Spent in rydeing to the Burgh thence to Chorley and from / thence to the streetyate two dayes to fetch the old reference / of the judge of Assyzes	6s
Spent in going to the Assyzes and staying there till frydaye	6s 8d
paide for an horse that journey	5s
Charges of the horse that tyme	3s
paide to a counseller[23]	10s
paide to the bastardes nurse	40s
paide to Lawrence Bridge old churchwarden according / to my lords and the rest of the parish their direction	£5
paide for breade and wyne for a communion	21d
Spent in meeting two severall tymes, and making presentmentes / to the deane according to the booke of articles	2s
paide for writeing the same	1s
paide to a messenger to bring the same to Holland	6d
Spent in going to meete the deane at Wigan	12d
paide to the deane the same tyme	3s 4d
paide for bread and wyne for a communion	21d
paide for an hacke halme	3d
paide to the glazier for mending the glass windowes in / three whole paines and other broken places	6s
spent in one daye in taking broken glasses downe upon / the glazier and my selfe	8d
spent another tyme in setting them up	7...

[f.14v]

...t in meeting the deane at Childwall	12d
...yde to the deane the same tyme	22d
...aide for breade and wyne for acommunion	21d
spent in making presentmentes to the deane	12d
paide for writeing the same	6d
payde for washing the Surplesse twice	12d
paide to Christopher Shurliker for repayreing the / clocke with wyre and oyle and his labour	12d
paide to the glazier for this last great wynde for / repaireing the glasse windowes	7s
spent in takeing them downe and setting them up	12d
paide for dressing the leades on either syde the church	6d
payde for a plancke for the church doore	14d
payde for bringing from Liverpoole	2d
paide for nayles to repaire it with bandes and other / thinges	6d
spent in makeing presentmentes for the last assyzes upon / the churchwarden and sydeman and all the constables	3s

23 For legal help, perhaps in the suit concerning the bastard.

paide for writeing the same	12d
paide to Christopher Shurliker for mending the / church doore	12d
paide for mending the Communion cuppe	18d
paide to Lawrence Bridge for going to Master Bridgeman / twice, and staying one night hee being not at home / concerning the letter hee sent	3s
...aide to John Shurliker for writeing the names of / ...he communicantes	2s

[f.15r]

paide for the register being written in parchement	*x*...
payde for writeing myne accountes	12d

Disbursed by me Robert Boulton Churchwarden	£14
Received for two church leyes	£12
Disbursed more then received	33s
Received more for three ley stalles	7s
Received more for three ley stalles[24]	7s

Seen and allowed by us
Nevill Kaye Vicar of Walton
Thomas Legh   Alexander Molineux[25]
John Moore

[*f.15v is blank*]

[f.16r]

[*Days of the month from here and in the ensuing account are usually in roman numerals but sometimes in arabic.*]

April 26th 1633

By my lord Molineux Master Moore and Master / Legh Richard Johnson of Everton is / Elected Churchwarden of Walton / parishe and William Aspinwall Sideman / and a ley of £6 graunted to bee paid before / the 20th of may next according to / the usuall praportions in the parishe / to paye the ould Churchwarden to be / in the gardians hands for the parishe / use and other Layes to be by them / granted forth as the parishe occasions / shall require

Richarde Molyneux
John Moore
Thomas Legh

[*The first few letters of the second and third names have been copied alongside these signatures, as doodles or practice writing.*]

---

24 Added or copied in a different hand and not included in the calculation.
25 Not the former Rector, who had died in 1630–31. See also f.112v.

1633–1634

[f.16v]

The accountes of Richard Johnson of / Everton churchwarden for this year of /
our lord 1633

Receipts as Followeth

Imprimis of the bayliffes of Liverpoole	£8
Item of Robert Boulton for Darbye	£11 17s 10d
Item from the Churchwardens of Kirkeby	£4
Item from the churchwardens of Formeby	£4
Item from the Constables of Walton cum Fazakerley	£3 19s 5d
Item from the Constable of Kirkedall	30s
Item from the Constables of Linaker cum Bootle	30s
Item from the Constables of Everton	20s

Received for two measures of haire from Master Walley	6d
Item for three leystales Nicholas Bootle Thomas / Anderton and Anne Rose	7s
Item for <xx> twentye and fyve poundes of old iron	3s 1d

Summum totallis[26] £36 7s 10d

debtes oweing to the church

<...> Imprimis Mistress Moore for old Hugh Rose ground	7d
<...> Item Hugh Rydeing of the Ackers end for two leyes	15d
<...> Item for Richard Dawse	10d
<Item more oweing by William smyth>	<...>
Item Henrey Carter for a ley stalle	2s <...>d

Summum 5s <...>

[f.17r]

The disbursementes of Richard Johnson of / Everton Churchwarden of Walton for
this / yeare of our lord 1633 as followeth

*[Dots and small arabic numerals inserted on the right hand side during adding up
have not been transcribed but the totals added at the foot of most pages (mainly in
arabic numerals) have.]*

Imprimis for wryteing eight precepts	12d
Item spent in getting my lordes hand and Master Moores / hand to the preceptes	6d
Item spent in getting the preceptes delivered	3d
Item payd for the booke of Cannons the 25th daye / of Maye	16d

---

26 Scribe's dog-Latin version of *Summa totalis*, also on folios 27r, 28v, 35v, 42r, 46r, sometimes
contracted and possibly intended as *Summus*.

Item spent upon John Chantrell hee being at / Walton to take measure of a seate for the wardens / and a doore for the pulpit my selfe and some others	4d
Item payde to Edward Nicholson the 5th of June / for a bell roape	2s 9d
Item the sixte of June for three boardes and nayles / and for carrying them to Walton to mend the / belle house	3s 5d
Item spent in bying those thinges at Liverpoole / at two severall tymes	6d
Item payd to Shurliker and Layland for setting the / partition betweene the church and the bell house / the seaventh of June	2s
Item to Laylandes wife for carrying rubbish out / of the church the same daye	3d
Item my charge the same daye	8d
Item payd to Robert Boulton old churchwarden / that hee had layde downe	xx...

$$2 - 6 - 0$$

[f.17v]

... payde for a locke and keye and staple for the / ...ellhouse doore the 8th of June	14d
Item the 15th for bread and wyne for acomunion	1s 7d
Item for three lockes and keyes for the chest / and nayles	1s 9d
Item the 18th of June for eight preceptes for / a second leye	12d
Item the 19th of June for two tunne of lyme stones / to Edward Nicholson and for leading	<9s> 9s[27]
Item to Edward Strange for a new band to the / chest and makeing the other lyke unto it and / [?men]ding the church spade	1s 6d
Item payde to the nurse for the bastard	12s 6d
Item for coales to burne the lymestones	5s 7d
Item for <...ing> a petition about the bastard / to goe to the quarter sessions	12d
Item spent upon Lawrence Bridge and my selfe / and our horses at the quarter sessions being forth / three dayes, and for an order and warrand of the / quarter sessions and a coppye of the order	16s 8d
Item for wood and turfe to kindle the lyme kilne	10d
Item to Plombes mayde for carrying the coales into / Plombes stable	2d
Item to Master Ogles man for bringing the / Statute booke from Lathom[28]	4d
Item to John Formeby for breaking and burneing / the lyne stone	2s 6d
Item <to> for carrying the coales from Plombes / ... the lyme kilne	4d

$$2 - 15 - 2$$

---

27 *viiii* corrected to *ix*.
28 Seat of the Earl of Derby.

[f.18r]

Item payde to the joyner for the wardens seate and / fetcheing from Tarbocke and nayles	19s 9d
Item to John Wigan for worke done at the church	8...
Item spent the same daye upon the workemen my / fellow sydeman and my selfe	9d
Item to John Formeby for draweing of the / lyme kilne and wattering	10d
Item <for> to two women for carrying the lyme into / the church and water to watter it	12d
Item spent upon the old churchwarden and / sydeman constables and our selves in makeing / presentmentes for the Assyzes	2s
Item for wryteing the presentmentes faire over	12d
Item spent upon Robert Gorsuch sifteing lyme / and steeping it	2d
Item to two women for carrying in water	6d
Item for seaven measures of hayre and carrying / it to the church	2s
Item spent upon the bayliffes of Liverpoole in / receiving of the monye at twice	8d
Item spent at receiving Darby mony twice	4d
Item Formeby monye at twice	4d
Item Kirkeby monye at twice	6d
Item Kirkdall	2d
Item spent at Prescot meeting the head / constable upon old churchwarden constables / and my selfe with our horses	2s

1 – 12 – 8

[f.18v]

... spent >at< twice in going to Master Ireland and / Master Bridgeman about the bastard	1s 6d
...tem spent at the rushe bearing in seeing / who brought who made default	6d
Item my charges in being at the church to / see the lyme kilne layde, and three lockes / set upon the chest the 23th of July / and the 30th seeing the lyme carryed into / the church and watered	1s 4d
Item payde to John Butler for carrying the / rubbish and burying the bones that laye all / in the church	4d
Item payde to Robert Gorsuch for five dayes / for himselfe and a boye, and Foure dayes for / Edward Turner Edward Ryce and a boye	19s
Item payde for sixe measures of haire and one / to carrye it from Liverpoole to the church	20d
Item payde to the head Constable for the / maymed souldiers and an acquittance	17s 6d
Item spent at Prescot for my charges in / bringing it thither	8d
Item to Robert Gorsuch and his men for five / dayes more payd	21s 8d

3 – 4 – 2

[f.19r]

Item spent upon the workemen whyle they were / doeing the worke and for nayles	2s
Item given to Thomas Johnsons wife for dressing / the pillars and windowes	4d
Item my charges in attending them nyne / dayes	6s
Item for dressing the leades of the church	4d
Item spent upon the old churchwarden and / sydeman and our selves making presentmentes / to Yorke[29]	16d
Item for wryteing the same presentmentes	12d
Item spent at Wiggan at the visitation, of the / old churchwarden and sydeman and our / selves and the booke of Articles and assigneing / our presentmentes being forth all / night	14s 10d
Item for a bell roape for the second bell / and a board for the North doore	3s
Item for carrying them to the church	2d
Item to John Corker for mending the Church / leades and soder and Thomas Johnson for heating his / irons	3s
$1-12-4$	

[f.19v]

... spent upon John Corker and Thomas Johnson / the same daye	4d
Item for bread and wyne for a communion	2s 1d
Item the fifte daye of October for a comunion / table the clearkes seate, and fetching / them from Tarbocke	29s 4d
Item payd to John Wiggan the same daye / for stone worke	8d
Item payd to John Layland for mending / the church doore	4d
Item spent upon the workemen the same / daye	6d
Item to Edward Strange for hookes and staples / for Master Kayes the clearkes and churchwardens / seates	6d
Item payd to the vicar for the order of the / defectes in the churche that are to bee done	3s 3d
Item to Edward Turner for setting the clearkes / seat lower and Johnsons wife for carrying / sand	10d
$1-17-11$	

[f.20r]

Item to Layland and Shurliker for setting [?up] / the partition betweene the church and the / Chancell	4s
Item to a boye for going to the Smithye to get / bandes and nayles made	3d

---

29 Refers to the 1633 visitation of Archbishop Neile of York, see Introduction, p. xxi.

Item spent upon the workemen and masons / whyle the were about the part[i]tion and / joyner cutting the communion table / feete	14d
Item payde to Hughe Gibbons for goeing to / the joyner and painter	6d
Item my charges three dayes being with / the workemen	2s
Item payd Edward Strange for bandes / for the Chancell doore	15d
Item to Edward Turners man for filling / under the partition	15d
Item for candles being Saturdaye at night / to finish their worke	2d

0 – 10 – 7

[f.20v]

... spent upon the parishioners masons joyners / ... paynter meeting to agree about their <worke> / worke	3s 6d
Item payd to the mason joyner and paynter in / earnest severally for their worke	12d
Item spent at Liverpoole being there to / get leave to get stone for the church	6d
Item for the ringers to the church upon / the kinges holy daye	2s
Item payd more for wryteing eight preceptes	12d
Item spent in getting them assyngd and / delivered	12d
Item for bread and wyne for a communion / the 24th of November	21d
Item payd the 25th to the visitors at / Warrington	5s
Item the same tyme our charges being / out two nightes churchwardens and <syd...> / sydemen	8s 6d
Item spent upon the constable of Kirkedall at / receipt of the new leye	2d

1 – 4 – 5

[f.21r]

Item payde for cloath for makeing a surplesse / for the clearke threede and washing	15s 3d
Item my charge at Chester to buye a booke of / Common prayer and the cloathe	2s 8d
Item spent upon the bayliffes of Liverpoole / at the receipt of their new leye	6d
Item for a bosse for Master Kaye to kneele / upon	4d
Item payde at Childwall the 17th of / December for the kinges booke directions / to the vicar[30] and our charges with our / horses	2s 6d
Item spent at the receipt of Darbye / monye	4d
Item payd to Master Deanes sonne for a coppye / of the order of thinges to be done in the churche	6d
Item payde to Christopher Shurliker for makeing / the church yarde wall and mending the / north doore	2s 6d

1 – 4 <– 7   1 – 4 – 7>   1 – 4 – 7

---

30 James I's *The Book of Sports and Pastimes*, reissued in 1633.

[f.21v]

...tem spent upon the churchwarden of Kirkeby / ... Darbye and myself at receiving of the halfe ley / of Kirkeby meeting upon buisines at Walton / the first of Januarye	4d
Item spent at the receipt of the leye for / Fazakerley upon the constable	2d
Item payde to Thomas Johnsons wife for washing / the Church windowes	6d
Item payd to John Syre for tymber towardes / the making of the church Style	8s
Item payde to John Boates for going with mee / to choose tymber, and to see the rest of the tymber / for the same Style	12d
Item spent the same daye upon James / Boates the sydeman and Corker hee taking / downe the broken glasses at the church and / my selfe	18d
Item for cutting and leadeing the same <...> / tymber	8d
Item spent upon the joyner my selfe and / foure men to remove the great stone the / pulpit stoode upon	8d
Item payd to Corker for two and twentye foote / of new glasse and seaven foote of old glasse / and Fyve and twentye quarrells	14s 6d

$$1 - 7 - 4$$

[f.22r]

Item spent upon him	<6d> 3d
Item my charges the same daye being there to see / it set up and measured	8d
Item spent at the receipt of Lynaker and Bootle / whole ley	2d
Item payd to Thomas Meadow for foure spokes to / make pinns for the church Style	3d
Item payde to Thomas Johnsons wife and two / daughters for carrying rubbish forth of the church / and stones to the church style, and earth out of / the chancell to the bottome of the church	9d
Item payd to Robert Gorsuch for carrying the / tymber from John Syres to the church	12d
Item payd to Edward Strange for makeing a band / for the north church doore, and a bolte for the / second bell	10d
Item payde to James Boates for makeing the / church style his men and himselfe being seaven / dayes	26s 2d
Item spent [?up]on them whyle they were doing / the same worke	14d
Item my charges whyle they were doing that / worke	4s 8d
Item more spent upon them and two joyners beeing / there to agree for the cover of the pulpit	6d
Item payd to the joyners in earnest	4d

$$1 - 6 - 9$$

[f.22v]
[*Most of the page after the two entries is blank, with the total inserted at the foot.*]

...tem payde to Christopher Shurliker	4s
Item for an hundred of Slate and leading to / the Church	3s 6d

7 – 6

[*f.23r is blank. It is not clear why this and the previous page were not fully used, nor whether folios have become out of sequence, but checking the addition of totals indicates that they do belong with 1633–34.*]

[f.23v]

... for six yardes of stone for the style and / leading from the quarrye	2s 6d
Item for three bushells of lyme and fetcheing it / from Liverpoole	18d
Item spent at the receipt of Kirkeby Leye	2d
Item payd to Christopher Shurliker for setting / a band on the north church doore and boardes that / were loose, and a plate for the yate	2d
Item payd to Edward Turner for worke at the / church Style and walle his men and him selfe / five dayes	10s 7d
Item spent upon them whyle they were doing / that worke	10d
Item payd to Thomas Johnson and his wife a daye / and an halfe for carrying stones to the / style	16d
Item charges for attending 4[31] dayes / >and the syde man one<	3s 4d
Item payd for removing earth where they / set the wall on both sydes	3d
Item payd to Edward Strange for nayles and a / plate for the yate	<3d> 5d
Item payd to Robert Gorsuch for mending / the church where it was blowne out	12d
Item payd for lyme to mend it withall	4d
Item spent when I payd the workemen	6d

1 – 2 – <9> 11

[f.24r]

Item payde to Christopher Shurliker for mending / seates in the church when wee removed the / pulpit	6d
Item payd to Edward Turner the same daye in / setting up the pulpit and other worke	12d
Item spent the same tyme at removing of it <the> / upon the workemen, sydeman and others	9d
Item payd to Edward Turner in earnest to make / another new style	4d
Item the 15th daye of Februarye for bread and / wyne for a communion	2s 1d
Item payde to Landesdale and Wiggan the same / daye in part for flagging	12s

31 Arabic numeral.

Item for fetching the cover of the pulpit / from Halewoode	2s 4d
Item for bandes and nayles for the pulpit doore	7...
Item for double single and stone nayles	6d
Item spent at the receipt of Walton ley	2d
Item to Edward Turner for laying stones for Master / Kayes and the clearkes seate and steps to the / pulpit for two dayes	2s
Item spent upon them whyle they were doing / that worke	4d
Item payde to the joyner for the pulpit cover	22s

2 – 3 – 7

[f.24v]

... payd to John Wiggan for Flagges and leading / that are in the wall by Shurlikers	2s 2d
Item payde to him <for> in part for flagging	7s
Item payde to the joyners for cutting the vicars / seat and setting it up, and making stayres for / the pulpit	2s <...d>
Item spent on them whyle they were doing that / worke, and setting up the cover for the / pulpit	8d
Item to Thomas Johnsons wife and his daughter for / carrying stones to the churchyard wall	3d
Item my charges three dayes there with the / masons and joyners	2s
Item spent at the receipt of Liverpoole / monye the 19th daye of Februarye	4d
Item to Edward Strange for the rod hoope / gudgeon and staple to hang the cover of /the pulpit	3s
Item payd Thomas Johnsons for carrying rubbish / out of the church when the vicar and clearkes / seates were removed	3d
Item spent in going to Tarbocke to looke / for the seates and church doore	6d
Item payd for carriage of them	8s <6d>
Item spent when they were brought to the church / on Hugh Gibbons Shurliker and others	6d

1 – 7 – 8

[f.25r]

Item spent at the receipt of Darby monye	...
Item the first of March for nayles	10d
Item for bandes and nayles for the vicars seate	6d
Item for wryteing presentmentes to the head constable / to the Assyzes	12d
Item spent the same daye in meeting about the / presentmentes upon the constables	16d
Item payde Henry Tyrer for the seates and / church doore	£6 10s <d>
Item for three hundred of spike nailes for the / seates	2s

Item payde for chalke for the paynter to wash / with	15d
Item for whyte patches carring them and the / chalke to the church	8d
Item spent at \<by\> buieing these thinges	4d
Item to Edward Turner for cutting the wall to take out / old gudgeons and laye new in	2s
Item spent upon the joyner and Edward Turner / whyle they were doing this worke	18d
Item to Edward Strange for bandes and gudgeons and / nayles for the new church doore	12s
Item to two boyes for carrying them from the / smithye to the church	4d

\<6 – 14 – 1\> 7 – 14 – 1

[f.25v]

... to Thomas Johnsons wife for carrying the / rubbish that was cut out of the church wall / when hee layde in the gudgeons	2d
Item for seaven poundes of leade to laye the / gudgeons in the wall \>and carrying to church\<	16d
Item to a boye for going to Liverpoole for more / nayles	2d
Item my charges when \>the\< joyner and mason set / up the seates and church doore five dayes	3s 4d
Item the twelveth of March for a dyall for / the churchyard	18d
Item my charges at Chester to have bought a / booke of common prayer when I bought the / dyall	2s
Item given to the joyners man for barrage	4d
Item spent at Prescot in meeting the / head constable with presentmentes to the / assyzes	8d
Item payd for parchement and wryteing the / register	16d
Item spent the 19th daye of March upon / the paynters and masons	6d
Item payd the same daye to Wigan	2s
Item payde to the paynter in parte	20s
Item to Landesdall and his man	7s 6d

2 – 0 – 10

[f.26r]

Item payd to Landesdale the 28th of March	2...
Item payde to Wiggan	4s
Item spent upon them and the paynter the same daye	6d
Item to Landesdale and Wiggan the 29th of March	12d
Item the last of March to Landesdale	2s 8d
Item to Corker the first of Aprill for two foote of / glasse	12d
Item the third of Aprill for a measure of stone lyme / and fetcheing it from Liverpoole	10d
Item to Edward Turner in parte for the / new style	29s
Item to the paynter the same daye	10s

Item more the same daye to Landesdall and / Wigan	18s
Item spent upon the workemen the same daye	4d
Item payd to Landesdale and Wigan upon / Easter Eve	22s
Item to Shurliker for writeing the names / of the communicantes	2s
Item for a dyall post	2s
Item to Edward Turner in full payment for / the new Style towardes the towne	14s 4d[32]
Item payd to the paynters sonne for whyteing / the church that was not in our agreement	*xi...*

$$5 - 10 - ... <4 - 16 - 4>$$

[f.26v]

...tem payde to the <payde> painter in full satisfaction / for his worke	20s
Item given the paynters two sonnes for barrage	12d
Item spent upon the workmen the 10th of / Aprill to see them set up the new Style	4d
Item the sydemans and charges and myne owne / the same daye	8d
Item payde to Christopher Shurrliker for / making the church wall towardes the / towne	2s
Item payde for writeinge these accountes	2s 6d
Item payde to Landesdale	6s 6d
Item payde for washing the Surplesses and / table cloath	2s
Item payde to Landesdale and Wigan for / flagging	16s 10d
Item to Thomas Plombe for claye	3d
Item to his wife for a potte the painter / brake	4d
Item spent upon the workemen that / daye	4d
Item payd to John Corker for soddering / the communion cuppe	6d

[f.27r]

Item payde to Christopher Shurliker for setting / the postes for the little gate towardes the / towne, and hanging the yate, and setting the / dyall poste	6d
Item payd to Thomas Johnsons wife for carrieing / claye to set the dyall post in	1d
Item spent the same daye	6d

Summum totallis of disbursementes / £12 4s 3d

More payde then received / £5 16s 5d

Received of Richard Dowse	10d
From Hughe Rydeing of the / Aickers end in parte	8d

more payde then received £5 14s 11d

32 Pence given as arabic 4.

[f.27v]

april the 25th anno Domini 1634

itt is concluded and ordered a laye of Eighteene / pounds by equal portions to be layed and collected / for the Churche use repaire and adorning / according to the Custome of the parishe / and paid to Nicholas Cooper at or <the> / before the feast day of Pentecost / next and that therby the orders given / out by the deputed Commissioners in the / Metropoliticall visitation of >the< Lord / ArchBishopp of Yorke may be observed / and performed

Thomas Legh
Robert Fazakerley

1634–1635

[f.28r]

The accountes of Nicholas Cowper of / Kirkedall Churchwarden for this / yeare of our lord 1634

Receipts as followeth

Imprimis of the bayliffes of Liverpoole	£12
Item of the Churchwardens of Kirkeby	£6
Item of the Churchwardens of Formebye	£6
Item of the Constables of Darbye	£18
Item of the Constable of Walton	£2 19s 8d
Item of the Constable of Fazakerley	£2 18s 3d
Item of the Constables of Bootle cum Linaker	£2 5s
Item of the Constables of Kirkedall	£2 5s
Item of the Constables of Everton	30s
Received of Gilbert Balshawe for one ley stall	2s 4d
Received of Thomas Rothell for 46 poundes of / old Iron being all the old clocke	7s 8d
Received of old Mistress Moore for a leye shee did owe / to the church in the old churchwardens tyme	7d

[f.28v]

Debtes oweing to the church

Roger Bryares gentleman a leystall for a child	14d
Hugh Rose for two leyes	21d
Edward Tarleton two leyes	1d
William Ryce two leyes	1d

Summum totallis of the receipts
fyftye foure poundes <eight> nine shillinges / <sixe> eight pence[33]
Owing to the parishe 23d

[f.29r]

[As in the previous account, subtotals have been added at the foot of each page in arabic numerals, and this practice continues in most of the succeeding years.]

Disbursementes 1634

Payde for wryteing eight preceptes	12d
Spent in getting my Lordes hand Doctour Leghes and / Master Moores unto the preceptes	6d
Spent in getting the preceptes delivered unto / the Constables	6d
Spent upon the old and new Churchwardens and / sydemen, the deane his fees, and the apparitor, and / for our oathes	2s 10d
Payde for spyke nayles to amend the seates in the / Church, and for amending them	12d
Payde unto the paynter in earnest to laye the pulpit / and the partition in colours	6d
Spent upon him when wee bargayned about the same	2d
Payde unto Landesdale	16d
Payde for breade and wyne for a communion	2s 1d
Payde unto the payneter	10s 6d
Payd unto Christopher Shurliker for walling	7s
Payde to John Corker for two foote of new glasse / and for sixe quarrells	18d
My charges being with him to see the broken glasse / taken downe, and the new set up	8d
Payde to the paynter	8s
Spent upon the glazior and paynter	6d
Spent at the receipt of Walton leye	2d
Payd unto Thomas Boulton for leading flaggs	10s ...

2 – 8 – 3

[f.29v]

Spent upon the parishioners at the cast of myne / accountes when the new churchwarden was chosen	2s
Spent at the removeing of the new seates / a little lower to set the wardens seate	2d
Payde unto Landesdale	9s
Payde un Wigan	10s

33 Corrected in a different hand, which has also added the following line.

Payde unto the paynter in full satisfaction for his / worke at the pulpit partition and Fonte	13s
My charges being with the paynter whyle hee was / doeing that worke nyne dayes	6s
Spent upon the paynter and his two sonnes and my / selfe when I payde him the last monye for / his worke	12d
Spent at the receipt of Darbye leye	4d
Payd unto Master Johnson what hee had layd out	£5 14s 11d
Payd unto John Butler for getting stones for the / churchyard wall	4s
Payd for leading the stones	4s
Spent at the receipt of Kirkedall leye	2d
Spent at the receipt of Formeby leye	4d
Payd at Wigan at the visitacion for the booke / of Articles and orders	3s 6d
Spent at the same visitacion upon the old and new / Churchwardens sydemen and our horses	9s 6d
Spent at the receipt of Liverpoole leye	6d
Payd unto Master Johnson which hee spent in lying out / all night at the visitacion	15d
Payd unto John Butler for getting / more stones	12d
Payd for bread and wyne for a communion	2s 1d
Payd unto Landesdale	8s

£9 – 8 – 7

[f.30r]

Payd unto the maymed souldiers by mee to the head constab... / and for an acquittance	17s 6d
spent in bringing the same to Hyton	8d
Payde for takeing the fringe from the bottome of the / pulpit cloath setting it at the top and for silke	10d
Payd for taynter hookes and holders for the same	2d
<payd> Spent for making our presentmentes to the Bishops visitacion / upon the old and new Churchwardens and sydemen	2s 2d
Payd for wryteing the presentmentes	12d
Payd unto John Butler for getting more stones	4s
Payd for leading the same stones	5s
Payd unto Christopher Shurliker for keeping the / bell roapes in repayre	6s 8d
Spent at the rushe bearing in seeing who brought rushes / and who made default	8d
my charges with the workemen at the church fyve dayes	3s 4d
Payd unto John Chantrell for atable for <the> my / lord Bishops orders	12d
Spent at the fetching it from him	2d
Payd for abooke of common prayer	9s
spent at the makeing of our presentmentes / to the Assyzes >the constables and ourselves<	2s

Payd for wryteing the presentmentes	12d
Payd unto Thomas Johnsons wyfe and his daughter / for carrying rubbish out of the church	6d
Spent upon the constables and ourselves at Hyton at / at the delivering of the presentmentes	2s 2d
Payde for wryteing eight precepts for a second / leye	12d

2 – 18 – 10

[f.30v]

...pent in getting them assigned and delivered	12d
Paide for a new church spade	2s
Payd unto the head Constable for the prisoners at / Lancaster, and for an acquittance	8s 6d
Spent in bringing it to Hyton	8d
Payde for getting more stones for the church >yard< wall / and leading them	8s
Payde for bread and wyne for a communion	2s 1d
Payd unto Wigan	30s
Payd unto Landesdale	3s
Spent upon the masons	6d
Spent at the receipt of Walton second leye	2d
Spent at the receipt of Kirkbye second leye	4d
Spent at Wigan at my lord bishops corrections / upon the sydemen and my selfe and our horses for our / appearance fees and the order	9s 2d
Spent at the receipt of Darbye leye	4d
My charges being with the Masons eight dayes	5s 4d
Payde unto Landesdale	8s
Spent at the receipt of Formeby leye	4d
Payd unto Landesdale	5s
Payd unto Thomas Johnsons wyfe and his daughter / for carrying rubbish out of the church	6d
Payd unto Landesdale	5s
spent upon the masons and others that did worke / in the church	6d
Payd unto John Butler for more stones	12d

4 – 11 – ...

[f.31r]

Payd unto Landesdale	12d
Payde for one measure of stone lyme and bringing it to the / church	9d
Spent in going to standish to view the rayle about the / communion table	12d
Spent upon John Chantrell when hee came to / take measure how to make the rayle	6d
Spent upon the sydeman and my selfe when wee / agreed with him to make the rayle in Liverpoole	4d

Payd unto him in earnest	4d
Payde unto Landesdale	7s
Payd unto Wigan	6s
Spent upon the masons	6d
Payd for bread and wyne for a communion	2s 1d
Payd unto Thomas Johnson and his wyfe for carrying / rubbish out of the church	6d
Payd unto John Butler for more stones	15d
Payd for leading the rest of the stones	8s 4d
My charges <my> with the workemen twelve dayes	8s
Payd unto Wigan	6s
Payde unto Landesdale	12d
Payde unto the deane and apparitor	8d
Spent the same daye upon the sydeman and my / selfe and our horses	23d
Payde for wryteing our presentmentes	12d
Payd unto the masons	£2 14s

5 – 1 – 9

[f.31v]

spent upon the masons the waller the stonegetter / the sydeman and my selfe	12d
Payde unto Landesdale	2s
Spent upon the clockesmyth and my selfe in / goeing to Prescot to take a paterne of the clocke	12d
Spent upon another clockesmith which came to / looke upon the old clocke	4d
Spent upon the sydeman and my selfe when I / agreede for the new clocke	5d
Payde unto Thomas Rothwell in earnest	4d
Payd unto Christopher Shurliker for walling	7s
Payd for wryteing eight precepts for / a third leye	12d
Spent in getting them sygned and delivered	12d
Payd unto Landesdale	3s
Payde unto Edward Martyn[34] for leading flagges	9s
Payde unto Wigan	8s
Payde unto Landesdale	4s
My charges being with the masons foure / dayes	2s 8d
Payd for bread and wyne for a communion	3s 1d
Spent at the receipt of Liverpoole second leye	4d
Spent in goeing to Chester to deliver / the certificate into the registers office	3s 2d
Payd for one bushell of Slecke lyme and one pecke / ...e lyme and the carriage	12d

2 – 7 – 4

34 Or *Mortyn*.

[f.32r]

Payde for wryteing the Certificate	6d
Payd unto the ringers upon the kinges holy daye	3s
Payd unto Landesdale	2s
Payde unto Thomas Johnsons wyfe and his daughter / for carrying rubbish out of the church	6d
Payd unto Myles Waddington for walling one roode	12d
Spent at the receipt of Kirkeby third leye	2d
Payd unto deane and apparitor the third tyme that / wee were before him, for the order, and the sydmans / charges and myne owne	3s 2d
Spent upon John Chantrell when hee tooke / the last measure for the rayle	6d
My charges being with the masons eight dayes	5s 4d
Spent at the receipt of Formeby third ley	2d
Spent at the receipt of Darby third leye	4d
Spent at the receipt of Liverpoole third leye	<...d> 6d
Payd for washing the Surplusses the first tyme	18d
Payd unto Landesdale	12d
Spent in going to Liverpoole to looke for the rayle / and to agree for hinges for the same	<7d> 4d
Payde for the hinges	14d
Payd unto Landesdale	6s
Payd for bringing the rayle from Liverpoole to / Walton	3s 6d
Payd unto Landesdale	[?12]d

$$1 - 9 - 8$$

[f.32v]

Payde unto John Chantrell for the rayle, and for / cutting the communion table shorter, and makeing / a deske to laye Byshoppe Jewelles workes[35] upon	£3
Payd for nayles	8d
Spent at the paying of the monye	6d
Payd unto Landesdale	6s
My charges being with the masons three dayes	2s
Spent upon John Chantrell his sonne and his / man when they set up the rayle	8d
My charges the same daye being with him	8d
Payd for bread and wyne for a communion	4s 11d
Payd unto Thomas Johnsons wyfe and his daughter / for carrying rubbish out of the church	6d

35 *Apology of the Church of England.*

Payd unto Master Johnson the old churchwarden / for his appearance Fees before the / Archbishops visitors at Warrington the sydeman / and their charges	8s 6d
Payd for wryteing the Certificate	6d
Spent upon the masons	6d
Payd unto Wigan	6s
Payd for wryteing our presentmentes to the deane / according to the order wee had from him	8d
Spent at the makeing of the presentmentes / my selfe the sydeman and others	22d
My charges <iii> three dayes with the workemen	2s

$$4 - 15 - 1$$

[f.33r]

Payd unto Landesdale	3s
Spent when I delivered the presentmentes to the deane	8d
Payd unto Landesdale man	3s
Payd unto Thomas Johnsons wyfe and his daughter / for carrying rubbish out of the church	6d
My charges with the masons seaven dayes	4s 8d
Payd for fyve bushells of lyme and carrying it to / Walton	2s 7[or 8]d
>Given to the paynters man for barriage	4d<[36]
Payd unto Landesdale	12d
Payd unto Landesdale	4s 8d
>Given to the joyners man for barriage	4d<
Payd unto Wigan	11s
Spent upon the masons	6d
Payd unto Landesdale	12d
Payd unto Christopher Shurliker for walling	12d
Payd unto Edward Strange for iron and workmanshippe / at the little bell clapper	4s 8d
Payd for carrying it from the Smithye	2d
Payd unto Christopher Shurliker for amending the sills / of the seates in the church	10d
Payd for nayles	12d
Payd unto Landesdale	12d
my charges with the workemen nyne dayes	6s
Payd unto John Corker for eight foote of new glasse / and seaven foote of old glasse, for nayles and wyre, and thirtye / quarrells and his wages and for poynting the wyndowes	9s x...

$$2 - 16 - 10$$

36 Inserted between the two lines of the previous entry.

[f.33v]

My charges being with the glasier to see / the broken glasses taken downe, and the new glasse / set up being about that worke three dayes	2s
Spent upon the glasier those dayes the / masons and others working in the church	14d
Payd unto Thomas Johnsons wyfe and his daughter / for carrying rubbish out of the church	6d
Payd unto Landesdales man	7s
Payd unto Wigan	10s
Payd unto Landesdale	2s
Spent in going to Thomas Rothwell his / house to looke for the clocke	6d
Payd for bread and wyne for a communion	3s 10d
Payd unto Landesdale	12d
Payd unto John Corker for sodering the font	2s
My charges being with the masons seaven dayes	4s 8d
Payd for wryteing our presentmentes to the / head Constable for the Assyzes	12d
Spent at the makeing of our presentmentes / upon the Constables and our selves	1s 10d
Payd unto Thomas Johnsons wyfe and his / daughter for carrying rubbish out of the / Church	6d
Payd unto Landesdale	12d
spent upon the masons	5d

1 – 14 – 5

[f.34r]

Spent in going to Hyton to deliver the presentment... / unto the head Constable upon the constables and / our selves	18d
Payd for tymber and boardes for the clocke house and / carrying them to Walton	14s
Payd for spyke nayles	18d
Spent at the buyeing of those thinges	4d
Payd unto Wigan	5s
Payd for a locke and keye for the clockhouse doore	14d
Payd for bandes and gudgeons, and a staple for / the doore, and for 30[37] nayles	1s 10d
Payd for carrying them from the Smithye	2d
Payd for carrying the clocke to the Smithye / to bee weighed and backe agayne to the church	4d
Payd unto John Layland for working five / dayes at the clocke house	5s

---

37 Arabic numeral.

My charges being with him	3s 4d
Payd unto Thomas Johnsons wyfe and his / daughter for carrying	
rubbish out of the church	6d
Payd unto Landesdale for cutting the stayes / of the seates somewhat shorter	4d
Payd unto Landesdale	6s
My charges being with the masons seaven dayes	4s ...

2 – 5 – 8

[f.34v]

Payd unto John Amond in earnest for a new style	6d
Payd for two bushells of Lyme and bringing it / to Walton	14d
Payd for measu[r]eing the whole church after it / was flagged	2s
Payd unto the masons	£5 1s 6d
Spent the same daye when it was measured upon / the sydeman and my	
selfe, and they that did measure it / and the masons	18d
Payd unto a boye for fetching oyle from Liverpoole / for the clocke	2d
Payd for the oyle	2d
My charges with the masons three dayes	2s
Payd unto Thomas Johnsons wyfe and his daughter / for carrying	
rubbish out of the church	6d
Payd for beesomes to sweepe the church	1d
My charges being with Thomas Rothwell two / dayes when hee brought	
the clocke, and set it up	16d
Payd for a board to laye in Master Kayes seate and / carrying it to the	
church	1s 9d
Payde unto Christopher Shurliker for putting one / old seate amongst the	
rest and <b...> boarding Master / Kayes and the clarkes seate in the	
bottome	12d
My charges being with him the same daye	8d

5 – 14 – 4

[f.35r]

Payd unto Thomas Rothwell for a new clocke	£5
Payd for washeing surplesse and table cloath the / latter tyme	21d
Payd unto Christopher Shurliker for walling the churchyard / wall	13s
Payd for a locke and keye for the font	6d
Payd for wryteing the names of the / Comunicantes	2s
<Payd for wryteing myne accountes all yeare	...>
>Pay for wryteing the accountes my selfe	2s<
My charges in buyeing all the lyme for the churche / use, and bread and	
wyne for all the communions	2s
Payd unto John Amond for a new style which is not / yet set up, the	
monye remayneing <yet> in my / handes untill hee bring the same	30s
Payd unto Corker for sodering the communion cup	6d

Payd unto Edward Strange for a cheyne for byshop Jewells / workes >and two staples and some other thinges for that booke<	16d
Bishop Jewelles workes provided, and the pryce	30s
Payd unto Christopher Shurliker for takeing the dyall / of the post and setting it there againe	2d
Payd unto Edward Strange for mending the dyall	4d
Payd for parchment and wryteing the register	16d
Payd for wryteing myne accountes	2s ...

[no total]

[f.35v]

...ayd unto Thomas Johnsons wyfe and his daughter for / carrying rubbish out of the church	6d
Payd for boardes and carrying them to Walton	2s
Payd for nayles	4d
Spent upon Thomas Rothwell when hee brought / the clocke	6d

9 – 8 – 9

Summum totalis of all disbursementes / £55 15s 5d

More payde upon all accountes then / received <sixteen shillings eleaven / pence>[38] as by the books appeareth	£1 5s 9d

Accounts of Nicholas Cooper / admitt[e]d £12 Lay graunted
James Richroft [of Derby] and William Bouellton [of Walton][39] / gardian and sideman / aprill 3d

[f.36r]

Richarde Molyneux
Thomas Legh Rector

[*f.36v is blank*]

1635–1636

[f.37r]

The accountes of James Rycraft of Westderbye / Churchwarden for this yeare of our lord / 1635

---

38 A different hand has struck through this sum and has written all the subsequent matter on the page.
39 Superscript *D* and *W* above the names have been taken to indicate township of origin.

Received from the parish at two severall / leyes one being £12 another £6   £18
Received for a Childs leystall   22d[40]

[*f.37v is blank*]

[f.38r]

Disbursementes 1635

Imprimis spent upon the old and new Churchwardens / at the makeing of their presentmentes to the deane	12d
Item payde for wryteing the presentmentes	12d
Item spent at the receiveing of two church leyes	4d
Item spent upon the old churchwardens and the new / and their horses when they went to Childwall to the deane and for their oathes	3s 7d
Item payde to the high Constable for the prisoners / at Lancaster	8s 4d
Item for an acquittance	2d
Item for wryteing eight preceptes for a church leye	12d
Item payde to the old Churchwarden	25s 10d
Item payde to Wigan for flaggeing	10s 6d
Item payde for bread and wyne for a Communion upon / whitsondaye	2s 9d
Item spent at the receiveing of two leyes	4d
Item payd to Christopher Shurliker	6s 8d
Item payd to Nicholas Boulton	13s 4d
Item payd for wyre for the clocke	2s 4d
Item spent at the same tyme	2d
Item payde to Edward Strange for nayles and / workemanshippe	6d
Item spent at the a mending of the clocke	6d
Item payd for woode to amend the seates and the workemanshippe	6d

£3 18s 10d

[f.38v]

...m payde to Rodger Heye for going twyc[e] to come to / amend the clocke	6d
Item for two bushells of lyme and the carriage from Liverpoole towardes the setting of the new style	12d
Item spent at the setting up of the same style	6d
Item more payde to John Wigan	5s 1d
Item payde to Norres when hee and his sonne set the / style	4s 6d
Item payd to Nicholas Boulton for two dayes worke / at the setting of the same style	12d
Item payd to Raphe Burgesse for Blinstones / Children[41]	20s

---

40 Entry added in a different hand, arabic numeral.
41 Orphans requiring maintenance.

Item for bread and wyne for a Communion	3s 9d
Item payde for one bottle for the parishe use	18d
Item my charges being with Wigan when hee / was workeing in the porch 5 dayes	3s 4d
Item two dayes with Norres when hee set up the / new style	16d
Item payd to Thomas Mercer for filling Rubbish	6d
Item payd for leadeing Rubbish out of the / church porch and sand to laye the flagges	1s 4d
Item payde to John Wigan	5s
Item for stayeing with him one daye	8d
Item bestowed upon the Mason and others in drinke	6d
Item payde for carryeing sand in to the bellhouse	2d
Item payd to Wigan	5s
Item my charges being with him two dayes	16d
£2 16s 8d	

[f.39r]

Item spent at the flaggeing of the bell house	...
Item spent at the measureing of the bellhouse and porch	6d
Item payd to Wigan	30s 6d
Item my charges	8d
Item payd which was oweing in Nicholas Cowpers tyme / being spent at the b[?y]ing of a new style	6d
Item payd for wryteing presentmentes to the high Constable	12...
Item payd to Thomas Meadow for goeing to the Chappell / for the Chappellwarden	2d
Item spent at the makeing of presentmentes to the / high Constable	2s 6d
Item payde to Thomas Bridge	15s
Item spent at the bringing of the presentmentes upon / the Constables and myselfe	2s
Item for bread and wyne for a Communion	3s 8d
Item payd for bringing the Rayles for the porch	6d
Item for mending the byble	6d
Item payde to the high Constable for the / maymed souldiers and for an acquittance	16s[42] 6d
Item spent upon my selfe and my horse the same / tyme	12d
Item payd to Edward Strange for Iron ware / for the porch	4s 8d
Item spent at two severall tymes in setting up / the Rayles at the porch upon the workemen	12d
Item for lead for the same worke	14d
Item spent in goeing to the deanes Court / and his fees	2s
Item payde for the yates	12s
£4 15s 7d	

42 Possible mistake for *17s*.

[f.39v]

...m spent at the meeting of the Constables and / Churchwardens and other honest men of the / parish \<at\> on two severall dayes concerning / Recusantes goodes and landes[43]	6s
Item spent upon ourselves and our horses in goeing to / Wigan to the inquisition	4s
Item given to Faringtons Clarke for setting his / hand to the presentmentes	3s 4d
Item for wryteing the presentmentes to the / inquisition	12d
Item payd for Blinstons children to Burgesse	20s
Item for makeing presentmentes to the deane	12d
Item spent at makeing the presentmentes	12d
Item for bread and wyne for the fourth Communion	3s 2d[44]
Item spent at the Receiveing of Liverpooles / second Church	4d
Item payde to the Ringers upon the Kinges / holy daye	2s 6d
Item more for wryteing eight precepts for / a Church leye	12d
Item payd to Robert Turner for dressing the / pillar and dressing the leades	12d
Item for my expences the same daye / in seeing him finish the worke	8d
Item spent at the receiveing of Forbye / leye	4d
Item spent at the receveing of Bootle leye	3d
Item for oyle for the clocke	4d
Item payd to the glazier	18d
Item spent the same daye	8d

£2 7s 9d

[f.40r]

Item spent at the receiveing of Darbye leye	i...
Item spent at the Receiveing of Kirkebye leye	4...
Item spent upon the old Churchwarden and Rothwell / to amend the clocke, and to make leade Plumines[45]	6d
Item for a locke and nayles for the bellhouse doore	18d
Item for a Communion	3s 6d
Item payd to Burgesse	20s
Item payde unto the glazier	6d
Item bread and wyne for acommunion	4s 10d
Item spent at makeing of presentmentes to the / high Constable	1s 8d
Item for wryteing the presentmentes	12d
Item for mending the wyndowes and putting in / quarrells	2s 6d
Item for myne owne charges the same daye	8d
Item for goeing to the high Constable to deliver / the presentmentes	2s 2d

43 For the 'inquisition', see also f.49v and Introduction, p. xviii.
44 Arabic numerals.
45 Or *Plummes*, presumably referring to plumbs (clock weights).

Item payd to Nicholas Boultons wyfe for / washeing the surplesses   3s
Item unto Widdow Pendleton   1s
£2 3s 8d

[f.40v]

...m for parchment   6d
Item payde for mending the churchyard walles   2s
Item payd for the iron ware belonging to / the bell frame   12d
Item payd for amending the glasse wyndowes   1s 6d
Item myne owne charges being three severall / tymes <tymes> there   12d
Item payde to Raphe Burgesse for Blinstons / children   20s
Item payd to John Shurliker for wryteing / the names of the communicantes   2s
Item for wryteing myne accountes   2s 6d
Item for wryteing the Register   8d

[*The rest of this folio and the next are in different hands and employ arabic numerals except for the sums of £6, £1 and 20s on f.41r.*]

Rec[ei]pt in toto £18 22d
Due to the parish 8s 2d
and paid to the Gardian
May 20 1636
Reade over and allowed the day and yeare above written / by us
Thomas Legh Rector
John Moore
Robert Fazakerley
Nicholas Fazakerley
Nevill Kaye vicar

[f.41r]

Thomas Mercer Gardian 1636 May 20th

a ley of £6 allowed and £4 to Blinstones Children / per £1 a quarter. To
Christopher Sherlaker 6s 8d / for Bellropes et cetera. To the Clark for the Clock for
/ Curfuer and Sweeping the Church 20s. And that the / Schoolle bee pointed by a
ley from the parishe / and itt is ordered that the Churchwarden for this yeare / shall
bee Schoole Reeve the next and that course / continue to be observed hereafter

Thomas Legh
John Moore
Robert Fazakerley
Nicholas Fazakerley
Nevill Kaye vicar

[*The whole of the above passage is marked in the left margin by a large X, keying to a footnote in a later hand reading* The School to be pointed etc. *See p. 176.*]

[*f.41v is blank*]

1636–1637

[f.42r]

The accountes of Thomas Mercer / of Walton churchwarden for this yeare /
of our lord 1636

Received from the parish at two severall leyes / one being £12 and another six pound	£18
Received from the executors of Robert Worrall for a / leye stalle	2s 4d
Item from Master Lawrence Bryares for another leye stall	2s 4d
Item more received from William Glover / of Thingwall for a leye stalle	2s 4d

Summum   7s

[*f.42v is blank*]

[f.43r]

Disbursementes 1636

Imprimis spent upon the old and new churchwardens at / Childwall	2s 4d
Item for their oathes	1s 8d
Item spent upon the old and new churchwardens at makeing / presentmentes to the deane	1s 6d
Item for wryteing presentmentes	12d
Item spent upon the parishoners at the takeing of the / old churchwardens accountes	2s
Item spent at the receiveing Liverpoole leye	4d
Item payd for wryteing the precepts	12d
Item for two tunne of lyme stones	6s
Item for leading	4s
Item for coales to burne the lyme stones	5s
Item for carrying the coales into Plombes house, and / from thence to the lyme kilne	4d
Item for woode, turfe, and leading the claye, and makeing / the lyme kilne readye	12d
Item payde to Christopher Shurliker for repayreing / the lyme kilne	6d
Item spent at the receiving Formebye leye	2d
Item payd to the clarke	20s

<46s 9> £2 – 6s – 9d

[f.43v]

Item spent upon Christopher Shurliker and Formeby and / Johnsons wyfe at the carrying of the coales, and laying / of the lyme kilne	6d
Item payde to Formeby for drawing the kilne	12d

Item payde for carrying the lyme from the kilne into / Shurlikers house, and water to water it	12d
Item my charges being with them when the kilne was / layde and taken up agayne two dayes	1s 4d
Item spent at the receiving Kirkeby leye	2d
Item payde for bread and wyne for a communion upon / Whitsondaye	5s
Item payd leading water	10d
Item payd for a second appearance in fees to the / deane upon a scytacion	1s 10d
Item payd for sixe bushells of hayre	12d
Item spent at the receipt of Darby leye	4d
Item spent at the receipt of Walton leye	4d
Item payd for nayles to repayre the church seates	2d
Item payd to Raphe Burgesse for Blinstons children	20s
Item payde to Shurliker	6s 8d
Item spent upon the churchwarden Master Kaye and / other neighbours of the parish in searching / Darby Rolles[46] upon St Peters daye	2s

£2 – 2s –2d

[f.44r]

Item payd for mending the Communion cuppe	5s 8d
Item payd to Edward Strange for one band gudgeons, and / nayles to mend the Steeple doore	4s 9d
Item payde for three pound of leade	6d
Item for beame filling the schoole[47] for leading of / claye and strawe	3s
Item payde to the deane in fees and my charges the 5th daye / of July	3s
Item payd to William Turner and Christopher Shurliker for / setting the gudgeons in the Steeple wall, and bandes upon the Steeple doore	12d
Item my charges the same daye	8d
Item for a communion the last of July	5s
Item spent at the Filling of the bottles	4d
Item payd for wryteing preceptes for a second church / leye	12d
Item payde for mending the glasse windowes	2s
Item >for< my attendance the same daye	8d
Item for twelve bushells of lyme	4s
Item payd for fetching it	12d
Item for tenne bushells of hayre	2s 6d
Item for fetching it	6d
Item for an hundred of slates	2s 6d
Item for fetching them	2s 6d

£2 – 0s – 7d

---

46 Probably West Derby Hundred's assessment for county taxes.
47 Has been annotated with a large X inserted here keying to a marginal note subsequently obliterated by thickly striking through. See notes on annotations, p. 176.

[f.44v]

Item more for nyne bushells of lyme	3s
Item for fetching	12d
Item for patches for syzeing	6d
Item payde to John Wigan for two rigdgeinges	12d
Item payd Robert Gorsuch and his men	55s
Item more worke at the church	9s 4d
Item for blecke	9d[48]
Item for one bushell of <lyme> stone lyme	8d
Item for Foureteene dayes staying with the / workemen both at the church and schoole	10s
Item payde for washeing the glasses and formes	3d
Item more for hayre	6d
Item spent at the ending >their< worke when they were / payde their wages, and given them in drinke	3s
Item spent at makeing the presentmentes to the / high Constable against the Assyzes	2s
Item payde for wryteing	1s
Item spent at <makeing> delivering the presentmentes upon / my selfe and my horse	2s
Item payde to the high Constable for the maymed souldiours	17s 4d
Item for an acquittance	2d

<£5 – 6 – 6>   £5 – 7: 6

[f. 45r]

Item spent at the delivering of the same	1s 8d
Item for being assyted before the deane	12d
Item spent the same tyme	1s 6d
Item spent at the makeing presentmentes to the / Chancellour and deane	2s
Item payd for wryteing	8d
Item payde to Raphe Burgesse	20s
Item spent at the delivering presentmentes to the / deane	12d
Item spent at receiveing all the last church leyes	12d
Item payd for bread and wyne for a communion / October the 16th	5s
Item for oyle for the clocke	3d
Item payde to Edward Strange for mending / the beare	4d
Item payde to William Strange for mending / the little bell clapper	12d
Item spent there	4d
Item spent upon the ringers upon the kinges / holy daye and the night before	5s
Item payd to John Corker glazier	6s 9d
Item my charges being with him two dayes	1s 4d
Item payd for two bookes for the Fast	2s

£2 – 10s – 10d

48 Arabic numeral.

[f.45v]

Item for a Communion on Christmas daye	5s
Item for washing the surplesses the whole yeare	3s
Item payd to Christopher Shurliker for mending / the great bell wheele for nayles and staples	2s
Item for my charges two dayes	1s 4d
Item payd to Edward Strange for gudgeons for the / churchyarde yate, and his journey hither	6d
Item spent the same tyme	3d
Item payde to Raphe Burgesse	20s
Item payd for mending the church walles	2s
Item for my appearance being cyted before the / deane concerning briefes	1s 6d
Item payde unto John Layland an hack halm	4d
Item for a Communion the First sunday in lent	5s
Item spent at filling the bottells >at< foure severall / Communions	1s 4d
Item payd for wryteing presentmentes to the / Assyzes	12d
Item spent upon the Constables and others of the / severall towneshipps the same tyme	2s 6d
Item spent at delivering the presentmentes to the / high Constable against the Assyzes	2s 3d
Item payde unto John Butler for foure / loade of stones	12d

$$£2 – 9s – 0d$$

[f.46r]

Item for leading	12d
Item for mending the surplesses	8d
Item payd for repayreing the windowes	2s 6d
Item my charges the same daye	8d
Item payd to Christopher Shurliker for mending / the little bell wheele and seates in the church	1s 2d
Item payde for makeing the style and the wall at / the schoole end	2s
Item for woode for the one syde of the style	6d
Item for takeing the schoole floore up and laying / new claye	1s
Item for wryteing the names of the communicantes	2s
Item payd for parchment and wryteing the / register	1s 8d
Item wryteing myne accoutes >for the whole / yeare<	4s
Item payde to Raphe Burgesse	20s

$$£1 – 17 – 2d$$

Summum totalis	£18 – 13s – 7d

Seene and allowed by us

Thomas Legh   John Moore

Nevill Kaye vicar / Walt...

[*f.46v is blank*]

1637–1638

[f.47r]

The accountes of John Mercer of / Westderbie Churchwarden of Walltone
For this yeare of our Lorde god 1637

[*Rest of folio blank. In this account all numerals appearing within the text of entries, including days of the month but not years, are roman, and there are no added totals at the page foot.*]

[f.48r]

Imprimis for wryting eight preseptes for a Church ley	1s
Item spent uppon the oulld and newe Churchwardens /at Chilldwall being syted thither	2s 3d
Item payd for theire Oathes there	1s 8d
Item payd woode and bordes andd nailes for the great / bell wheille being broken in Thomas Mercers tyme	4s 6d
Item payd Kerster Sherliker for three dayes worke / For making of this bell wheille	2s 6d
Item for my owne attendance three 3 dayes	2s
Item payd to William strange[49] for Iorn worke for / the bell wheille	1s
Item spent upon the workmen and others which did / hellpe to gett up the great bell wheille	4d
Item spent at at the Receipte of Derbie leye	4d
Item spent at the Recepte of Leverpoll leye	4d
Item payd for wryting a note of the names of / all those that were to goe to the visitacione	6d
Item payd that was spent at the agrement maide / betwixt Master Dockter Leigh and the parishe[50]	4s 8d
Item payd to the visitor at the visitacion at Wigane / for the booke of articles and our Oathes there	3s 6d
Item payd the same tyme for a boocke of penance	1s
Item spent upon us and our horses in goeing / to the visitacione being seaven personns	6s 11d
Item payd for a horse hyer to the visitacione	1s 2d
Item payd Kerster sherliker for mending of twoo bell / wheills and for nailes and woode for the same	2s 3d
Item payd William strange for Clapes and bandes for the same	1s
Item for my Oane attendance for a daye	8d
Item payd Nicolas Boulltone for his waiges	20s

---

49 Or perhaps *straunge*, as there is a mark of contraction.
50 Not identified, perhaps concerning his paying towards the building works.

[f.48v]

Item spent upon the Oulld and newe Churchwardens / and other parishiners at making the presentmentes to / the Lorde Bishope at the visitacione	2s 6d
Item payd for staving and mending of a lader	4d
Item spent the 22th daye of maye uppon the oulld / and newe Churchwardens and other parishioners att / making presentmentes to the lord bishop at the visitacion / to goe to Chester	2s 6d
Item payd for wrytinge of the presentmentes	1s 4d
Item payd for Casting of Clay and leading the same / and for strawe for it and for workmanship	2s 6d
Item payd to twoo laborers for Caring water and for / serving the workmen w[i]th[51] Claye and morter	1s 2d
Item my owne Charges For twoo dayes to / gett that worke finished and donne	1s 4d
Item payd for Iorne bandes for Master Key his seate	8d
Item spent at the Receving of formbie leye	2d
Item spent at the Recept of Wallton Cum fazakerley leys	4d
Item spent at the Receving of Kerkbie ley	2d
Item spent at the Recept of Kerkdole Cum boutel[52] leys	2d
Item payd Master Keyes for his Charges in delivering / the presentments for the visitacion at Chester	2s 8d
Item payd for bread and wyne for a Communion / uppon whitt sondaye	4s
Item payd for wyer for the Clock at whitsontyd	1s
Item payd for Oylle for the clock the same tyme	6d
Item payd Kerster shirliker for bell Ropes	6s 8d
Item payd for blinstons Chilldren at midsomer	20s
Item payd for Marie Adamsons Chilldren	10s
Item payd to the high Constabell For / the mained solldiers and for aquitance	17s 6d

[f.49r]

Item spent att the payment to the high Constabell / of the money For the mained solldiers	1s
Item payd William Strange for Iorne geare to hange / the littell bell withall the 20th of June	2s 6d
Item my Owne attendance For that dayes worke	8d
Item payd For bread and wyne for a Comunion the / sixth daye of August	4s
Item payd for wryting presentmentes against the assises	1s

---

51 Several contractions of similar type in this account show little sign of superscription but have generally been expanded.
52 Apparently a mistake for Kirkdale and/or Bootle-cum-Linacre.

Item spent upon the Constabells and others of severall / tounships being 2 severall dayes about that busines	3s
Item spent upon the Constabells and my sellfe / at the delivering the presentmentes to the high Constabell	2s
Item payd Nicolas boulltons wyfe For washing of / the surplesses for the wholle yeare	3s
Item payd to the oulld Churchwarden that hee / had disbursed more then hee had Received	6s 2d
Item payd For a horse hyer to the Correccion at Wigan	1s 6d
Item payd to the Chanseler for an Order att Wigane	4s
Item spent upon us and our horses in our Journey / to Wigan and againe the 23th of Auguste	3s 6d
Item payd for wryting presentments for the Coreccion / the 21th of Septembar	1s
Item spent at making of the presentmentes accor / ding to the Order uppon the Churchwardens and sydmen	2s 7d
Item spent at the delivering of those presentments att / Chester and my Journey thither and backe againe	2s 8d
Item for a horse hyer 2 dayes for that Journey	2s
Item payd for a Copie of the warrent Con / cerning the Inquisicon the 24th of septembar	5...

[f.49v]

Item payd the 29th of Septembar for the / keeping of Blimstones Chilldren	20s
Item payd the same day for William Adamsons Chilldren	15s
Item payd for wryting of 8 preseptes for the / second ley the 7th of Octobar 1637	1s
Item spent att a meting of the Churchwardens / and Constabells Concerning the Inquisisione	2s
Item spent at an Other meting the fyrst of / Octobar where the Churchwardens and all the Consta / bells of the parish came bringing 4 men apeise / with everie Constabell for praysers	4s
Item spent uppon the same Companie at a / meeting at Darbie Chapell the 6th of Octobar / by the appointment of the high Constabell to put / theire handes to the boocke	5s 2d
Item payd for the presentmentes and praismentes	2s
Item payd Master Keys for his Journey to Chorley with / the Constabells att the inquisicionn	3s 4d
Item payd to the Constabells that they layed downe / to the Comissioners Clarke at Chorley	2s
Item payd the 7th of Octobar to the high Constabell / for the Releife of the prisoners in Lancaster gaille	17s 6d
Item spent att the payment thereof the same tyme	6d

Item payd for bread and wyne for a Communion / the eighth daye of Octobar	4s 10d
Item payd the 17th of Octobar being syted to / the deanes Corte the deans feeis and our expences	2s 6d
Item spent the 21th of Octobar in making / the presentmentes to the Deeane	1s 6d
Item payd for wryting the presentmentes	1s

[f.50r]

Item spent at the delivering of the presentmentes	...
Item payd the 17th of Novembar to the deane for / an Order being syted thither to appeare	3s 4d
Item spent uppon our sellves the same tyme	1s 6d
Item payd for a Flagone for the Churches use	6s
Item payd for mending a locke and key of the Church / Chist beinge broken in the Oulld Churchwardns tyme	6d
Item spent att the Recept of Leverpoll latter leye	4d
Item spent att the Recept of Derbie latter leye	4d
Item spent at the Recept of Walltone and Kerkdall ley	2d
Item payd to the Ringers uppon the Kinges hollidaye	1s 6d
Item for fyve dayes travell before I Coulld gett / leverpolle ley whereof one daye was to seftone to Master / Dockter Leigh my Expences in all[53]	1s 6d
Item payd John Corker for making newe glasse and / mending of the Church windowes after the greate / wyndes the 16th of Novembar in all	5s 10d
Item payd to Robart gorsige[54] for mending the slats / that were blowen doune and for making Clene the leades	1s 4d
Item for my Owne attendance 3 dayes to see this / worke finished by by the glaisier and slater in all	2s
Item spent at the Recepte of Kerkbie leye	3d
Item spent at the Recept of formbie leye	3d
Item spent the 21th of Novembar at making / presentmentes to the deane according to an Order / geven us in Charge the 7th of this month / to bee Retorned to him before this months ende	2s
Item payd for wryting of theise presentmentes	1s
Item spent at the Resept of fazakerleye	2d
Item spent at the Recept of butell Cum liniker ley	...

[f.50v]

Item spent att Delivering of the presentmens to the deane	1s
Item payd for wyer and nailes for the Churche / glasse windowes to fasten the glasse with all	10d

53 Entry marked in left margin with a rough + sign.
54 Gorsuch.

Item payd for 38 quarels of glasse mending / and putting in newe glasse	2s
Item for my attendance there that daye	8d
Item payd for the keeping of blimstons Chilldren / the 24th of Desembar for this quarter	20s
Item payd Marie Adamsone the same daye for / the keping of her Chilldren by an Order from the Justis	10s
Item payd for wyer for the Clock the 24th of desembar	1s
Item payd for bread and wyne for a Comunione / for newe years daye and for Caridge of it	5s
Item payd for 6lb and hallfe of Cording for the / Church Clocke and I left the oulld Cordes in the Church Chest	3s 3d
Item payd William Torner for making of weights / for the Clocke	1s 2d
Item payd for leade and Iorne huckes for the same	6d
Item for my attendance there that daye	8d
Item payd the 10th of februarie for breade and / wyne for a Communion and for Caridge of the same	5s
Item spent the 22th of februarie at the making / of the presentments to the high Constabell	2s 2d
Item payd for wryting of the same presentmentes	1s
Item spent at the delivering the presentmentes to the / high Constabell upon the other Constabells and my sellfe	1s 8d
Item spent at the bargaine made w[i]th Robart gorsige for solating the Churche	6d

[f.51r]

Item payd For 24 bushells of lyme for the Church use	8s
Item payd for the Caridge of the same to Walltone	1s 8d
Item payd for Caridge of water to laye the lyme in stipe	3d
Item payd for 4 bushell of heare for the same	1s
Item payd for 2 thousande of stone nailes	5s
Item payd for 4 hundered of dubell and singell spikes	2s 6d
Item payd for a hundered of lathes for the Church	3s
Item payd for 17 bushell of lyme more for the Church use	5s 8d
Item payd for Caridge of water to stipe the lyme	2d
Item payd for plankes to make seates in the Church	6s 5d
Item payd for Caridge of 17 bushell of lyme and the planks	1s 8d
Item payd for 4 hundered of slates for the Church	10s
Item payd for leading of the same slates	8s
Item spent upon the Carters that brought all this stuffe	6d
Item my Owne attendance 4 dayes in bying and / getting this stuffe to the Church	2s 8d
Item payd Robart gorsige for a daye and hallfes / worke in dressing slates att the dellfe	1s 6d

Item payd Kerster sherliker for a daye and a hallfes worke / in setting up the seates in the Church	1s 2d
Item payd Thomas Corker the same daye for soderinge / and mendinge the leads in the Church gutters	2s
Item payd him more for mending glasse windous	1s
Item spent upon theise 2 workemen	4d
Item payd for the keeping blimstons Chilldren	20s
Item payd Marie Adamsone for keping her Chilldren	10s
Item payd John shurliker for taking the names of / all the ComuniCates against easter	2s
Item payd for mending the Church yorde wall / that fell doune in the grete froste	2s

[f.51v]

Item payd for parchment and wryting the Register	2s
Item payd Nicolas boulltone for washing the glasse / windowes and Caring Rubish out of the Church	1s
Item payd for whytwashing the piller betwine the / Chancells and the south syde of the Churche	1s
Item payd Robart gorsige for 15 dayes worke / for him sellfe and his man in slating of the Church	28s 9d
Item payd more for eight dayes worke to Edwarde / Ryce working with Robart gorsige at the Church	8s
Item payd that I gave gorsigis man at finishing the work	4d
Item spent uppon the workemen in the tyme / that they weare adoeing of this worke	2s
Item for my attendance with the workmen 15 / dayes in seeing the worke donne and Finished	10s
Item payd for an Order from the deane the / 3 of aprill Concerning sertaine brifes	8d
Item payd for wryting my accountes for the / wholle yeare	4s

Receved from the parish	£24
More for a leystall for William smiths wyfe	2s 4d
More Receved from Master More for his part / of worke donne over his seate in the Church	3s 4d
Disbursed in all	£24 16s 6d
Soe I have Layd out more / then I have Receved	10s 10d

[f.52r]

Aprill the [?6]th anno 1638

The accounts of John Mercer anno Domini / 1637 >seene and allowed< and To Richard Greaves Churchwarden / anno 1638 a laye of £12 alowed for / the Church use and those many other / matters of Charge enjoyned to bee / paid out of the

Church Laye and the said / some to bee paid by the Constables unto / the said
Richard Greaves att or before the / feast day of Pentecost next[55]

Thomas Legh   John Moore

Nevill Kaye / vicar Walton

1638–1639

[f.52v]

[In this account numerals in the text are once again arabic, with arabic totals at each page foot in the disbursement section, but the itemised sums remain in roman numerals.]

The Accomptes of Richard Greaves of / Everton Church-Warden of Walton' for / this year of our Lord God: 1638

Received from the parish	£18
for an old spade	6d
for a ley stale for William fazakerley sonne / of Edward fazakerley of Kerkby	14d
uxor Johannis Mosse her ley stalle	2s 4d
Richard Woodes his buriall place[56]	2s 4d
the Mother of Edward Strange her ley stale	2s 4d
Richard Woollfall his ley stalle	2s 4d
Thomas Woolfall his ley stale	2s 4d
uxor Thomas Poole his ley stale	2s 4d
Receiptes	£18 15s 8d

[f.53r]

Disbursmentes 1638

Payd to Master Lewis[57] when wee tooke our Oathes	8d
to the Parreter	4d
for our expences then att Childwall	14d
when wee received the old Church-wardens / Accomptes spent	4d
payd to Henry Thomasson' the high Cunstable / Aprill 8 for the mantaynance of two Children / per precept	5s 8d
Acquittance	2d
for makeinge eight preceptes for the first / Ley	12d
spent in getting them signed and delivered	6d

---

55 Memorandum using arabic numerals throughout.
56 Entry marked in left margin with cross or hash sign.
57 The Dean.

spent att the makeinge of our presentmentes / upon the new and old church-wardens et alii	2s 2d
for writtinge of the sayd presentmentes	12d
his charges in bringeing the presentmentes to / Childwall	8d
payd for an order to the Deane to rectifie our / presentmentes	2s 3d
our expences then att Childwall	7d
payd to the old church-warden which hee hadd / disbursed over and above his receiptes	10s 10d
	1 – 7 – 4

[f.53v]

Payd for oyle for the Clocke	1d
for wyne and breade for the first Communion / beinge att Whitsontyde	4s 2d
spent upon the new and old Church-wardens / att the makeing of our presentmentes by an order / from the deane according to the booke of Articles	2s
for drawinge of them	12d
for sendinge of them to the Deane spent	4d
payd for wyne and bread for the seacond Communion / beinge the third sonday after whitsontyde	3s 6d
payd to the Clarke for his whole yeares / wages	20s
to Christopher Shurliker for his yeares wages	6s 8d
to Mary Gorstich for her quarterage att / Midsomer	10s
payd for wyne and bread for the third Communion	2s 6d
spent upon the Church-wardens and Cunstables / when wee made our presentmentes for the Assizes	2s
for engrosinge of them	12d
my Charges in goeinge to Farneth[58] to deliver / the presentmentes to the high Cunstable	12d
for a horse hyre to farneth	12d
spent when wee rectifyed the same presentmentes / beinge retorned upon us againe	6d
	2 – 15 – 9

[f.54r]

Payd to the high Cunstable for maymed souldiers / per precept	15s 4d
Acquittance	2d
spent on the Joyner when he tooke measure of some / worke donne in the Church	4d
spent on sixe men att the takeinge up of the / great Bell	10d
payd to Edward Strange for mending the hoope / about the great bell heade and for 5 wedges	6d

58 Farnworth, near Widnes.

spent att the layinge againe of the great bell / upon certayne men	12d
my Attendance about the same for one day / att the least	8d
payd for a horse hyre to Ormeschurch when / I went to prevent any	
forther Order / touchinge Blinstons childeren att the / sessions	16d
for my dinner and expences	18d
payd for a peece of wood to mend the East / steele	1d
to Christopher Shurliker for putting in the steppe	1d
payd to the deane September 18 wee beinge / sited to Childwall	8d
My dinner and expences then	9d
when I was called to Childwall by Master Moores / warrant concerning	
the poore, my expences	8d

£1 – 3s – <...>1d

[f.54v]

spent att the Receipt of Darby ley	4d
att the Receipt of Liverpoole ley	3d
att the Receipt of Formby ley	2d
att the Receipt of Bootle ley	2d
att the Receipt of Walton ley	2d
att the Receipt of Kirkby ley	2d
spent att the makeing of our presentmentes againe / accordinge to the	
booke of Articles	12d
for drawing of them	12d
payd for wyne and breade October 7th beinge / the Fowerth Communion	3s 8d
when wee were syted againe to Childwall / for my expences and horse	
hyre	12d
paid to Mary Gorstich for her quarterage / att Michalmas	10s
to the Ringers for ringinge upon the / Kings hollyday and the night before	5s
paid to Robert Gorsuch for puttinge upp / certayne slaytes that were	
taken off / the Church with the great wynd and for / <s...inge>	
Clensinge the gutter	6d
my Attendance then and charges	4d

1 – 3 – 9

[f.55r]

Paid to Edward Strange for a new spade	2s 4d
for mendinge the old hacke, Iron and / workmanshippe	10d
payd to Edward Tatlocke for new formes / and other worke donne in the	
Church	32s
to John Runckhorne[59] for bringeinge them / to Walton	8d

59 Cf. Runcorn.

my Attendance there one day	8d
Paid to Thomas Corker for glaysinge, / nayles, and pointinge of other windowes	3s 10d
for one pecke of lyme	2d
my Attendance there one day	8d
bestowed on the Joyner, the glayser and other / workemen >in drinke<	12d
Payd to the high Cunstable towardes the / reliefe of the prisoners in his Majesties goale / of Lancaster	17s 4d
Acquittance	2d
for oyle to the Clocke	4d
Paid to Mary Gorsuch for her quarterage / att Christmas	10s

$$3 - 10 - 0$$

[f.55v]

for makeinge eight preceptes for the seacond ley	12d
spent in gettinge them signed and delivered / with a horse hire to Sephton, and Bancke / hall[60]	12d
payd to the Clarkes wife for washinge the / surpesses the whole yeare[61]	4s
paid for wyne and breade December 30th / beinge the fifte Communion	3s 5d
for a horse hyre to farneth when I / delivered the names of >all able men of< every Towneshippe / to the high Cunstable per warrant	12d
for my dinner and expences	12d
for engroseinge their names in parchment / for <...> all the Towneshippes	2s
payd to Thomas Corker for glaysinge, when / great wyndes had broken the windowes	3s 9d
my Attendance and helpeinge him one / day	8d
spent at the Receipt of the seacond ley of / Walton	2d
att the receipt of Kirkby ley	2d
att the receipt of Kirkdall >ley< bootle cum lyniker >ley<	2d

$$0 - 18 - 4$$

[f.56r]

att the receipt of Liverpoole ley	3d
Payd to John Layland for a hacke halme / and putting itt in	3d
spent att the receipt of Darbie ley	4d
paid to James higginson for keepeinge / one of Blinstons childeren for the / haulf yeare endinge att our Lady day	12s 6d

---

60 Respectively the homes of Thomas Legh (Rector of both Sefton and Walton) as well as the Molyneux family, and of John Moore.
61 Entry marked in left margin with double hash sign.

to Jane Rose for keepeinge an other of / Blinstons children the same tyme	7s 6d
Spent upon Deane Lewis when hee / preached twice on sabboth in Master / Vickars Absence	8d
payd for a locke for the stiple doore	12d
for setting itt on	2d
payd march 10th for wine and bread for the sixt / Comunion	3s 1d
to Mary Gorstich for her quarterage att / our lady day	10s
spent when wee made our presentmentes to / the high Cunstable for the lent Assises	2s 8d
for drawinge of our presentmentes	12d
	1 – 19 – 5

[f.56v]

My charges in goinge to Farneth to deliver / the presentmentes	12d
horse hire	12d
payd for a church ladder which was >not< / finished	7s 2d
more for staveinge itt	12d
spent when I bought the ladder	2d
for carryinge itt from broad greene[62] to / Walton	12d
payd to Edward Tatlocke for a new beare / and cover	12s
spent when I agreed for the same	2d
for wyre for the clock	10d
payd to Christopher Shurliker in augmentacion / of his former wages and in regard of / his great charges of <...> bell roapes	3s 4d
for carryinge the new beare from Liverpoole / to Walton	6d
for a new hinge for the pulpitt doore, nayles / and settinge itt on	6d
	1 – 8 – 8

[f.57r]

Payd for a napkine for the Communion	3s
for a new stay for the church steele	8d
for wrytinge a coppie of the Register / booke for the whole yeare and for parchment[63]	2s
payd to John Shurliker for wrytinge / the names of all Communicantes att Easter	2s
to Christopher Shurliker for putting in two / new stayes to the bell wheeles which / were decayed and <for> expences	5d
Payd to Master Banister for >parchment which< is putt into the / register booke, there being a great want / thereof	4s

---

62 Broad Green near Childwall.
63 Entry marked in left margin with double hash sign.

spent on him when I bought the same	1d
>More for cuttinge the parchment, and settinge itt in the booke	2d<
for wrytinge theis Accomptes	4s
spent att the Eleccion of the new church- / warden with certaine gentlemen and others of the / best of the parish	4s
more spent when John Mercer delivered upp / 16 bondes concerninge the schoole Moneys / a vew thereof beinge taken[64]	6d
payd to the Clarke for washinge the Church / windowes	12d
	£1 – 1s – 10d

[f.57v]

Payd to John Chantrell for a litle table whereon / to sett childrens corpes that come to bee buryed	3s 4d
spent on him when I agreed with him	3d
payd to John Laylande for worke which / hee did to the church steele	2d
for bringing of the litle table to Walton	2d
Payd unto Master Key which hee distributed / <...> unto certayne decayed Ministers some / <decayed> maymed souldiers and to other / poore people in my Absence	4s
payd <fo> more to him which hee payd for / repayring and mendinge of the church >yard< walles	3s
	10s 11d[65]

Receiptes	£18 15s 8d
Disbursmentes	£15 19s 11d
Rem[ains]	55s 7d

John Moore

Robert Fazakerley   Nevill Kaye vicar / Waltouen

1639–1640

[f.1r]

[Pasted out of place at the beginning of the book, and inserted here rather than after the disbursements because the 1640–41 account begins on the reverse of the last folio of 1639–40, leaving no space for it. The page is very untidy, with many interpolations, crossings out, alterations and doodles, apparently made at different times. Numerals are a chaotic mixture of arabic and roman.]

---

64 Entry marked in left margin by X, fainter than the above mark, see notes on annotations, p. 176.
65 Altered from 10d, originally in arabic numerals. The three following sums are in roman.

The accountes of Nicholas Goore / Church Warden of Waltone for the / yeare
of our lorde god 1639

Recved Frome the parishe at twoe / severall Leis	£18
<Item paide for bred and wine f... / Comunion	4s 1d>
<...ing ... unto the p...>	
Receved more Frome Rycharde greaves	<41s> 55s 7d
Receaved more of hugh Rose / for a ley stone	2s 4d
Remaines in the old churchwardens / handes to be payd to the new churchwarden / 1640	54s[66] 10d

John Moore
Robert Fazakerley[67]

<Receved by	22s ...d>

Nevill Kaye vicar
...rd that 54s 10d is paid by N[icholas] Goare
... Riding guardian anni 1640   the 21th of June ... / S[?um] of ..s 10d ... Riding is to ...

[*f.1v is blank*]

[f.58r]

[*Although the page appears to start mid-account, there is no sign of missing pages, nor of missing amounts in the total of disbursements, and the entries deal with dates early in the accounting year. Possibly the first four words were originally a heading. Days of the month as well as amounts are in roman numerals except that the totals added at the page foot are mainly in arabic figures.*]

the bocke of accountes >concerninge< the deane for his >F...< /	20d
<...> and For owre expences	20d
the firste of maie for makinge presentmentes / to the deane Rurall and for wrytinge theime	18d
and spent upon the owlde churchwardens / and new churchwardens and cunstales	2s
Item paide for eighte precepes for the firste / churche leye	12d
and spent	2d
the 7th of maie for goinge to the deane / at childwall spent upon the owlde / churchwarden and new churchwarden	12d
the Firste >of June< paide For breade and wyne / for a communione	4s
and spente <and> and for Carige	6d
the 24th of June spent one the / wrightes and sclaters in takinge a / a vewe of the churche	6d
paide for a Jare of oyle for the / churche Clocke	6d

66 The *4* is uncertain but agrees with the note at the foot of the page. This line is marked with a marginal cross.
67 Around and above these signatures are various semi-legible deleted scribbles.

the 25th of June paide to Ellyn strange[68]	20s
	some is 34s 6d

[f.58v]

I[te]m the Forth of July paide to Thomas Rothwell / For mendinge the clocke and expences of	3s
paid for breade and wyne for a communion the / 7th of July	3s 6d
paid to christofer shirlyker for bell ropes	10s
paide to Thomas Booden for a Firste for the / churche and For the workemanshipe of / hime and his sone	14s
spent upon the workemen the saime daie	6d
spent at drainge up the Firste	4d
spent upon the cunstables Churchwardens / and syde men the 12th of Auguste	2s
and For wrytinge presentmentes to the / hie Cunstable	2s
spent in bringinge theime to Rainforde	22d
paide for presepes for the Firste <ly> churche / ley	12d
and spent at the Receite of theime	2d
Item paide to Robarte gorsuche and his / three men For nailes lates and sclatinge / the churche	24s
and spent one theime	6d
Item for mosse for the sclater	6d
and geven to twoe pre[n]tisses for cleringe / the leades	6d
	some is £3 3s 10d

[f.59r]

Item for the churche wardens attendance / sixe daies >of the wrightes and sclaters<	4s
the thirde communion the 8th of september / paid for breade and wyne	4s
paide to Rychard Tarltone for Fower bushell / of lyme for the church and heire	4s 6d
the 22th of september at childwall paide / to the deane for his Fies and cale	12d
and For owre expences	12d
Item paid to Ellyn strange the Fifte[69] october	20s
spent the thirde of October at makinge presentmentes	12d
paide for writinge presentmentes the saime tyme	18d
Item spent at the accountes of the owlde / churche warden and parissioners	12d

---

68 For the upkeep of children.
69 Written *fiste* and occurs several times in this account, but used for 5 November so is transcribed as *fifte* not *firste*.

the 22th of October paide to the deane / for an order owet of the courtes	3s 4d
and for the pariter	4d
and spent the saime tyme	12d
paide for Claspes for churche boockes	8d
Item paide for glasses for the scole house	3s
Item paide for glasses for the churche and / byinge wyre and nailes	4s
spent upon the glasier	6d
and for my attendance >twoe daies<	12d

some is £2 12s 10d

[f.59v]

Item the Fifte of November paid to the Ringers / and for candles	5s 1d
Item paide for boordes and nailes for the <for> / scholers and Fetchinge theime	7s 7d
and for the workemanshipe of theime and / the scole boorde	4s
and For my attendance	16d
the <...> 17th >november< of the Fifte communion paide for / breade and wyne	4s 6d
the 14th of december paide for oile for / the clocke	6d
at the receite of Darbie ley spent	2d
and at the receite of Kirkebie spent	3d
at the receite of Formebie ley spente	2d
at the Receite of Walton and Fazakerlay spent	2d
paide to Ellyn strange the firste of Januarie / for her towe childeren	20s
Item paide to Catie Key for a quarter / of hollandes for mendinge the church surplus	12d
spent at the receite of Lyverpoole ley	3d
spent at the receite of Bootle Kirkdall / and Evertone leyes	4d
paide to Edwarde strange for / makinge a key for the steeple doore	4d
paide for wyre for the clocke	8d

some is £2 6s 9d

[f.60r]

Item for Fifte of Januarie paid For breade / and wyne for a Communion	4s 8d
Item paide to Marie Adamsone wyfe of / William Adamsone the 21th of Januarie / in a full discharge for her and her towe / children From the parishe the some / of Fiftie	of Fiftie shillings
Item paide for mendinge the walles / abowte the churche yardes beinge / Fower Roodes and a halfe	4s 4d
Item paide for eighte precepes For / the later ley	12d
and spente	2d
Item paide to James higinsone For / Blinstones children	40s
Item paide For three Fote of >glase< at the north / end of the churche	18d

Item paide For three Fote one the north / syde above	18d
Item one the easte syde above	18d
Item in another paine above / twoe Fote	12d
Item behinde the churche doore / Fyve Fote new glasse and Fower Fote owlde	4s

some is £5 9s 8d

[f.60v]

Item for wyre and nailes	6d
Item for pointinge the glasses / with morter	6d
Item paide for lyme for morter	<4d>
Item for my attendance at / three severall tymes	12d
the 23th <off> of Februarie paide / for breade and wyne for a Communion	5s
Item spent at the Receite of Formbie ley	2d
Item spent at Kirkebie ley	2d
Item spent at Walton cum Fazakerley ley	2d
Item spent at Receite of Darbie ley	2d
Item spent at the Recite of Lyverpole ley	2d
Item spent at the Receit of bootle lynaker / and Everton	4d
Item paide for mendinge the Clocke / to Thomas Rothwell and for one to Fetch / hime From Ince	2s 8d
and spente one hime at twoe / severall tymes	7d
and For my attendance those daies	6d
paide For wrytinge presentmentes / againste the syses	2s
and spente upon the cunstables and / Churchwardens	2s

some is 16s

[f.61r]

Item spent in delyveringe presentmentes / to the hie connstable at prescote	8d
<Receved For hue Roose of the Clube / moore[70] for a ley stall	2s>
and paid to John laylande for / For mendinge the Formes and nailes	4d
paide to William Turner for layinge / Fower flages which were shorkene	12d
Item paide to John shirlyker for the / the names of the comunicantes	2s
For wrytinge the boocke of / accountes	4s
paide to Master key for parchmente / for the <comunicantes> register and ingrosinge / theime in the boocke	2s
paide to Nicholas Boltone for / his yeares wages	20s
paide for washinge the churche / surplussies at severall tymes	5s

70 Clubmoor, in the Anfield/West Derby area.

paide hime more For karringe / Rubbishe owte of the churche	12d
Item to Blinstons children	20s

some is £2 16s[71]

some totalis of this accounte is / £18 13s 6d

[For the receipts and audit of this account see insertion between f.57 and f.58.]

1640–1641

[f.61v]

The Accoumptes of Thomas Rydinge / of Westderbie Churchwarden of /
Walltonne For this year of our / Lorde god One thousand six hundered /
and Fortie as Followeth videlicet

Imprimis Re[iv]ed[72] From the parish	£18		
Received for a ley stall of a Chilld of Anthony Johnson		1s	2d
Received for a ley stall for the wyffe of John / Roose of prescott Leane		2s	4d
Received of Edward Fazakerley for a Ley stall / for his wyffe		2s	4d
Received by the handes of Nicolas goare the / oulld Churchwarden which Remained in his / handes in perfecting his accoumptes[73] some of	£2	14s	10d
Received of Raffe Johnsoon for a ley stall		2s	4d
Received for a ley stall for Richard Roose of Evertoun[74]		2s	4d
Receiptes	£21	5s	4d[75]

[f.62r]

[Totals at the page foot in this account are given in arabic numerals.]

Disbursmentes by Thomas Rydinge 1640

Imprimis Disbursed and payed att the / visitacion at Wigain for Article bookes / and other expences there upon our / horses and our Sellves and others	10s
Item spent att a meetinge att Walltone / att making presentmentes to the bishope / by the oulld and new Churchwardens / the Connstabells and Others	3s
Item payd for wryting those presentmentes	1s 4d

---

71 Or *10s.*
72 Number of minims makes actual spelling uncertain.
73 Or *accomnptes.*
74 Or *Evertonn.*
75 Also the same total as a rough note in arabic numerals in the left margin.

Item payd in Charges laid out in bring- / inge of the presentmentes to
  the Bishoppe   <6s 8d> 5s
Item payd for bread and wyne for A / Comunion had at Wallton upon
  whittsonday   4s 2d
Item spent at the bying of the same   6d
Item for the Caridg of the same payd   2d
Item payd for Oylle and wyer for the / Church Clocke which was oat of
  Order   1s 6d
Item paid Thomas Rothell for mending / of the Clocke being out of
  frame   2s
Item my expences and attendance 2 dayes   1s 4d

                                 01 – 09 – 00

[f.62v]

Item payed to the high Constabell for / the use mained Solldyers   17s 4d
Item payd for aquittance for dischare therof   2d
Item spent in bringing the money to the high constable[76]   4d
Item spent upon Master Feilldinge wich / Did preach att Wallton the
  21th of June   10d
Item payd for abooke apointed for the / Fast by Com[m]and from the
  Kinges Majestie   1s 2d
Item paid for wryting of preceptes for / the payment of a Church Ley   1s 6d
Item paid For bread and wyne For A / Comunion had the seacond day
  of August   4s 2d
Item payd for Caridg of the same to Wallton   2d
Item spent at bying of the bread and wyne   6d
Item paid For 30tie[77] bushells of >stone< Lyme / For the use and
  Repaire of Wallton Church   20s
Item payd for Caridge of the lyme From / leverpoulle in twoo severall
  Dayes   4s 4d
Item my owne Charges and attendance / twoo severall Dayes about that
  busines   1s 4d

                        <2 – 1s – 10> 2 – 11 – 10

[f.63r]

Item payd for wryting presentmentes / to the Assyses the 7th of August   1s 4d
Item spent att making presentmentes to / the Assises upon the Constables
  and others   4s
Item payd to Nicolas Boullton for / tending the Clocke sweiping the
  Church / and Ringing Corfue for the wholle yeare   20s

76 Or *connstable*, as there is a mark of contraction.
77 Written *xxxtie*.

Item payd that was geven to Ellin strang[e][78]	10s
Item payd Christofer >Sherlacaker< for the Repayer of / the bellropes and other busines in the Church	5s
Item payd for three bookes and an order / had from the Chanceler at the <visitacon> Corecion / att Wigian the 11th of Auguste	4s 6d[79]
Item spent in our Journey to Wigain / at the visitacion upon our horses and our sellves	5s
Item payd John Corker for Repairinge / the glasse windowes in Wallton Church	2s 6d
Item payed for a Covering for a booke / Caled Jewells workes which is kept in the Church	2s 6d

02 – 14 – 10

[f.63v]

Item payed Robarte Gorsige for himsellfe / and his men for Fiftine dayes workman / ship in poynting and Repayring where / neede was in Walltone Church	£2 8s 2d
Item payd hugh gibbins for Carring / water to sleck and lay the lyme in steipe	1s 6d
Item paid for 6 bushel of hewer / for lyme morter to pointe with	2s
Item payd for Carridg of the heauer	8d
Item my owne Charges in six dayes / in Attendance with the workemen	4s
Item payd for bread and wyne For A / Comunion had the fowerth day of octobar	4s 2d
Item spent at bying of the bread and wyne	6d
Item payd for Carridg of the bread and / wyne From Leverpolle to Wallton	2d
Item paid at Chilldwall being syted to / apeare at the deans Court Concerning presentmentes	1s 6d
Item payd for wryting presentmentes to / the Deane	1s 6d

<2 – 8 – 02> 3 – 4 – 2

[f.64r]

Item spente att making of the pre / sentmentes to the Deans Courte	1s 6d
Item paid James higginsonne the 19th / of Octobar for blimstons Chilldren	£1
Item paid to Elline strange the / Nintinth daye of Octobar	10s
Item paid to Edwarde Strange for / mending of the bell Clapper	6d
Item payd more to Edward Strange / for Claspes for the Church booke and for / bandes for the pooars box and for men / dinge of the Church Spade	2s 6d

78 Appears as *strang* with mark of contraction.
79 Altered to or from 11d, but has been counted as 4s 6d in the total.

Item paid to the Ringers the fifth of / November being the Kings
  majesties holliday   5s
Item paid Master Key for wrytinge / of preceptes for a Church Ley   1s 6d
Item paid Christofer shorlaker for / mending the bell Roopes and other /
  busines donne about the Church   5s

02 – 06 00

[f.64v]

Item payd for bread and wyne for A / Comunion had att Wallton the
  27th of Decembar   4s 2d
Item my owne Charges and for bringing / of the bread and wyne from
  leverpolle to Wallton   8d
Item spent at sondry tymes in taking notes / of the severall disbursmentes
  of my accoumptes   1s
Item paid for wryting notes at severall / tymes of my disbursmentes
  Concerning the Church   1s 6d
Item payd for wyer For the Clocke   1s 3d
Item payd for glasinge and Reparinge of the / glasse windowes of the
  Church and scoullehouse   11s
Item my owne attendance there twoo dayes   1s 4d
Item paid for expences of the Constables / and others at making
  presentmentes by / direccions from the assemblie of the Court / of
  parlement directed to his majesties / Justices Concerninge
  Recusauntes   3s 4d
Item paid for wryting presentmentes to bee / delyvered to the Justices
  Concerninge / the same busines   1s 4d

01 – 05 . 7

[f.65r]

Item my owne expences in bringinge / the same presentmentes to
  Ormschurch / to the Justices according to warrent   1s 6d
Item payd for bread and wyne for A / Communion had the 10th of
  februarie   4s 2d
Item paid for brining the same to Walton   2d
Item my owne expences in bying the sam[e]   6d
Item paid Elline strange the 10th of February   10s
Item spent at making presentmentes / to the Assyces upon the Constabls
  and others   3s
Item payd for wryting of the presentmentes / to the Assises and for
  ingrosinge of them   1s 4d
Item payd in my owne expences twoo / severall dayes in delyvering
  those pre / sentmentes to the high Constabell for / to bee delyvered
  att the Assyses   8d

Item spent upon Master Feillding that did / preach and Reede servise at Wallton the / 21th of martch	1s
Item spent upon Master Lewes that did / preach and Reeide Servise at Wallton / the twentie eighth day of martch	1s 4d

$$01 - 03 . 8$$

[f.65v]

Item spent in apperinge at Ormschurch / before his majesties Justices by vertue of / a warrent Directed From the Court / of parlement Concerning subsidies[80]	1s 6d
Item spent uppon Master Feillding that / did preach and Reeid servise att Wallton / the Fowerth daye of Aprell	1s 6d
Item spent and payd att the Recept / of the parrish money being twoo Leys / and for geving quittances for discharg / of the same att severall tyms in all	3s 4d
Item payd in expences of the high / Constabell and others in goeing thrugh / the parish in Disarming and takinge / notise of all the Armor weaponns / and Furniture belonging to Recusantes / by vertue of A warrent directed From / the Lordes of his majesties most honorable / privie Counsell to his majesties Justices / of this Countie for the execucon therof	2s
Item to Katherin Key For mending of / the Church surplesse and For new cloth / bought for the same	1s
Item payd to James higginsonn For / blimstonns Chilldren the 17th of Aprell	20s

$$01 - 09 - 4$$

[f.66r]

Item paid the 18th of Aprell	10s
Item payd to John Corker For sodering / the Leades glasinge and Repairing the / glasse windowes in and about the Church	4s 8d
Item my owne expences in attendance / about that worke twoo deyes	1s 4d
Item spent uppon the workmen	4d
Item spent more att severall tymes in / taking notes of my severall disbursmentes	1s 4d
Item paid for a new spaede for / the usse of the Church	2s 6d
Item payd For the washing of the / Church Surpllesses For the wholle yeare / to Nicollas Boulltonn	6s
Item payd For wryting my accoumptes / For the wholle yeare and Ingrossing / them in the boocke and for paper for the boocke	4s 4d

80 Probably the 'pole monie'; see f.68v and Introduction, p. xxxii.

Item paid For parchment For / the Register	1s
Item paid For wryting of the / Register	1s
Item paid For mending the Church / wall	1s

01 – 13 . 06

[f.66v]

Item paid Master Key in his Charges / in getting the poores money att
    London[81]   1s[82]
Item for writing names of the Com[munican]ts / att Easter   2s[83]

Receptes £21 – 5s – 4d
<Disbursmentes £18 11d 2s 11d>[84]
<Rem[ains] £3 6s 5d>[85]

disbursed £19 11d[86]
manet unpaid £3 4s 5d

1641–1642

[*The following loose and apparently re-used folio has been misplaced in the book,
but the dated material on it belongs here. The handwriting of the first two lines on
f.84r and the side note on f.84v is the same as the first entry on f.67r, all three being
dated 25 May 1641. The signatures on f.84r, however, may relate to earlier entries,
as they appear to include that of Thomas Legh (died 1639), though the form does
differ from earlier examples of his signature so it may not be the same man. The list
on f.84v, apparently a list of recusants or 'converted recusants', could be the list
referred to on f.70v or could relate to an earlier exercise, such as that mentioned on
f.64v. See also Introduction, p. xxxii. The numerals used are arabic.*]

[f.84r]

May 25th 1641
John Whitfelld had paid for 5 Sunday past

Nevill Kaye Vicar of / Walton
Thomas Legh
Edward [?Henshaw][87]

---

81 Refers to Thomas Berry's 'bread money'.
82 *1s* also written in left margin by way of a subtotal.
83 This entry added in a different hand, using arabic *2*.
84 Amount altered (using arabic *2*) and then the whole entry deleted.
85 *6s* altered to *4s* and then the whole entry deleted.
86 This and the next line added in a different hand, using arabic numerals.
87 Unclear, possibly intended to have been erased.

[f.84v]

Robert Fazakerley gentleman
Anne his wife
Maria Fazakerley vidua
Maria Fazakerley spinster
Anne Boulton spinster
Emam[88] Chorley vidua
William Chorley gentleman
Ailic[i]a his wife
John Hawkes a[nd] Katherine his wife
Ailica Hawkes spinster
Katherin ux[or] Thomas Marsh
Robert Tarleton nicholas his son
Edward Tarleton
Anne vxor orugiall[89] Flitcroft
Brichet vxor Raphe Marcer
Alic Harper vidua
Eline Molineux vidua
Mari vxor Richard Bridg
Richard Fazakerle
Elizabeth vxor Hener Wyndle

[*Page also contains practice words scattered about, including the name* John Whitfild, *a sketch of a ?wax seal next to the word* Noverint, *and the following memorandum written down the left side:*]

Recpt per John Whitfeild[90] of Thomas / Riding May 25th 1641 £3 4s 5d
[?Gardian] presentibus et vicario

[f.67r]

[*Several hands have contributed to this page: the first and last entries and the amended amount in the fourth being by the same scribe, who uses arabic numerals.*]

May 25th anno 1641
Recpt by John Whittfeild gardian of Walton from / Thomas Riding late gardian
    £3 4s 5d

The accomptes of John Whitfield / of Fazakerley Churchwarden of / Walton for this yeare of our lord god / one Thowsand six hundreth Fowertie / and one, as Followeth, videlicet,

---

88 Apparently for *Emma*.
89 Name appears as *Originall* in parish register entries.
90 Possibly *Receptum* and *Johannem*. The whole sentence is a contracted mix of Latin and English, and transcription is tentative.

Inprimis received from the / parish two six pound leyes	£12
Received for foure lestalles / twoo shillings four pence a peec	<...> 9s 4d
Recpts by John Whittfeild Churchwarden / of Walton anno domini 1641	£15 13s 9d

[*f.67v is blank*]

[f.68r]

[*In line with the general style note given under f.13v, still in force, the main numerals used in this account are roman, here including days of the month, but totals added at the page foot and the figures in the final calculation are arabic.*]

Disbursmentes made by John Whitfield / for this yeare one thowsand six hundreth / Fowertie and one videlicet

Inprimis spent att Chyldwalle upon the / ould and new Churchwardens and for our oathes / five shillinges	
Item paied for a matte for / the Churchwardens pew	4d
Item >spent< att Walton upon the ould and / new Churchwardens aboute making / presentmentes unto the deane	2s
Item paied unto Master Kaye for writing / the said presentmentes	1s
Item spent att delivering them unto / the deane	1s
Item paied to Master Kaye for writing / eight preceptes for a church ley	1s
Item spent att delivering the preceptes / unto the Constables	6d
Item paied for bread and wine for / acommunion upon whitsunday	4s 10d
Item paied for lead for hengling / of the portch gates	3s 8d

14s 4d

[f.68v]

Item paied to William Torner for hengling / the yates of the porch	1s
Item my expences for being with / him one whole daie	8d
Item paied for turves and Coales to melt / the leade	2d
Item paied for carring the leade / from Liverpoole	2d
Item paied to John leyland for / mending the south Church style	3d
Item paied to Elin strange	10s
Item spent at receiving the church / ley att severall tymes	1s 4d
Item paied to Christopher shorlyker	10s
Item paied to nicholas Boulton	20s
Item my expences of my horse and / my selfe at OrmeChurch being / called by the virtue of a warrent / of his majesties Commissioners con / cerning the great pole monie	1s 6d
Item spent att Walton upon the Constables / and our selves att makeing presentmentes to the / assyzes	3s

Item paied to Master Kaye for writting them	1s 4d
Item spent att Prescott of my horse and / my selfe in goeing to deliver presentesmentes / to the High Constable	2s
Item paied to the High Constable	17s 4d

£3 8s–9d

[f.69r]

Item paied for aquittance	2d
Item spent of my horse and my selfe / in goeing to paie the monie to the / High Constable	1s 8d
Item paied for bread and Wyne / for a communion upon the eight daie / of August	4s 10d
Item spent att making presentmentes unto / his majesties Commissioners of all / that paied unto the pole monie within / our liberties	1s 6d
Item paied to Thomas Hodgson for / bynding and Clasping one of the / Church bookes	2s 6d
Item spent at fetching of it from / Liverpoole	2d
Item spent upon the fowerth daie of / september upon the ringgers	5s
Item paied for bread and wine for acom / munion upon the 26th daie of / september	4s 10d
Item spent att takeing downe the rayles / and removeing the Communion table / and other Occasions of the Church	8d
Item spent att takeing downe the / glasses	8d

£1 2s

[f.69v]

Item payed to the ringgers upon the / fift of november	5s
Item paied for bread and wine for / a communion upon the seaventh day / of november	4s 10[91]
Item paied to Master Kay for writting / preceptes for a church ley	1s
Item paied to Master Kaye for writting / a certificate unto the parliament howse	1s
Item my expences of my horse and / my selfe in goeing to gett my lord / to put his hand to the preseptes	1s
Item spent in goeing to deliver the / certificate unto the knight of the / shyre	8d
Item spent in goeing to Master Moore / to get his hand to the preceptes	8d
Item spent att Liverpoole in goeing / to deliver preceptes to the Constables	6d

91 Sic, no *d*.

Item for bread and wine for a com / munion upon the 22th daie of november	1s 6d
Item paied for wyre and oyle / for the clocke and my expences	2s 6d
Item spent upon the Constables and / our selves att makeing presentmentes unto / Master Moore and Master Oagles of all the re / cusantes	3s

£1 – 1s – 8d

[f.70r]

Item paied to Master Kaye for writting / them	1s
Item spent att Childwall in goeing / to deliver the presentmentes to the / justisies of peace	1s 6d
Item spente at severall tymes being / promised paiemt of Liverpoole ley / and disapointed of it	2s
Item paied unto Elin strange	10s
Item spent at receiving the second / Church ley att severall tymes	10d
Item paied unto Master Ireland for wood / for the new style and boardes and gyfes / for the tunnell for the clocke stones	28s
Item att >spent< buying of the same of the / workmen and my selfe	1s 4d
Item paied for leading wood from / Liverpoole	2s
Item paied unto William Mercer for / leading stones from the breacke[92] / for the style and for leading the / style and boardes from Kyrkdale to / Walton	3s
Item paied unto Edward Turner / for stones for the style and worke / menshipe of them and lyme	7s

£2 – 16s – 8d

[f.70v]

Item spent att sondry tymes in / tymes in takeing notes of the severall / disbursmentes of my accomptes	2s
Item spent of the workmen att setting / of the new style	6d
Item paied unto Thomas Boeden for / makeing the new style	8s
Item for my attendance att setting of the / style	8d
Item paied unto John Butlor for / mending the Churchyord wall	3d
Item paied to James higginson / for Blinstones children	20s
Item paied for bread and wine for / acommunion the third daie of / January	4s 10d[93]
Item spent att amitting[94] att Walton / to make certificates to Master Moore / of all the Converted recusantes bee / twixt Michaelmas and Chrismas	1s

92 The Breck.
93 Entry marked with pencil cross in left margin.
94 i.e. *a meeting*: this account has several examples of running the indefinite article together with a noun.

Item paied for cloth to bee a bag for / the silver bowell and for making /
of it   6d

Item in charges of mending abell / wheell for workmenship wood and /
nailes and my being with the work / men att doeing of the same worke   1s 2d

£1 – 18s – 11d

[f.71r]

Item paied for aplanke and more wood / for the tunnell   1s 6d

Item paied for nailes for tunnell and / for the seates   1s 6d

Item paied unto Edward strange / for two paire of Iron bandes and
[3[95]] / plaites of Ioron for the tunnell   1s 8d

Item paied for writting notes / att severall tymes concerning / my
accomptes   2s

Item paied to Thomas Boeden for / making the Tunnell and mending /
the seates and the particion betweene / the two chancells[96]   6s

Item paied unto William Turner for / making mortisies in the wall and /
dressing the clocke stones   1s

Item spent of the workmen att doeing / of the same worke   6d

Item for my attendance and charges / fower severall daies about the
same / worke   2s 8d

Item paied for bread and wyne for a / communion upon the 20th daie of /
February   4s 10d

£1 – 8d

[f.71v]

Item paied unto Master Kaye for writting / certificates of all the
Converted recu / santes betweene Michaelmas and Chris / mas   8d

Item spent of our selves and our horses / in goeing to Ormechurch being
appoin / ted of Sir Thomas standley to take / the protestacion[97]   3s

Item paied to the clarke for the pro / testacion   8d

Item spent in our attendance a whole / day and parte of some other daies
att / Walton when the parishoners / tooke the protestacion   1s 6d

Item spent att being with Corker / att taking downe the glasse and /
taking measure for new   8d

Item paied for slates to mend the / Church >and for leading of them<   2s 2d

Item paied to Robert Gorsuch / for himselfe and his man one / day in
repaireing the slates / of the Church and pointing in / other places
where wanted   1s 10d

Item paied to John Mercer for / two bushell of Lyme >for< the slates   1s

11s – 6d

95   Appears to be an arabic *3*, but could be an extra bracket between lines.
96   See Introduction, p. xx.
97   See Introduction, p. xxxiii.

[f.72r]

Item paied for sifting it and / Carrying it into the church	2d
Item for my attendance one day / about the same worke	8d
Item spent of the workemen	4d
Item paied to Master Kaye for writting / the names of those that did take / the protestacion, and likwise of / those that refused	1s
Item spent of my selfe and my horse / att Ormechurch in delivering the / names unto sir Thomas standley / of those that did take the protestacion / and alsoe of those that did refuse	1s 6d
Item spent att meeting att Walton / to make presentmentes to the high / Constable, of the Constables and our / selves	3s
Item paied to Master Kaye for writting / presentmentes to the assyses	1s 4d
Item in Master Kayes Charges in goeing / severall tymes unto my lord Mo / lineux about getting of Liverpoole / ley	2s

11s

[f.72v]

Item spent att Prescott in / delivering presentmentes to the / high Constable of my selfe and / my horse	2s
Item paied to Corker for tenn / foote of new glasse and fower foote / of ould and for twelve Quarrells	7s
Item for my attendance att the setting / up of the glasse	8d
Item spent of Corker att takeing / downe the ould glasse, and setting / up the new two severall daies	1s
Item paied for twelve bares / of wood for the glasse and nailes	6d
Item spent of the Overseers / and my selfe in gathering mony / for the poore of Ireland[98]	3s
Item paied for writing of the / names of the givers	1s 6d
Item spent in my travell unto / Prescote to paie to the high con / stable the monie which was ga / thered for the poore in Ireland	1s 6d
Item paied for aquittance	2d

17s – 4d

[f.73r]

Item in charges in repairing a windowe / standchion which was readie to fall downe / in stufe and workmanship	1s 6d
Item paied for twelve pound of lead / for waightes for the clocke and my spences / att buyinge of the same	2s
Item paied to William Torner for meltinge / lead for the waightes and my expences	1s
Item paied for aladder for the bell howse	1s

---

98 See Introduction, p. xxxii.

Item paied to John shorlyker for writting / the names of the communicantes att easter	2s
Item paied to Ellin strange which was / granted hir <att> by the Kynges majesties justices	10s
Item paied for putting afoote in the new / beare	2d
Item paied for parchment and writting the / register	2s
Item paied to John Leyland for a hame / for the church hacke	2d
Item paied to William Mercer for mending / the churchyord wall	3d
Item paied to Nicholas Boulton for / washing of the surplyes for the / whole yeare	6s

[*No total given*]

[f.73v]

Item paied for engrossing my accomptes / in the booke	3s 9[99]
Item paied in getting the poores / monie att London	1s
spent att receivinge the church / wardens accomptes	18d
payed unto Ellin strange / which was granted hir by by his / majesties justies	4s

[*Here a blank area with pen-testing marks*]

summa Totalis of disbursmentes / £16 – 4s – 11
more disbursed then received / <u>10s 2d</u>

[*There is no record of the audit or election, and no further accounts until 1649.*]

1649–1650

[*The format of this and the following year's account is the same: a left margin is ruled, the abbreviated word* Imprimis *being the only writing in it.* £ s d *abbreviations are used only in occasional column headings (as shown), otherwise denominations are indicated by the laying out of amounts in columns separated by the = symbol. Amounts under 20s are indicated by 00 or 0 in the pounds column except where the entry leaves insufficient space. All numerals in the accounts are arabic from this date on unless noted.*]

[f.74r]

The Accompts of John Whitfeild / of Fazakerley Churchwarden of / Walton for the yeare 1649

Receiptes	£	s	d
Imprimis Received From the Executor of John Ellison	01	6	5
Received from the Cunstables of Darbye	04	0	0
Received from the Cunstables of Kirkebye	01	6	8

---

99 Sic, no *d*.

Received from the Cunstables of Formebye	01	6	8
Received from the Cunstables of Bootle cum Linaker	00	10	0
Received from the Cunstable of Kirkdall	00	10	0
Received from the Cunstable of Everton	00	06	8
Received for a ley stall for John Ellison	00	02	4
Received For a ley stall for Henry Pendleto[n]	00	02	4
	09	= 11	= 01
Oweinge to the parishe for two / Church leyes by the Cunstables / of Walton Cum Fazakerley	01	6	8
Oweinge by the Towne of Liverpoole / for the same[100]	2	13	4

[f.74v]

Disbursmentes by John Whitfeild Anno domini 1649

Imprimis spent in goeinge to Darbye 2 severall dayes / Concerneinge the money in the old Church- / wardens handes	00	00	8
paid the Ringers the 3d of November being / a day of thankesgiveinge for the Victorye / in Ireland	00	02	0
paid the Ringers the 5th of November	00	04	6
For my attendance those two dayes	00	01	4
paid for two new bellropes	00	06	0
spent two severall dayes in goeinge to / Liverpoole about the ropes in regard / of the necessitie because of the day of / thankesgiveinge	00	00	8
paid for writeinge notes of my Accomptes	00	00	2
spent at a meeteinge at Liverpoole / about the money which was in the old / Churchwardens handes	00	00	8
paid for writeinge 8 precepts	00	01	0
paid for the Cariage thereof to the / severall Cunstables	00	00	4
spent at a meeteing at Walton / when Collonel Moore[101] and the parishioners / Came to veiw the Church Concerne- / inge the repaire therof	00	02	0
spent in goeing to Collonel Moore / to gett his hand to the precepts	00	00	4
	00	= 19	= 8

[f.75r]

	£	s	d
spent at a meeteinge at Walton / when John Ellisons Executor Came to / deliver up his Accompts and to pay the / moneyes which was in his handes[102]	00	01	8

100 Entry added in a different hand.
101 John Moore had become military governor of Liverpool.
102 See Introduction, p. xiii.

spent at Receiveinge of Formebey ley	00	0	2
paid to Sarah Govett for keepeinge / a Child	00	15	0
paid to Thomas Wiggan for mendinge / the Churchyard Wall	00	0	4
spent at receipt[103] of Darbye ley two se- / verall times	00	00	4
paid for writeinge notes of my Accomptes	00	0	2
paid For six bushells of lime	00	5	0
paid For Cariage of it from / Liverpoole	00	1	0
paid For writeinge 8 precepts	00	1	0
paid For six Bushells of / Heire and the Cariage of it	00	2	0
paid For a hundred of slaytes	00	2	6
For my Teame and my selfe in / gettinge them to the Church	00	00	10
	01 =	10 =	00

[f.75v]

	£	s	d
Payd for twelve Bushells of lyme	00	10	0
paid For Cariage of it	00	02	0
For my selfe in goeinge to Liverpoole / two severall dayes to buy the same	00	1	4
paid to Sarah Govett for keepeing / a Child	00	15	0
paid for writeinge notes of my Accompts	00	00	2
Spent uppon my selfe and partener / at Prescott beinge warned thither / about the engagement[104]	00	1	6
paid For Wood to mend a bell / wheele withall	00	1	10
paid To Edward Ryce for himselfe / and Two men ten dayes	01	10	0
For my attendance uppon the / worke those 10 dayes	00	6	8
For one day goeinge to Liverpoole / to agree with the wrights and glasiers	00	0	8
Spent uppon them at that time	00	00	4
	03 =	09 =	6

[f.76r]

Spent uppon Gyles Corker and his / man when they Came to sett up / the glasse	00	00	6
Paid to Henry Stananought for / 9 barrs for the scoole windowes	00	01	6
Paid to Gyles Corker for fiftye / Foote of new glasse >and six score quarrells putt in< for the Church / and scoole	01	12	0
Paid For lyme and heyre for point- / inge the same	00	00	6
For my attendance uppon the / workemen two dayes	00	01	4

103 Or *receiving*: the abbreviation *rec* is used.
104 See Introduction, p. xxxiii.

Paid to William Turner and / Nicholas Mercer for one dayes worke	00	02	0
paid to John Bridge for <the> stones / for thacktables for the Church	00	00	4
paid for Carijnge[105] the wood from / Liverpoole that made the wheele	00	00	6
paid for Iron worke for one bell	00	00	4
Payd to John Amond for a peece / of Timber to bee two supporters / for the Church	00	10	0
	02 =	09 =	0

[f.76v]

	£	s	d
Paid for fetchinge that timber from / the Clubmore	00	01	0
Paid for writeinge notes of my / Accompts	00	00	2
Paid for swines grease for the bels	0	00	6
Spent uppon Fryday in the Easter / weeke uppon the parishoners, beinge more in Number then formerly / use to bee for Chuseinge Church- / wardens	00	06	0
Paid to William Boates and his man / for 4 dayes worke about the makeing / of a bell wheele and puttinge the / rest of the bells in order, which were / much out of frame, and likewise for / puttinge uppe a peece of Timber / for a supporter in the Church	00	10	8
paid to a laborer for helpeinge them / to lifte and worke those 4 dayes	00	2	8
paid For nailes for that worke	00	1	6
paid for wyre for the Clocke	00	0	6
	01 =	03 =	00

[f.77r]

For my Attendance of the workemen / those fowre dayes	00	02	8
Paid to Nicholas Boulton	01	00	0
Paid to Edward Strange for / Iron worke for the bells	00	02	3
paid for writeinge notes of / my Accompts	00	00	2
paid for ingrosseinge my Accomptes	00	01	0
due to mee uppon arreare since / the last time I served Church- / warden as may appeare by / my Accompts	00	3	6
	01 =	9 =	7

105 Editors' transcription of a spelling used in this and the following account, employing a *y* with both arms dotted.

The totall sum of all the disbursmentes is	11 = 00	=	9
The totall of all the money received is	09 = 11	=	1
More disbursed then Received	01 = 9	=	8

These Accompts read and published in the parishe / Church of Walton <Aprill> May the 3d 1650 Coram

Henry Hokenhoils   Edward Strange
Nevill Kaye / vicario et ministro ibidem

1650–1651

[f.77v]

The Accompts of John Whitfeild / off Fazakerley, Churchwarden of / Walton for the yeare 1650

Itenpr[imis][106] Receipts

Received of the Cunstables of Walton Cum / Fazakerley for there proporcion of a / Church ley due the last yeare	01	6	8
Received from the Cunstables of / Darbye for a Church ley	04	00	0
Received from the Cunstable of / Kirkby the same ley	01	6	8
Received from the Cunstable of / Kirkdall the same ley	00	10	0
Received from the Cunstable / of Everton	00	06	8
Received from the Cunstable of / Bootle cum Linaker the same	00	10	0
	8 = 00		= 00

[f.78r]

Received from the Cunstable of / Formeby the same ley	01	6	8
Received of the Cunstables of Walton / Cum Fazakerley the same ley	01	6	8
Received of George Standish for a / ley stall	00	2	4
Received of Mistress Moore for a ley stall	00	2	4
Received of Cuthbert Halsall for a / ley stall for a yonge Child	00	1	2
Received of Master Bree>r<s for the same	00	1	2
Received for a ley stall for Margery / Goore	00	2	4
Received for a ley stall for William Woodes	00	2	4
Received for a ley stall for Dorathy / Woofall beinge buried in St / Pauls Chappell[107]	00	2	4
	3 = 7		= 4

---

106 Appears to be amalgam of *Item* and *Inprimis.*
107 See Introduction, p. xx.

[f.78v]

Disbursments: by John Whitfeild / Anno domini 1650

Imprimis due to mee uppon Arreare the / last yeare	01	9	8
Spent at the deliveringe upp / of my Accompts the last yeare	00	1	4
Spent at a meeteinge when the / parishoners Came to view the decay / of the Church and Concluded uppon / a ley for the repaire thereof	00	1	6
paid for wryteinge 8 precepts for / the Church ley	00	1	0
paid for sendinge the said precepts / to the severall Cunstables	00	0	6
spent at Walton when I went to / meete the overseers for the poore	00	0	8
spent at a meeteinge at Darbye / uppon the same occasion	00	0	8
	1 =	15 =	4

[f.79r]

paid for Carrijng 100 of slates into / the Church	00	0	2
spent at Childwell beinge Calld / by a warrant Concerneinge the poore	00	0	6
spent at Walton at a meeteinge / Concerneinge the same	00	0	4
spent at Liverpoole in goeinge / thither 2 severall dayes and one day to / Kirkbye Concerneinge the poore	00	1	0
paid for a new spade for the Church	00	1	6
spent at Liverpoole at a meeteinge / Concerneinge the poore	00	0	6
paid for Carijnge an order and Coppies / thereof unto the severall Cunstables	00	1	0
paid the Attorney for his Fee for / mooveinge for the said order	00	3	4
paid the Clarke of the peace for the / said order	00	1	4
	0 =	9 =	8

[f.79v]

paid for a new bellrope	00	03	0
paid to Sara Goovett for the / nurse of a Child	00	15	0
paid the Ringers the 5th of November	00	05	0
for my attendants that day	00	00	8
spent in goeinge to a Justice of peace / to Free the parish from keepeinge a / blynd man, beinge sent hither by / a warrant	00	0	8
paid for wryteinge notes of my Accompts		0	2
paid to Nicholas Boulton for Ringe- / inge the Corphye, sweepeinge the / Church and lookeinge to the Clocke	1	0	0

paid to Thomas Rothwell for mendinge / the Clocke and stuffe for the same	0	3	6
for my attendance uppon the worke / the same day	0	0	8
paid to Gyles Corker for 4½ foote of / new glasse and 20 quarrells	00	3	6
	2 =	12 =	2

[f.80r]

For my attendants	0	0	8
spent at Receipt of Darbye ley	0	0	2
paid for 2 dayes worke in mendinge / the formes and Churchyard Styles	0	2	0
paid for nayles	0	0	3
for my attendance uppon the worke		0	8
paid for a new belrope	0	2	6
spent in buyinge thereof	0	0	2
paid for wryteinge notes of my accompts	0	0	2
paid for 20 yards of stronge wyer / for the Clocke	0	1	6
spent uppon the Ringers January / the 29th beinge a day of thanksgive- / inge for severall victories	0	2	0
For my Attendants that day	0	0	8
paid to Sara Goovett for nurseinge / a Child	0	15	0
	1 =	5 =	9

[f.80v]

paid for oyle for the Clocke	0	0	6
spent at Receiving the Formebye ley	0	0	2
paid Michaell shurliker for / mendinge the Churchyard wall	0	1	0
for wryteinge notes of my accompts	0	0	2
paid to William Kirfoote for mendinge / two formes neare Collonel Moores pew / and for wood	0	2	0
for my Attendants	0	0	8
paid for 10 bushells of lyme	0	8	4
paid for fetchinge it from Liverpoole	0	2	0
paid for 10 bushells more lyme	0	8	4
paid for Fetchinge of it	0	2	0
For my goeinge to Liverpoole / to buy the lyme	0	0	8
paid to Edward Ryce for 3 dayes / worke in sleckinge siftinge / and layinge the same in steepe	0	3	0
	1 =	8 =	10

[f.81r]

paid a laborer for Carijnge water	0	1	0
For my attendance 3 dayes	0	2	0
paid for nayles for mendinge the / formes, and for new key	0	0	6
paid for 7 bushells of hayre and the / fetchinge of it	0	2	0
paid for 8 bushells of lyme	0	6	8
paid for the Carriadge of it / from Liverpoole	0	1	6
paid for two peeces of Timber / for the Roofe of the Church	0	9	0
paid to William Boates and his man for / theire worke 3 dayes	0	8	0
For nayles for the said worke	0	0	8
For my attendance uppon the / worke 3 dayes	0	2	0
spent of the workemen	0	0	6
	1	= 13 =	10

[f.81v]

paid for 4 bushells of hayre	0	1	0
paid for wryteinge notes of / my Accompts	0	0	2
paid for wood for eve poles for / the Church porch and >for< nayles	0	0	4
paid for two flagges, for the fetch- / inge and layinge them and mendinge / others in the Church	0	1	2
paid for leadinge Rubbish for of / the Church	0	0	4
paid to Edward Ryce for 33 dayes / worke at the Church	1	13	0
For my attendance 13 dayes	0	8	8
paid to Gyles Corker for glasseworke / and soderinge the leads	0	3	0
spent uppon the workemen 3 severall times		1	6
paid for ingrosseinge my accompts		2	0
	2	= 11 =	2

The totall of all the / disbursments this yeare is	11	= 16 =	9

[f.82r]

The totall of all the disbursments / for this yeare is	11	= 16 =	9
The totall of all the receipts / this yeare is	11	= 7 =	4
oweinge by the Towne of Liverpoole / for this Ley	2	= 13 =	4
more disbursed then received / is	0	= 9 =	5

Aprill the 4th 1651

These Accompts were Read in the / Church, before many parishoners /
and allowd of by Nevil Kaye vicar

[f.82v]

Aprill the 4th 1651

It is this day agreed uppon by severall / of the parishoners, that Thomas Rose / of Walton shall beē paid eight shillings / for keepeinge a poore man 8 dayes, and / two shillings to William Tatlocke of / Kirkbye which hee laid out about the remoo- / vinge of the said man, forth of the first / ley, which ley is to bee a twelve pound / ley, likewise Sarah Guffett is to bee / paid all the money that is due to her for / keepeinge a Child

Nevill Kaye vicarius et minister

[f.83r]

Churwarden for Walton parish Church / anno domini 1651 Edward henshall de Darby
<Sideman John Wigann de Kirkdale>
John Bankes Sydeman

[*f.83v is blank*]

[*f.84 is transcribed in its most appropriate place, before f.67 in 1641*]

1651–1652

[f.85r]

[*In this account figures of pounds, shillings and pence are usually separated by single dashes, and columns are headed by* £ s d *as shown.*]

The accomptes of Edward Henshawe of Westder... / Churchwarden of Walton for the yeare of our Lord / God 1651

Receiptes	£	s	d
First received from the Constables of Derbye	10	0	0
Alsoe received from the Constables of Kirckbie	3	6	8
Alsoe received from the Constables of Formbie	3	6	8
Alsoe received from the Constables of Walton / cum Fazakerley	3	6	8
Alsoe received from the Constables Bootle / cum Linaker	1	5	0
Alsoe received from the Constables of Kirckdall	1	5	0
Alsoe received from the Constables of Everton	0	16	8
Alsoe received from Master Ward[108] Towardes the / Cleansinge of the Chancell	0	3	0
Summa	23 –	9 –	8

---

108 William Ward, Rector since about 1645 (Pastor in Commonwealth terminology).

Received from Edward Moore Esquire[109] / towardes the glazing of his Pue	0	2	0
owing to the parish by the Mayor Bayliffes / and inhabitantes of Liverpoole	5	6	8

[f.85v]

Disbursmentes 1651

	£	s	d
First spent att Prescott the 24th of Aprill / being Called thither by the Constables about / the parish businesse the sydeman being with mee	0	0	6
Alsoe paid for a peticion >which was preferred< to the Justices for / the removiall of a bastard Child out of the / parish	0	0	4
Alsoe spent att Prescott the 26th of May / being Called thither by the Constables / to appeare att the sessions	0	0	6
Alsoe spent att Liverpoole when wee brought / the Bastard Child thither	0	0	6
Alsoe paid to Ellen Kenion for keeping the / said Child before itt was brought to / Liverpoole	0	4	0
Alsoe spent att Prescott the 29th of June / being Called thither by the Constables / to appeare att the sessions	0	0	4
Alsoe spent att the receipt of Formbie ley	0	0	2
Alsoe spent att the receipt of Kirckdall and / Bootle Leye	0	0	2
Alsoe paid to Sarah Govett for keeping / a Child Layd upon the parish in the ould / Churchwardens tyme	1	10	0
Alsoe spent att a meeting att Raph Hilles / about the parish businesse	0	1	0
	1 –	17 –	6

[f.86r]

	£	s	d
Alsoe paid to Nicholas Boulton Clarke of Walton	0	10	0
Alsoe paid to Thomas Rose of Walton for / keeping of a blynd man	0	8	0
Alsoe spent att the receipt of kirckbie Leye	0	0	2
Alsoe paid to William Tatlocke of kirckbie	0	2	0
Alsoe spent att Prescott being Called thither / by the Constables to appear att the sessions	0	0	4
Alsoe paid to Sarah Govett for keeping of / a Child Laid upon the parish	1	10	0

109 Son of Col. John Moore, who had died in 1650.

Alsoe spent att a meeting when the overseeres / of the poore met about Marye Higginsones / Children	0	2	4
Alsoe spent upon the Ringers the 10th of September	0	2	6
Alsoe spent in going to Sir Thomas Stanley / upon my self and my horse	0	1	0
Alsoe paid to a woman for Carrying a Lettre[110]/ to the Marshall <whe> to Liverpoole when the / Towne Was infected[111]	0	0	2
Alsoe spent att a meeting att Walton about / the removing of the prisoners out of the / Church[112]	0	1	0
Alsoe paid for the Wryting of 7 preceptes and / other notes of my account	0	1	4
Alsoe spent att Walton att a meeting / about Mashams Wife and Children	0	0	6
	2 – 19		– 4

[f.86v]

	£	s	d
Alsoe paid to John Hyton for dressing / the Church	2	0	0
Alsoe paid to John Hyton for making a hole / to putt in the strawe and pelf that was in the / Church	0	1	0
Alsoe spent att a meeting att Walton /about the parish busines	0	2	6
Alsoe spent upon the dressers of the Church / and my self	0	0	4
Alsoe paid for a Locke to sett upon the Church / doore	0	1	4
Alsoe paid to William Fleetwood of Knowsley / for glazing the Church and schoolehouse[113]	1	2	6
Alsoe paid for <Wy...> Wyre to mend the Clocke / and for franckinsence and pitch for the Church	0	0	6
Alsoe paid for oyle for the Clocke	0	0	6
Alsoe paid for Two Belropes	0	5	4
Alsoe paid for Rushes to strowe in the / Belhouse	0	0	2
Alsoe spent att the buying of the belropes	0	0	2
Alsoe spent upon the ringers the foure / and Twentith of October	0	1	6
Alsoe spent upon the Carpenters smith / and dressers of the Church when itt was / in Cleansinge	0	1	0
	3 – 18		– 10

110 Editor's expansion of *Lre* with mark of contraction.
111 Plague was endemic at the time.
112 Following the Battle of Worcester; see Introduction, p. xxxiii.
113 Entry marked with a cross in the left margin; see notes on annotations, p. 176.

[f.87r]

	£	s	d
Alsoe paid for a peticion which was preferred <to> / to the Justices att Wigan	0	0	6
Alsoe spent upon the overseeres of the poore / and dressers of the Church att a meeting about / the parish businesse	0	1	6
Alsoe paid to Margerie Lidgeat	0	1	0
Alsoe paid to the Ringers upon the fyfte of / November for ringing	0	5	0
Alsoe <paid> spent in going to Collonell / Ireland upon my self and my horse	0	0	9
Alsoe paid to Collonell Irelandes Clarke	0	1	0
Alsoe paid to Margerie Lidgeat	0	1	0
Alsoe spent in going to Sir Thomas Stanley / upon my self and my horse	0	1	0
Alsoe spent upon the Carpenters when / they Wrought att the Church	0	1	0
Alsoe for my attendance there Three dayes	0	2	0
Alsoe for my attendance one daye when / the Church was in Cleansing	0	0	8
Alsoe spent in going to Crosbie to the / Clockmaker	0	0	6
Alsoe paid to Margerie Lidgeat	0	1	0
Alsoe paid to the Clockmaker for mending / the Clocke and setting itt in frame	0	2	6
Alsoe spent upon the Clockmaker and other / Workmen att the Church	0	0	6
Alsoe for my attendance the same daye	0	0	8
	1 –	0 –	7

[f.87v]

	£	s	[d][114]
Alsoe paid for Workmens dyett when the / Church was in <Cleansing> glazing	0	4	6
Alsoe paid to Nicholas <Bolton> Mercer for poynting / the glasses and mending a place where itt rayn'd / into the Church	0	1	0
Alsoe spent when the Franckinsence and pitch / was >burnt< in the Church	0	0	3
Alsoe paid unto the Workemen for their / wages and Timber for the Church	1	6	<8>
Alsoe paid to John darbishire for nailes for / the Church	0	4	0

114 Omitted, £ and s forming part of the first entry instead of appearing as column headings.

Alsoe paid to Sarah Govett for keeping a / Child Laid upon the parish	0	15	0
Alsoe spent upon the overseers of the poore / and my self att Prescott the 12th of december	0	0	11
Alsoe spent att the receipt of Kirckbie Leye	0	0	2
Alsoe spent the 14th of Januarie att the sessions / att Prescott	0	0	8
Alsoe spent att the receipt of Bootle cum / Linaker Ley	0	0	2
Alsoe paid to Sarah Govett for keeping a / Child Layd upon the parish	0	15	0
Alsoe paid to Nicholas Bolton Clarke of / Walton	0	10	0
Alsoe spent in going to demaund Liverpoole / Ley	0	0	4
Alsoe paid to Thomas Strange for making / an Iron shovell and mending a Locke to sett / on the Church doore	0	2	6
Alsoe paid for glue Linseede oyle and redd / Lead for the Church and a botle to put the same in[115]	0	7	3
	4 –	7 –	9

[f.88r]

	£	s	d
Alsoe spent att the buying of the same	0	0	4
Alsoe spent att the receipt of Walton cum Fazakeley Ley	0	0	2
Alsoe paid for Eighteene Bushelles of Lyme for / the Church	0	14	0
Alsoe spent when I went to Liverpoole to buy / the Lyme	0	0	6
Alsoe paid for Carring the Lyme from Liverpoole / to Walton	0	2	0
Alsoe spent att the Carrying the Lyme	0	0	6
Alsoe paid for fetching a Ladder from kirckdall	0	0	3
Alsoe for my attendance the 9th of March	0	0	8
Alsoe spent in going to Liverpoole two severall / dayes to fetch the Lyme itt being not readie	0	0	4
Alsoe paid unto Richard Blackmore for / Lyme to poynt the glasses With	0	0	6
Alsoe paid for beesoms for the Church	0	0	1
Alsoe for my attendance the 10th of march	0	0	8
Alsoe paid for an order to Clear the parish of / an ould blynd man the which was due in the old / Churchwardens tyme	0	2	4
Alsoe paid for a spade for the Church	0	2	0
Alsoe paid for a horse Loade of Coales to / boyle size with	0	0	8
Alsoe paid to Edward Ryce and his men for / Worke att the Church	1	0	0
Alsoe for my attendance the 13th of march	0	0	8
Alsoe spent upon the Workemen when / the Church was in Whitning	0	0	6

115 Recipe for paint.

Alsoe paid to William kerfoote for Timber / to mend two formes with and his workmanship	0 0	4
Alsoe paid to John darbishire for nayles for / the same	0 0	1

$$2 - 6 - 7$$

[f.88v]

	£	s	d
Alsoe spent upon the Workemen the 17th of / March	0	0	6
Alsoe for my attendance the 16t and 17t of march	0	1	4
Alsoe more paid to William Fleetwood for / glazing the Church and sothering the Leades	0	11	0
Alsoe paid for the workemans dyett when / the same was in doing	0	2	9
Alsoe for my attendance the 9th daye of march	0	0	8
Alsoe <for> paid to Edward Ryce and his men	1	3	0
Alsoe paid for a horse Load of Coales	0	0	8
Alsoe spent upon the workemen 24th of march	0	0	4
Alsoe paid for glazing the schoole[116]	0	3	2
Alsoe for my attendance the 24th of march	0	0	8
Alsoe paid to Edward Ryce and his men	0	19	0
Alsoe spent upon the workemen when I paid / them their Wages	0	0	6
Alsoe for my attendance the 26t of march	0	0	8
Alsoe paid to Master Kaye for the Carriage of Twoe / Letters to Landon to gett the bread money	0	1	0
Alsoe spent upon the Workemen the 3d of Aprill	0	0	6
Alsoe for my attendance the 3d and 7th of Aprill	0	1	4
Alsoe paid Richard Leyland for mending a forme	0	0	2
Alsoe spent upon the workemen the 6t of Aprill	0	0	2
Alsoe paid to Edward Ryce and his men for worke / att the Church	1	1	2
Alsoe spent upon the workemen when the worke / was finished	0	0	6
Alsoe paid to Sarah Govett for keeping a / Child Laid upon the parish	0	7	6
Alsoe paid for haire for the Church	0	1	3
Alsoe paid to Thomas Strange for worke att / the Church	0	0	10

$$4 - 18 - 8$$

[f.89r]

	£	s	...
Alsoe spent when I sett the Worke att the / schoole	0	0	4
Alsoe paid for rowles for the schoole Lofte	0	0	6
Alsoe for my attendance upon the Worke / men	0	0	8

116 Entry marked with a cross in the left margin; see notes on annotations, p. 176.

Alsoe paid for Leading Clay unto the / schoolehouse	0	3	9
Alsoe for my attendance the 15th of Aprill	0	0	8
Alsoe paid to John Wigan for slates	0	0	6
Alsoe paid to Michaell shurliker for Laying / the schoolehouse Loft floare	0	8	0
Alsoe spent upon the workemen when the / worke was finished	0	0	4
Alsoe paid for Leading slates and sand unto / the schoolehouse[117]	0	1	0
Alsoe paid to John Banckes for going to / Sefton with an order to the Justices	0	0	6
Alsoe paid to John Banckes for a daye and a / halfes attendance when I cold not bee there / myself	0	1	0
Alsoe paid to William kerfoote for Barres for / the schoolehouse Windowes	0	0	6
Alsoe paid for Carrying the Ladder from / Walton to Kirckdall	0	0	3
Alsoe paid for an acquittance for the bread / money	0	0	2
Alsoe spent att the receiptes of the Latter Ley / from Formbie	0	0	2
Alsoe paid for a sive and a mugg	0	0	5
Alsoe paid for ingrossing my accountes	0	2	0
	1	– 0 –	9

[The following three entries are added as an afterthought and squeezed alongside the reconciliation, but are shown separately here for clarity. They employ roman numerals.]

Alsoe paid for straw to make dobe with		11d
Alsoe paid to Sereh Gofitt for keeing / a Child laid upon the paris...	7s	6d
Alsoe spent upon the parishnors when / the New Church warden was / Chosenn	2s	2d

received / the somme off	23 – 11 – 8
disbursed	22 – 10 – 0
remayning <...> undisbursed	1 – 1 – 8

[f.89v]

The accounts of Edward henshawe / Churchwarden of Walton 1651 / Rec[eive]d and approovd the 23 of aprill 1652

Nevill Kaye vicar Waltone

Robert Mercer

117 Entry marked with a cross in the left margin, which may be intended as a note for the whole page, with its other references to work at the school. See notes on annotations, p. 176.

	£	s	d
	2 =	12 =	5
	1 =	15 =	7[118]

Richard Johnson
John Boulton
Thomas Boulton

Thomas Martin and Richard Boulton of / Walton cum Fazakerley Churchwarden and Sideman / Elect for the yeare 1652
Item a Ley of six pounds proportiatly to bee / paid unto the Churchwarden for the Church / use att or before the 24th of June next / by the parishioners ordered

[f.90r]

alsoo wase disborsed and un sed doune   £0   0s   6d
wich was spent the 11th[119] dey of mey / at the seshons Coled
    thither by the Constebeles

                                                                         £23 – 1s – 1d[120]

1652–1653

[f.90v]

[In this account and the next, figures of pounds, shillings and pence are separated by the = sign, and columns are headed by £ s d as shown (heading lost on f.92r and not entered on f.97v).]

June the 4th 1652
Received the day and yeare above said of and from / Edward
    Henshawe late Churchwarden   11s   1d[121]

[f.91r]

The Accomptes of Thomas Martin / of Fazakerley Churchwarden of Wallton /
            for the >yeare< of our lord 1652[122]

---

118 Amount probably added subsequent to the signatures, followed by other smudged figures includ-
      ing a 5, possibly deliberately erased.
119 Or possibly *14th*.
120 Written at extreme foot of page, representing total disbursements for 1651 including the above
      and the additional entries on f.89r.
121 Remainder of page blank except for the word *for*.
122 Spaces around the heading contain doodles and other characters, also a sum representing 1732
      minus 1652 = 80, apparently in the same handwriting as the account. A forward calculation of
      years may be intended.

Receiptes

	£	s	d
Imprimis Received of Edward Henshawe late / Churchwarden of moneys which he had in his hands	0	11	1
Allsoe Received of the Constables of / Wallton cum Fazakerley	1	6	8
Allsoe Received of the Constables of Kirkeby	1	6	8
Allsoe Received of the Constables of Formeby	1	6	8
Allsoe Received of the ley layers of Derby	4	0	...
Allsoe Received of the Constables of Kirkedale	0	10	...
Allsoe Received of the Constables of Bootle cum linaker	0	10	...
Allsoe Received of the Constables of Everton	0	6	8
Totum	£9 =	17 =	...
>oweinge by the towne of Liverpoole	2	13	4[123]<

Other Receiptes

	£	s	d
Imprimis For a ley stall for Widow Woods	0	2	...
Allsoe for a ley stall for Thomas Boulton	0	2	...
Allsoe for a ley stall for his wife	0	2	...
Allsoe for a ley stall for widow Stones	0	1	2
Allsoe for a ley stall for Richard Straunge[124]	0	2	4
Allsoe for a ley stall for William Rose	0	2	...
Allsoe for a ley stall for George Woods	0	2	...
Totum	£0 =	15 =	...

[f.91v]

Disbursed

	£	s	d
Imprimis Spent att the privy sessions att / Prescott being called thither by the Constables	0	0	6
Spent when we mett att Wallton to Consider / how Robert Higginsons Child should be kept	0	1	2
Payd for writting Articles of Agreement betwixt / Thomas Higginson and his daughter in law concer / ninge the keeping of the Child	0	0	4
Allsoe for A Bond for performance the said / Articles, And a discharge for the Parish / from the said Child	0	0	6
Payd for Eight preceptes for the Church ley	0	1	4
Spent att the sessions at Prescott the 23th / of June being called thither by the Constables	0	0	6

123 Amount unclear: the shillings appear to have been altered to or from *16*. Entry added by a different hand.
124 Exact spelling intended is uncertain due to a dot over one minim.

Spent when I went to provyde a house for / William Swift and his sonne according to Order	0	0	8
Spent the 27th of June when I mett the Overseers / to Enlist the poore of the Parish	0	0	4
Payd for writting A lyst of the poore, and par / ticularizing the Impotent, Apprentizes, and / such as were able to worke	0	0	6
Payd for Copyinge A note delivered by the Justices / which declared the office of Overseers and whatt they / ought to doe Concerninge their office	0	0	6
Payd for Nayles for the Church July the 15th	0	0	6
Totum	£0	= 6s =	10d

[f.92r]

For Writting notes of my Accompts	0	0	...
Payd for Wood to William Kerfoote July 13th	0	2	0
Payd for his worke att the Formes in the / Church July the 13th	0	0	10
For my Attendaunce upon the worke	0	0	8
Spent with the Overseers of the poore / att the second meetting	0	0	2
Payd for two Bellropes July the 22th	0	6	0
Spent when I bought them	0	0	2
Payd for Wyre for the Clocke	0	0	10
Payd for Sallet oyle for the Clocke	0	0	4
Spent when I went to the sessions att / Ormschurch July the 19th	0	0	6
Payd to Sara[h][125] Govett July the 26th	0	15	0
Payd to the Glazier for glazing att / the Church October the 11th	0	1	8
Payd for provision for the Glazer and spent	0	0	1...
For my attendance upon the Glazer October the 11th	0	0	8
Payd for writting notes of my Accompts	0	0	...
Payd for Mending the third bell Clapper	0	0	...
Earnest to the stone getter in parte of his wages	0	0	...
Totum	£1	= 10s =	...

[f.92v]

	£	s	d
Spent upon the Masons Smith and Carpenter / that came to view the great Bell	0	0	9
Payd to Thomas Bowden for / hanginge the great Bell	0	5	0
Payd to the Ringers the 5th November / and for Candles and Tobacco for them	0	5	2
Spent upon the Masons and Glazier November 8th	0	0	8

---

125 Written *Sara:*, as if contracted.

	£	s	d
Spent upon the Workemen when they / made the steele November the 9th	0	0	9
For my attendance two dayes when the bell / was taken downe and hung up againe	0	1	4
Payd for Soder and three dayes worke / att the leades	0	8	0
Payd for his provision the three dayes	0	2	0
Payd for fyre to heatt the Irons to Soder / and for a quart of beare for him	0	0	6
Payd for my attendance the three dayes	0	2	0
Spent upon the Masons working att the steeles	0	0	5
Payd to Thomas Straunge for Iron / and his worke about hanging the great Bell	0	8	6
Payd to John Butler for getting stones	0	13	10
Totum	£2	= 8s	= 11d

[f.93r]

	£	s	d
Payd to William Turner for his worke- / manshippe att the 3 Steeles and for / engravinge upon them	1	10	6
Payd to Richard Boulton for leadinge / eighteene loades of Stones	0	7	6
Spent upon the Masons att the finishinge / of their worke	0	1	4
Payd for Copijnge[126] two Orders and writting / notes of my Accompts	0	0	6
Spent upon the Parishoners december the 7th	0	1	0
Payd for Writting Eight precepts	0	1	0
Spent upon the Masons when the steeles were / all three measured	0	1	6
Payd to Nicholas Boulton for Tendinge / the Clocke sweepinge the Church and ringinge Curfu	1	0	0
Payd towards suppressing of the Quakers	0	6	8
Payd to the Atturney for pleading for an / Order that Liverpoole might be forced to pay / att the Sessions the 17th of January	0	3	4
Payd for the Order for Liverpoole to pay	0	1	4
Itt cost me of my horse and my selfe being / two dayes att the Sessions	0	2	8
Totum	£3	= 17s	= 4d

[f.93v]

	£	s	d
Payd to Sara Govett for keepinge the / child upon November the 11th	0	15	0
Spent att Formeby in demandeinge / the Church ley	0	0	4

126 Editors' transcription of dotted *y*; see notes to 1649-50 account, p. 76.

Spent upon two Fishermen that / brought Formeby ley to Liverpoole	0	0	4
Payd the 26th of January to John / Stukeley for releefe of Ten distres[s]ed / passengers which had an Order from the Generall	0	2	6
Spent in goeinge three severall times / to Liverpoole to demand the Church ley with / the arreares	0	0	6
Payd to Sara[h] Govett the 02th[127] February / for keeping the Child	0	15	0
Payd to Thomas Rothell for mendinge / the Clocke and for a quart of beare / and his dinner	0	2	10
Given to a man which Came with an Order / to have a colleccion	0	0	6
Payd to Nicholas Boulton for three Bushells / of lyme which lay in the Church	0	2	6
Payd for all most fower foote of Glasse	0	1	6
Totum	2 =	1 =	0

[f.94r]

	£	s	...
Payd for Engrossinge My Accompts	0	2	0
Payd for Walling at the Churchyard / to Thomas Wigan	0	0	10

	£	s	d
Received the some of	10 =	12 =	11
Disbursed	10 =	7 =	10
Remaining / undisbursed	0 =	5 =	1

[*The following lines concerning the election and ley are written alongside the above reconciliation but are shown separately here for clarity.*]

Thomas Boulton elected Church- / warden and Thomas Henshawe Sideman / for the yeare 1653

Allsoe A ley of Twelve pounds in the / parish to be payd unto Thomas Boulton Church- / warden att or before the last of May

Owing to the parish by the Maior Baylives / and Inhabitants of Liverpoole	2	13	4
Spent of the aforesaid some that was undisbursed / with the parishoners, at the eleccion of a nother	0	2	2

Read and Allowed by the parishoners / the 15th of Aprill Anno domini 1653

>Spent when I went to / Childwell for the parish 6d<

127 Overwritten correction with unclear intention.

Nevill Kaye/ vicar anno 1621[128]

          Edward Moore
          William Ward pastor ibidem
          Richard Johnson
          Thomas Boulton
          Richard Blackmore

1653–1654

[f.94v was apparently written out of sequence, and has been transcribed in its supposed chronological place between the end of 1653–54 and the beginning of 1654–55.]

[f.95r]

The Accomptes of Thomas Boulton / Churchwarden of Wallton for the /
yeare of our lord god 1653

Receiptes

	£	s	d
Imprimis Received of Thomas Martin late / Churchwarden of moneyes he had in his hands	0	2	5
Allsoe Received of the Constables of Walton cum Fazakerley	1	6	8
Allsoe Received of the Constables of Kirkeby	1	6	8
Allsoe Received of the Constables of Formeby	1	6	8
Allsoe Received of the Constables of Derby	4	0	0
Allsoe Received from the Constables of Bootle cum linaker	0	10	0
Allsoe Received of the Constables of Kirkdale	0	10	0
Allsoe Received of the Constables of Everton	0	6	8
Allsoe Received for two ley stalls for George / Standish and his wife	0	4	8
Allsoe Received for a ley stall for Master / William Fazakerley	0	2	4
Tot[um][129]	£9 =	16s =	1d

[f.95v]

Disbursements

	£	s	d
Imprimis paid for writtinge eight precepts	0	1	0
Itt cost me in gettinge them to / the severall Constables in the parish	0	1	4
Paid to the Glasyer the Fifteenth / day of October	0	5	0

128 His year of induction to Walton.
129 Expansion of *Tot:* in line with same scribe's spelling in earlier account.

	£	s	d
Paid to the Slator the same day	0	1	6
Paid for writtinge my notes	0	0	2
Paid for lyme	0	1	2
For my attendance upon the Glasyer and / Slator the 15° day of october	0	0	8
Given to a man that had a passe and / order for releefe	0	0	6
Payd to the man that mended the Clocke	0	1	4
For my attendance that day	0	0	8
Payd to Sara Govett for keeping the / Child this yeere	2	13	0
Itt cost me with the overseers of the poore 30° November	0	01	2
spent att the receipt of the moneyes from Walton / cum Fazakerley Derby and Bootle cum linaker	0	0	6
	3 =	8 =	0

[f.96r]

	£	s	d
Paid for a Warrant to collect the money / from Liverpoole	0	2	0
Itt cost me att the same time	0	0	6
Itt cost me allsoe att the sessions att ormschurch / upon my selfe and my horse being there 2 dayes	0	5	4
Paid to the Atturney	0	3	4
Paid to the Ringers the 5° of november	0	5	0
For my attendance that day	0	0	8
Paid to a man and eight persons that had / a passe and order for releefe	0	1	6
Itt cost me att Kirkby concerninge their ley	0	0	6
Itt cost me in December with the overseers	0	0	6
Paid to William Kirrfoote for ladder staves / and for stavinge itt	0	2	6
Paid to William Kirfoote for mendinge / the formes August the 11th	0	0	10
Paid to the Glasyer in August	0	3	4
Spent upon the Glasyer and his man	0	0	4
For my attendance three dayes	0	2	0
Itt cost me att Formeby upon my selfe / and my horse	0	0	6
Itt cost me the first time I went to Liverpoole / to demand their ley	0	0	6
	1 =	9 =	4

[f.96v]

	£	s	d
Itt allsoe cost me the second I went with / Richard Blackmoore to demand their ley	0	0	6

Itt cost me the third time I went to Liverpoole / when I delivered the order to the Maior	0	0	6
Given to a poore widow that had an order / for a Collection	0	1	6
Paid to the Clerke for tendinge the Clocke / sweepinge the Church and ringing Curfu	01	0	0
Itt cost me allsoe att severall other times / in goeing to Liverpoole and other wayes	0	0	8
Itt cost me when Master Moores man went / with me to Sir Thomas Stanley	0	1	6
Paid to the Glasyer the 10th day of November	0	5	6
Itt cost me when the side man went with me / to the Sessions holden att Wigan >3 daies<	0	5	4
Paid for wire and oyle for the Clocke	0	1	6
Spent another time att Liverpoole	0	0	6
For my attendance that day when the wire / and oyle was used to the Clocke	0	0	8
Paid to John Buttler for stone / towards the makinge of the Steele	0	3	0
	1 =	2 =	2

[f.97r]

	£	s	d
Paid for a Register Booke and cost / in procuringe itt	0	12	0
Paid to William Kirfoote for mend- / inge the formes 24° December	0	1	0
For my Attendance that day	0	0	8
Given to a man and his wife that had a passe	0	0	6
Paid to the Glasyer 24° February	0	3	0
Payd to the Clocke-smith the same day	0	1	6
Allsoe for oyle	0	0	6
For my attendance that day	0	0	8
Payd to the Mason for makinge a / weight for the Clocke	0	1	0
To Thomas Wigan for mendinge the Churchyard wall	0	0	10
To Richard Layland for settinge 2 Clapes on >the Church< ladder	0	0	2
Paid for mendinge the Churchyard gate	0	0	7
Paid John Shurliker for writtinge my notes	0	0	8
payd for a Bellrope	0	3	6
Spent upon William Mercer and them / that mended the ropes	0	0	6
Spent att the receipt of the moneyes from / Kirkeby Formeby and Everton	0	0	6

[*total missing*]

[f.97v]

I payd for an order att the / sessions holden att Ormschurch	0	1	4
Itt cost me when I went to Childwell / being summoned thither by warrant	0	0	6
Paid for the workmanship att the / Steele towards Bootle, and engraving on >itt<	0	10	10
Paid more to John Buttler for / stone to finish the Steele	0	1	8
It cost me of the Masons while they worked / att the steele and finished itt	0	1	0
Paid for two Bushells of lyme and / for Cariage of itt	0	1	10
Payd for leadinge Five loads of / stones for the Churchyard steele	0	2	6
For my attendaunce 2 dayes upon / the Masons att the steele	0	1	0
Paid to Richard Layland for / erectinge a Steele att the schoole / house end	0	0	10
	£1	= 1s	= 6d

[f.98r]

Payd for engrossinge my / Accompts	0	2	0
	<0	2	6>
Itt cost me when I finished / these reckonings	0	0	6
	0	= 2	= 6

The whole some dis- / bursed is	8	11	1
The some Received is	9	16	1
Remaininge	1	05	0

Owing by the Maior and Baylives / of Liverpoole	£2	13s	4d

Read and allowed by the parishoners / March the 31th 1654
George Smith   Edward Moore
                                William Ward pastor[130]
                                Ro[bert] Mercer
                                Richard Blackmoore
                                Thomas X Martin / his mark[131]

[f.98v]

Marcii 31° 1654

William Rydinge elected Churchwarden / and John Swift <sworn> side man

Allsoe it is agreed that a ley of £6 in the parish / shall be collected and paid unto William Rydinge / Churchwarden att or before Tuesday / in the Whittson weeke

---

130 Absence of the vicar's signature may indicate incapacity: he died in June 1654.
131 Mark blotted.

Disbursed of the aforesaid some that Remained in my / hands

	£	s	d
as followeth			
Imprimis more given unto Sara[h] Govett	0	7	0
more to Richard Layland	0	0	2
Spent upon the parishoners att the eleccion / of a new Churchwarden	0	3	6
For mendinge the Clocke twise and / spent upon him that mended itt	0	2	0
Received by William Rydinge from	0 = 12s = 4d[132]		

1654–1655

[f.94v]

[In the same hand as the 1654–55 account, though apparently written out of place in the book. Transcribed in its supposed chronological place.]

Received of the Old Churchwarden Thomas Boulton / By me William Rydinge
bondes for the use of schoole / att Waltoon this present yeare 1654

Imprimis William Cadicke for	£20
Item Thomas storie for	£13
Item Mistress Mollineuxe for	£3
Item hugh Rose of Walton for	£10
Item William Ascroft for	£5
Item John Tyrer of Alker for	£4
Ite[m] Master Kaye deceased for	£4
Item hugh Rose of Clubmore for	£6
Item Thomas Watmough for	£3
Item Thomas Tyrer of litherland for	£10
Ite[m] Nicholas Copple allsoe for	£5
Ite[m] William Aspineall for	£6
Ite[m] Robert Wright for	£7
Ite[m] Master Roger bryars for	£17
Item Raph Burges for	£2
Ite[m] Ann Turner for	£3
Item Elizabeth stones for	£7
It[em] Master Chorley schoolemaister for	£4
Ite[m] Thomas Martin for >n... bonnde<	17s
Ite[m] 2 bondes more one Master Allexander Mullinex >for £42< other William higinson >for £6<	

---

132 Pence possibly altered from *8*, the correct figure, to agree with the amount passed to William Ryding.

[f.99r]

[*Tabulation of amounts is somewhat variable in this account. The separator is usually a single dash, and there is occasional use of roman numerals, as indicated in the notes.*]

The Accountes of William Rydinge Churchwarden of / Walton for the yeare of our lord god 1654[133]

Receiptes

Imprimis Received of Thomas Boulton late Churchwarden / of monies he had in his hand	0	12s	4d
Rec[eive]d for a lose stone that was tacken / out of the Church wall or steele when / it was made new of John Knowles the dyer	0	0	6d
Received of the Cunstables of Walton cum fazakerley	0	13s	4d
Received of the Cunstables of formeby	0	13	4
Received of the Cunstables of Kerby	0	13	4
Received of the Cunstables of Darbie	£2	0	0
Received of the Cunstables of Kerdall	0	5	0
Received of the Cunstables of Bootle	0	5	0
Received of the Cunstables of Everton	0	3	4
Received for a ley stall for Edward / henshawe of Darbie	0	2	4

Receptes £5 >8s< 6d[134]

[*f.99v is blank*]

[f.100r]

Disbursmentes

Imprimis spent att the Receivinge of Oulde / Churchwardens acountes on him and others	£0	0s	8d
Item spent at twoe severall tymes in meetinge / some of the parishe att Walton about the Church / busines	0	0	10
Item paid for writinge Eight preceptes for the / Church ley and some other notes that the / schoolmaister writ	0	1	4
Ite[m] spente when I got the preceptes unto the / severall towenshipes	0	0	4
Item spent the 30th day of July beinge / the saboth upon my self the sydeman / and some others stayinge all the daye	0	1	0
Ite[m] spent att leverpoole Walton and / Kerckbie in laboringe to get Master finch / establised our vicaer att Walton	0	1	8
Item spent the 6 day of August beinge / the saboth att Walton about the vicar	0	0	8

133 Last digit appears to be corrected from *3*, and the date *1654* has been repeated, or added at a later date, below.
134 Roman numerals.

Ite[m] spent the 13 of August beinge the / saboth day att Walton	0	0	4
Payde to Sara govett for keepinge / the Childe this yeare and allsoe to free the / parishe hearafter John litherland of / breckesyde her pledge	£3	0	0

3 6 10

[f.100v]

Payd for mending Church walls	00	00	06
Payde unto nicholas Boulton for / tendinge the Clocke swipinge the Church / and Ringinge Corfie	£1	0s	0d
spent att the Receit of the Church ley	0	0	[?4]
spent in seeckinge Richard bibie / to mende the Clocke	0	0	6
payd for wyre to mend the Clocke	0	0	11
payd unto Richard bibie for mendinge / the Clocke and spent on him that day	0	3	0
payd for oyle	0	1	0
for my attendance that day	0	0	8
payd unto William Watmough the / smith for the locke <of> and key of steeple doore	0	1	0
payd unto the sydeman John swifte that he spent / att severall tymes in my absence and sicknes	0	2	4
James pye 2 fox heades[135]	0	2	0
William hallsall one fox head	0	1	0
Robert Mercer one fox head	0	1	0
Edward tamlinson 2 fox heades	0	2	0
Edmond Kerckebie five heades	0	4	6
Spent att the payment for the / fox heades	0	0	4
given unto a passenger that had Order for / Relife and sente frome Walton unto my house by Master fince our vicar	0	0	6

2...[136]

[f.101r]

[More than one hand has contributed to the reconciliation account, and all calculations following the initial entry on the page use roman numerals.]

paid To William Ward for writing a petition / and getting part of parish names	00	01	00[137]

The whole some disbursed	£5 <12s>9s 11d <£5 9s 11d>
The some Rec[eive]d is	£5 8s 6d

---

135 See notes on annotations, p. 176.
136 Running total unclear.
137 Or *06*.

<...>
Layd out more then received	17d
Owinge by Richard fazacarley for / Aley stall	
for his mother	2s 4d
Oweinge by the Maior and Baylives / of Leverpoole	
for the Church ley	£1 6s 8d

Aprill 20th 1655
Henry Halsall of Bootle Elected Churchwarden and / Thomas Knowles of Walton
sideman
Alsoe it is Agreed that >two< leys of £6 >aley< in the parish shalbe / Collected
and payd unto Henry Halsall Churchwarden / att or before Tuesday in
Whittsonweeke.

> John Heywood Pastor[138]
> Henry Finch vicar
> Richard Blackmoore
> Nicholas Cowper
> John X Much / his Marke
> Thomas X Ma...[139]

[*f.101v is blank*]

[f.102r]

[*This folio may be slightly out of order. The handwriting appears to match that of
1654–55, and the first item is referred to on the next page in the list of school bonds
handed over at the end of that year, but the total does not appear to have been
included in the reconciliation.*]

Disbursmentes Concerninge the schoole att Walton / agaynst the lorde	
Mullinex onelie and as yet untryed	12s 9d[140]
Imprimis spent att leverpoole uppon the Commicioners for pious uses /	
to gett some wittneses sworne Concerninge the schoole stockes[141]	10...
Item att prescot another tyme to advise with Master stockeley / howe I	
might Commence a sute against some we[r]cke men / Or tacke writes	
for their bodies	4d
spent the 3 day of October att prescot meetinge the / Commisioners	
there with Master Johnson of Everton	6d
Payde unto the sayde Master Johnson for the Carges / of him selfe and	
his man stayinge all night	2s

138 See Introduction, p. xii concerning his anomalous appearance. Ward had died during the year.
139 Or *Mo...* Marks are *IM* (John Much) and *TM* (Thomas Ma...).
140 Shillings expressed in roman numerals. This sum appears to be the total disbursed, those fol-
    lowing being its components; (if so, the first item must be pence, *7s* should read *7d*, and the
    addition is still inaccurate).
141 See Introduction, p. xxviii.

spent the laste of October att prescott	6d
spent the 20 of novenber att prescot havinge 2 wittnes / Richard blackemore and henry pemberton sworne before / the Commiconers spent on them and my selfe	18d
Payde unto John Parr for drawinge of theire / Depositions which they were sworne unto	16d
Payd for 2 preceptes to bringe Richard blackmore / and henry pemberton before the Commisioners	7s
spent the second of Januarie uppon Richard blackmore / Nicholas Couper and my selfe sent to assiste mee >att< / prescot by the parishe	9d
payde for 4 preceptes agaynste the lorde mullinex his father / granfather and Sir vivian theire executores	2s
payde unto Raphe burges for the deliverie of the preceptes	2s

12 [?9]

[f.102v]

Delivered in bondes and monie for the use of schoole att Walton by William / Rydinge unto henry halsall warden and schoole Rive for the yeare 1655

Imprimis William Cadicke for	£20
Thomas storie for	£13
Mistres Mollinex for	£3
hugh Ros of Walton for	£10
William Ascroft for	£5
John Tyrer for	£4
hugh Rose of Clubmore for	£6
Thomas Watmough for	£3
Thomas Tyrer for	£10
Nicholas Copple for	£5
William Aspinwall for	£6
Robert Wright for	£7
Roger Bryers for	£17
Raph burgesse for	£2
Ann Turner for	£3
Elizabeth stones for	£7
John Chorley for	£4
In monie delivered that was / oweing by vicarr Key[142]	£4
more delivered that was left / unspent, out of seaventeen / shillinges I Rec[eive]d frome / Thomas Martine	4s 3d
spent agaynst the lorde Mullinex	12s 9d[143]

142 *Hamlett Boulton* in margin next to this entry.
143 See f.102r.

[*Matter from here to the end of the page is written alongside and to the right of the above list in the original.*]

Delivered one bond of / Master Alexsander Mullinex / which
   debt is proved to / be Owing by the lorde / Mullinex
   deaceased /by Master Johnson late of Everton / beinge
   examined hath / tested the same and tenn years / use being
   unpayde   £42

I delivered a bond of / William higginson for / beinge a despert debt

1655–1656

[f.103r]

[*In this and the following accounts up to and including 1658–59 the symbols £ s d are almost always dispensed with by the scribe, who usually employs the = sign as a separator.*]

The Accomptes of Henry Halsall of Bootle / Churchwarden of Walton for the
yeare of / our Lord god 1655

Receiptes

	£	s	d
Received of Richard Fazakerley for >a< Ley stall / for his mother, beinge in Arreare	0	2	4
Received from the Cunstables of Kirkdall / for a Church ley	0	10	0
Received from the Cunstables of Walton and Fazakerley for theire Ley	1	6	8
Received from the Cunstables of Formeby	1	6	8
Received from the Cunstables of Bootle Cum Linaker	0	10	0
Received from the Cunstables of Everton	0	6	8
Received from the Cunstables of Darbye	4	00	0
Received from the Chappellwarden of / Kirkbie	1	6	8
Received for a Ley stall for Margrett Worrall		2	4
Received for a ley stall for Captain Smithes Child	0	1	2
	9 =	12 =	6

[f.103v]

Disbursmentes For the yeare 1655

	£	s	d
Imprimis Paid to William Rydeinge late Churchwarden / beinge due to him uppon Account	0	1	5
spent on him and others at the receiveinge / the bookes and other thinges from him	0	0	8

Paide for wryteinge 8 preceptes for a Church / ley and for sendinge them abroade	0	1	4
Paid for new Coards for the Clocke	0	2	2
spent in goeinge to William Bibbie	0	0	6
Paid him for mendinge the Clocke and / for his dyett	0	3	6
For my Attendance one day	0	0	8
paid to >Robert< Robinson for wood to mend the formes		0	10
paid for nayles for the same	0	0	6
paid to him <and him> and his brother for a dayes / worke	0	2	0
for my Attendance one day	0	0	8
paid for wryteinge Coppies of my Accountes	0	0	2
spent in goeinge to Prescott beinge / warned by the Cunstable, at a privie / sessions	0	0	6
spent uppon Master Finch and my selfe in / gatheringe money for the poore / protestantes in Savoy[144]	0	0	8
	0 = 15	= <9>7	

[f.104r]

spent at a meetinge of severall parishoners / aboute the parish busines	0	1	0
spent in goeinge to Formeby to demand / the Church Ley	0	0	6
Paid to Darby Keyton for a fox head	0	1	0
Paid for wryteinge Coppies of my Accountes	0	0	2
Paid to Thomas Pemberton for a fox head	0	1	0
Paid to John Syre for a fox head	0	1	0
Paid to Robert Robinson for a Ladder / for the Church	0	11	0
Paid for Carrijnge[145] the same and the / >Church< beere in a Cart	0	0	6
paid for wryteinge Coppies of my Accountes	0	0	2
Paid to Richard Bridge wyfe for one / quarters keepeinge for a bastard Child	0	9	0
Paid to John Hoogreave for makeinge / the Beare and all materialls therto / belongeinge	0	8	0
paid him for mendinge the pulpitt deske, one forme and the Clocke box	0	0	10
For my Attendance one day	0	0	8
	1 = 14	= 10	

[f.104v]

Paid for Lead for the Clocke waights	0	1	0

144 Government-ordered national collection following a sectarian massacre in the dukedom.
145 For this form, see notes to 1649-50 account, p. 76.

spent uppon the Plumer for his / viewinge the Leades	0	0	6
>paid< For makeinge Keyes, and mendinge / two Stocke Lockes	0	1	0
paid for writeinge Coppies of my Accountes	0	0	2
Paid for a horse for Master Finch two / dayes and his expences in goeinge / to a Counseller	0	3	0
Paid for quart of wine to give to / the Justices at Liverpoole about the Church ley	0	1	0
For Rydeinge two severall tymes to the / Justices at the parke about the parish busines	0	0	8
spent at Receiveinge Kirkbie Ley	0	0	2
paid for writeinge Coppies of my Accountes	0	0	2
Paid for Lyme and hayre to mend the / slates, and >pointinge< the Leades and for Carrijnge / it from Liverpoole	0	3	8
spent at the buyinge of it	0	0	2
	0 = 11	=	6

[f.105r]

Paid to the Carpenter for settinge on / two stockes Lockes, mendinge two formes and / for nayles for the same	0	0	8
Paid to Michaell Shurlikar for mendinge / the Churchyard wall	0	0	6
Paid to Edward Ryce for 2 days worke in / pointeinge the Leades about and rayseinge them	0	2	4
For my Attendantes those 2 dayes	0	1	4
paid to John Tarleton for goeinge on a / message for the parishe busines	0	0	2
paid for wryteinge Coppies of my Accountes	0	0	2
Paid for 18 yardes >of wyre< and oyle for the Clock	0	2	2
Paid to Thomas Carr for two new belropes	0	5	0
<spent> For goeinge on a weeke day on purposse / to buy the same ropes	0	0	4
spent uppon William Mercer and others in / puttinge to lye new ropes, and peeceinge / two old ropes, with other thinges about / the wheeles	0	0	6
For my Attendantes that day	0	0	8
For wryteinge Coppies of my Accountes	0	0	2
	0 = 14	=	00

[f.105v]

Paid for 2 sackes of Starr for the / belhowse floare to save the Ropes	0	0	6
Paid to the Ringers uppon the / 5th of november	0	5	0

Paid to a boy for goeinge twyce to / fetch Michael Shurlikar to mend the / Clapper hangers	0	0	2
paid to Thomas Strange for makeinge / a new eye for the bell Clapper	0	1	0
paid to Thomas Alkar of Kirkbie for / two fox heades	0	2	0
paid for writeinge Coppies of my Accountes	0	0	2
Paid to Nicholas Boulton his / wages	1	0	0
Paid to Henry Alkar Master Fox / man for a fox head	0	1	0
spent uppon the glasier when / hee Came to take measure of the / worke	0	0	4
Paid for 7 smale window barrs / for the scoole howse	0	0	10
Paid to William Fleetwood for new / glasse and mendinge the old for the / Church and scoole as appeares by his bill	1	19	0
	3	= 10 =	00

[f.106r]

Paid for his and his mans dyett for / 5 dayes while they did the worke	0	5	0
Paid for fyer for theire use	0	0	6
paid for wryteinge Coppies of my Accountes	0	0	2
Paid to Edward Ryce for slates to mend / the Church porch and other places of the / Church	0	1	6
Paid to him for layinge the slates and point- / inge all the glasse about for Church / and scoole	0	3	0
spent uppon the glasier and the slater / when they had finisht theire worke	0	0	6
For my Attendantes 5 dayes	0	3	4
Paid to Thomas Hurdis for a / fox head	0	1	0
Paid to widdow Bridge for keepe- / inge a bastard one quarter	0	9	0
spent at a meeteinge with the overseers / of thee poore about the same[146] Child	0	0	6
paid for wryteinge Coppies of / my Accountes	0	0	2
	1	= 4 =	8

[f.106v]

Paid to Michaell Shurlikar / for mendinge the Church yard wall / in severall places and remooveinge the / style at the scoole howse end	0	1	0
Given to poore Travellors haveinge / a passe, at the request of Master Heaton[147]	0	1	0

146 Or *said* (contracted).
147 Robert Eaton, now Rector.

Given to other Travellors at the / request of Master Finch	0	1	0
Paid for a stocke locke for the / scoolhowse doore	0	1	0
Paid for a spade for the Church use	0	1	10
Paid to Richard Effrey for a / fox head	0	1	0
Paid to Robert Robinson for / mendeinge 3 formes in the Church / and for wood and nayles for the same	0	0	9
paid for wryteinge Coppies / of my Accomptes	0	0	2
	0 =	7 =	9

[f.107r]

Payde For Ingroseinge / theis Accomptes 2s[148]

The whole summe disbursed is	9	00	4
The summe Received is	9	12	6
more Received then disburst	00 =	12 =	2
>more spent at the election of the new Church- / warden, beinge a great Company there		4s[149]<	
Oweinge by the Maior and Bay lives / of Liverpoole for there Church ley	£2	13	4
Oweinge by William Boydall / for a Ley stall for his Child	00	1	2

>Received and Allowed by the parishoners[150] Aprill the 11th
    1656<

John Mather   Henry Finch pastor
John X Much   Richard Blackmoore
Roger X Hey   Nicholas Cowper
William X Mercer   John Whitfield
                                       Thomas X Boulton[151]

[f.107v]

<Recieved by Henry Halsall>
John Boulton of Newsham Ellected / Churchwarden, and Robert Pemberton of Walton / Sydeman

Henry X Halsall
Richard Blackmoore
John Whitfield
Thomas X Boulton
John Mather

---

148 Roman numeral.
149 Roman numeral.
150 Or *parishiners*.
151 Marks are *M* or inverted *W* (Roger Hey and Thomas Boulton), inverted *V* (William Mercer) and as f.101r.

John X Bridge
Roger X Hey
William X Mercer
John X Burges
John X Widdowson
James Heye[152]
William X Hey
Henry X Dobb[153]

[*The following is written alongside and to the right of the above list in the original:*]

It is agreed uppon that / a Church ley of £12 bee ga- / thered and paid unto John / Boulton elected Churchwar- / den, on or before Tuesday / in the Whitsunweeke / next.

[*f.108r is blank*]

[f.108v]

Delivered in bondes and money for the use / of the scoole of Walton by Henry Halsall / unto John Boulton Churchwarden and scoole- / Reeve for the yeare 1656

	£	s	d
Imprimis / William Caddicke	20	00	00[154]
Thomas Story	13	00	00
Mistress Mollineux	03	00	00
Hugh Rose of Walton	10	00	00
William Ascroft	5	00	00
John Tyrer	4	00	00
Hugh Rose of Darby	6	00	00
Thomas Watmough	3	00	00
Thomas Tyrer	10	00	00
Nicholas Copple	5	00	00
William Aspinwall	6	00	00
Robert Wright	7	0	0
Roger Breers	17	0	0
Raph Burges[155]	2	0	0
Ann Turner	3	0	0

152 Or *Pye*.
153 Marks are inverted *V* (Henry Halsall), *IB* (John Bridge), *I* (John Burges), inverted *V* with additional stroke as in an arrowhead (John Widdowson), *H* (Henry Dobb), an indecipherable abbreviation possibly *wm* (William Hey) and as previously noted.
154 Separators in this list are colons.
155 Entry marked by cross in left margin.

Richard Stones	1	0	0
Hamlett Boulton	4	0	0
delivered in Ready money that / was paid by John Chorley			£4

[*The following is written alongside and to the right of the above list in the original:*]

an old bill of Master / Allexander Mollineux [?executors] / for	£42
a desperate bond of William / Higginsons	6 4 9¾
delivered that was left / of the scoole money	4s 3d[156]

1656–1657

[f.109r]

The Accompts of John Boulton Church- / Warden of Walton For the yeare 1656

Receiptes

Received of Henry Halsall late Churchwarden / of moneyes that remaind in his hand	0	8	2
Received from the Cunstables of Walton / and Fazakerley for theire Church ley	1	6	8
Received from the Cunstables of Darbye / for theire Church ley	4	0	0
Received from the Chappellwarden / of Kirkbye for theire Church ley	01	6	8
Received From the Chappell Warden / of Formeby for the like	1	6	8
Received from the Cunstable of / Kirkdall for the like	0	10	0
Received from the Cunstable of / Everton for the like	0	6	8
Received from the Cunstable of / Bootle and Linaker for the like	0	10	0
Received for a Ley stall for Thomas / Woofall	0	2	4
	9 =	17	...

[f.109v]

Received for a Ley stall for Mistress / Mollineux	0	2	4
Received for a ley stall for a Child of / Margrett Ormes of Kirkdall	0	1	2
In all	10 =	0 =	8
Received of William Boydall for / a Ley stall for a Child of his which / was in Arreare the Last yeare	0	1	2
The totall of the Receiptes / this yeare is	10 =	1 =	10
Oweinge By the Towne of Liverpoole / for theire Church ley	2	13	4

156 Roman numerals.

[f.110r]

Disbursmentes for the yeare 1656

paid for wryteinge 8 preceptes / for the Church ley, and for sendinge / them forth	00	1	6
paid for wryteinge the Certificatt / and discharge for the bread money	00	0	6
Given to three poore Travellors with / a passe and power from 3 Justices of the / peace for a Collection	00	1	0
spent on Henry Halsall and others at / the Receiveinge of the Bookes and other thinges		1	2
paid to Darby Kayton for 2 fox heads	0	2	0
paid to Edward Strange for 5 fox heades	0	5	0
paid to William Tatlecke of Kirkbie / for 3 fox heads	0	3	0
paid for a gill of >sallett< oyle for the Clocke	0	0	5
paid for a Warrant at Prescott for / gatheringe the Church ley and my expences	0	2	...
paid to William Blackie for mendinge / the Clocke and makeinge a smale Iron barr	0	3	...
	1 =	00 =	...

[f.110v]

Paid to Robert Johnson one of the overseers / of the poore of Kirkbye, by an order from the / Justices for one Feildes Child	0	10	0
Paid to Thomas Rose for his yeares / wages	1	0	0
Paid to the Ringers uppon the 5th / of November	0	5	0
Paid to Richard Atherton of Kirkbye / for a fox head	0	1	0
Paid to Robert Ellison of Darby for / the lyke	0	1	0
Paid for a belrope	0	3	4
Paid to James Standish for / a fox head	0	1	0
paid to Thomas Strange for mending / the eye of a Clapper, and Michaell Shurliker for Carrijnge the same	0	0	8
paid to Edmund Kirkbie for a fox head	0	1	0
paid to Robert Mercer of Walton / for the lyke	0	1	0
paid to Michaell Shurlikar, for mend- / inge the Churchyard wall	0	0	6
paid to Margrett Johnson for 2 sackes / of Starr for the belfrie	0	0	6
	2 =	5 =	0

[f.111r]

Paid for a belrope	0	3	0
Paid for a pint of sallet oyle / for the Clocke	0	0	9
Paid to a minister his wyfe and / 4 Children, who should have had a Collecion		1	6

Paid to Roger Haddock and Robert Bald- / win Clearkes to the Commissioners for pious / uses for their Fees for the £40 for / scoole money[157]	1	0	0
spent on my selfe and Robert Pember- / ton the same day at Prescott	0	1	6
spent on my selfe and horse the first / Jorney to Preston about scoolmoney	0	3	6
spent on my selfe and horse 2 dayes ano- / ther tyme goeinge to Preston to gett / an order either to give bond or pay / forty Pound in to the Reeve	0	3	...
Paid to Master Wall for his Fee	0	3	4
paid for the order and the Coppie / of the decree	0	9	0
	2 =	6 =	...

[f.111v]

spent in goeinge to Croxsteth[158] two severall / times, to serve the order and to speake to / Master Hardin about the money	00	1	6
Paid to Master Langton for his Fee when / the Commissioners decree should have beene / Confirmed by the Chanclor[159]	0	10	0
Paid to Master Wall for his Fee	0	3	4
Paid for a Certificatt the same / tyme	0	0	8
spent on my selfe and horse at Preston / those two dayes	0	4	0
paid to Nicholas Mercer for layinge / even the flagges in the Church	0	1	6
Given to a ministers >wyfe,< another woman / and some others in there Company	0	1	0
spent on my selfe and horse the first / tyme I went to Lancaster against / the Towne of Liverpoole September the 3d	0	2	4
	1 =	4 =	4

[f.112r]

spent uppon my selfe and horse the 4th / of September	0	2	4
Paid for our Charges 6 dayes more / stayinge there and Comeinge home at / 2s 6d[160] day and night	00	15	0
Paid for the Coppie of an order / which I had out of the Crowne office	0	2	0
Paid Master Bootes a Councellor for / mooveinge the Judge for an order / for the Church ley	0	10	0

157 Entry annotated *Feb the 2d 1656* in left margin.
158 Croxteth Hall, Molyneux family home.
159 Entry annotated *March the 3d* in left margin.
160 Roman numerals.

given to the Hostlers and Chamberlaines at / Lancaster and Preston this Jorney	0	1	0
Paid to Nicholas Valentyne for / distrayneinge Master Maiors goodes for / for the Church ley	00	1	0
spent that day on our selves and Robert / Pemberton	0	1	6
paid to Michael Shurlikar for mendinge / the Churchyard wall	0	0	4

$$1 = 13 = \dots$$

[f.112v]

Paid for a Coppie of James Berries / will, about a dowle which hee gave to / the poore of Walton twise everie / yeare to bee dealt[161]	0	10	6
Paid to Master Turner a Councellor / for his Fee Concerneinge Liverpoole / Church ley this Assizes	0	10	0
Paid to Master Darwin another Coun- / cellor to assist him in his motion	0	10	0
paid for my selfe and horse Charges / three dayes to Lancaster	0	7	0
paid to an Attorney to Answer the / Replevin at the County Court against / to towne of Liverpoole	0	3	4
paid for ingrosseinge these Accountes	0	2	0

$$2 = 2 = 10$$

paid since to Alexander Mollineux / for a fox head	0	1	0
more I spent uppon all the parishoners / that were at this election	0	2	2
paid for writeinge a Coppie of this Account / for the Justices of the peace	0	1	0

...

[f.113r]

The totall of Receiptes is	10	1	10
The totall of the disbursmentes is	10	16	4
More disburst then Received	00 =	14 =	6

This Account was Read and Allowed of the 3d / day of Aprill 1657 By us
Edward Moore
Robert Eaton
Henry Finch
James Standish
Richard Blackmoore

161 See Introduction, p. xxvii for the Berry charities.

John Whitfield
Thomas X Boulton
Henrie Mercer
Robert Mercer
Henry X Halsall[162]

Thomas X Hughson
Roger X Hey

[f.113v]

Aprill the 3d 1657

James Standish Elected Churchwar- / den and Thomas Hughson sydeman
Alsoe It is agreed that a Ley of £12 / bee Collected and paid in the parish / unto
James Standish Churchwarden / on or before Tuesday in Whitsunweeke / next

Edward Moore
Robert Eaton
Henry Finch
John Boulton
John Whitfield
Richard Blackmoore
John Johnson
Henrie Mercer

Richard Henshaw
Thomas X Boulton
Robert Mercer
Henry X Halsall
Roger X Hey[163]

[f.114r]

Delivered unto James Standish Churchw... / den and scoole Reeve for the
yeare 1657 / By John Boulton in bondes and money / for the use of the Free
scoole of Walton

Imprimis / Edward Aspinwall and William Caddicke for	20	00	0
Thomas Story of Liverpoole	13	00	0
Hugh Rose of Walton	10	00	0
John Tyrer of Darbye	3	00	0
Raph Hill of Walton	5	00	0
John Tyrer of Alkar	4	00	0
Hugh Rose of Darbye	6	00	0
Thomas Watmough of the same	3	00	0
Thomas Tyrer of Litherland	10	00	0
Nicholas Copple of the same	5	00	0
William Aspinwal of Walton	6	00	0
Robert Wright of the Low	7	00	0
Master Roger Bryers	17	00	0
Ann Turner of Walton	3	00	0
Richard Stones of the same	1	00	0

162 Marks are *T* (Thomas Hughson) and as previously noted.
163 Marks as previously noted.

Hamlett Boulton of Bootle	4	00	0
Received in money which was Master Chorleyes and / Raph Burgesses	6	00	0
the same putt to Thomas Tyrer and Richard Stockley / by bond delivered to him of the scoole / stocke		4s	3d[164]

[f.114v has been used for jotted calculations only]

1657–1658

[f.115r]

The Accomptes of James Standishe / of Westdarbye Church warden of / Walton for the yeare 1657

Receiptes

Received from the Cunstables of Darbye / for there proporcion of 3 Churchleyes	12	00	0
Received from the Cunstables of Walton / with Fazakerley for the same	04	0	0
Received from the Cunstables of / Formebye for the like	04	00	0
Received from the <Cunstables> Chappellwarden of / Kirkbye for the like	04	00	0
Received from the Cunstables of / Bootle with Linaker for the like	01	10	0
Received from the Cunstables of / Kirkdall for the like	01	10	0
Received from the Cunstables of / Everton for the like	01	0	0
Received from the late Maior of / Liverpoole in parte of one Church ley	2	0	0

30 = 00 = 00

[f.115v]

Received from John Boulton for a Ley stall / for his mother	00	2	4
Received from Master Bryers for a ley stall / for his son	00	1	2
For a Ley stall for my owne Child		1	2

0 = 4 = 8

30 = 00 = 0

Received in all   30 = 4 = 8

[f.116r]

Disbursmentes for the yeare 1657

Imprimis spent at Receiveinge of the old Churchwar- / dens Accomptes	00	1	6
Item paid to the old Churchwarden which was / due to him uppon his Account	1	5	6
paid to Master Finch for his Charges to / London about the towne of Kirkbye[165]	3	10	0
paid to Thomas Rose for his yeares / wages as Clarke	01	00	0
>paid to Henry Woods overseer of the poore of Kirkby	00	10	0<[166]
paid to Master Andrewes for answeringe / the Replevin against the towne of Liverpoole	0	5	0
paid to Master Withington for a Coppie / of the decree from the Chancerie / Concerneinge scoole money	0	3	...
paid for writeinge a Certificatt for the bread mony >to London<	0	0	6
paid to Henry Woodes overseer for / the poore of Kirkby towardes the / maintaineance of Feildes Child	0	10	...
paid to William Blackie for dressinge / the Clocke and puttinge upp the pulpitt / Cover	0	6	...
	7^{167} =	11	...

[f.116v]

...tem paid to Thomas Rose for Blackies dyett and for / helpeinge him to worke	0	2	6
paid to Thomas Norberrie of Toxteth parke / for 3 fox heades	0	3	0
paid to Darby Keaton for one fox head	0	1	0
paid to John Fradsom[168] of Kirkbye for / Five Fox heades	0	5	0
paid to Thomas Boulton for plates to mend / the pulpitt Cover with	0	2	0
Item spent on my horse and selfe in goeinge to / Wiggan to Weigh the bell	0	5	0
given to the workemen in drinke and money / in all	0	2	6
Item spent on my horse and selfe 3 dayes / and 2 nights at Preston about the scoolemoney / in all	0	5	0
spent in goeinge to ormiskirke for / an order from the Chancerie about / the same	0	1	6
Item spent on Thomas Hughson and my selfe / at Prescott in makeinge presentmentes / of all recusantes	0	1	6
	1 =	9 =	00

165 Probably concerning the order to give it parish status.
166 Inserted in a different hand.
167 *8* corrected to 7.
168 Probably a version of *Frodsham*.

[f.117r]

Item spent at the takeinge downe the bell		1	0
paid to Thomas Boden for takeinge downe / the bell	0	1	0
Item given to a traveller who had a passe / for a Collection	0	1	6
spent at Prescott at the privie sessons	0	1	0
Item paid to Jane Pemberton of Kirkdall / by order from Justice			
fox for keepeinge / a poore >weake[169]< woman	0	12	6
given to her <...> to helpe her over the water / at Liverpoole	0	0	6
paid to William Houghton for distraineing / Master Maiors			
plate for the first / Church ley	0	5	6
spent then on the Apprysers	0	1	6
Item given to the Ringers November the 5th		6	0
Given Master Antwizle[170] for his opinion / about the			
distresse	0	10	0
spent in goeinge to ormiskirke / to him	0	1	6
	2 = 02	=	0

[f.117v]

paid for wyre for the Clocke	00	00	6
paid for oyle for the same	00	00	7
given to 4 poore travellers which / would have had a			
Collection	00	2	0
paid to Robert Wright for a fox / head	0	1	0
Item paid the Belfounder for exChange / and Addinge metle in			
Castinge the / bell	7	00	0
paid to William Ryleance for Carringe / the bell to Wiggan and			
back againe	0	9	0
paid to Thomas Boulton for Iron / Geare to hange the bell in	0	5	0
paid to Henry Haworth for hangeinge / the bell, and mendinge			
th'other wheeles	0	4	0
given to his man	0	0	6
paid to John Lurtinge for mend / inge a Clapper	0	2	0
spent in goeinge to Preston about / the scoole money	0	5	00
	8 = 9	=	7

[f.118r]

Item paid to Thomas Rose for the Belfounders / meate and			
drinke when hee hang'd it	0	5	8
given to a poore man with a passe	0	1	0
paid for 2 warrantes for 2 Church / leyes	0	2	0

169 Or possibly *worke*.
170 Version of *Entwistle*.

paid to Margerie Walls for 7 quartes / of wyne for the Sacrament	0	4	8
paid for a warrant for another / Church ley	0	1	0
paid for writeinge 24 preceptes / for the 3 Church leyes and for send- / inge them forth	0	4	6
paid Tom Meadow for Carijnge a letter / to the post howse	0	0	3
paid to Henry Woodes overseer of / the poore in Kirkbie for keepeinge / a poore Child, by order from the Justices	1	0	0
spent on 5 of the parishoners at a / treatie with Liverpoole about there / Church ley	0	1	6

$$2 = 00 = 7$$

[f.118v]

paid Henry Haward for mendinge the / Churchyard yate	0	2	8
paid Master Finch when hee went to London / against the towne of Liverpoole	1	10	0
paid him more towardes his Charges / when hee returnd	4	19	5
paid Ann Windle for the hyre of / his horse	1	6	8
paid Master Chapman for a Coppie / of Gilbert Formebies [?declaration][171]	0	1	6
paid him his Attorneyes Fee	0	1	4
paid Master Andrewes for a Certiorare / to remoove the suite from Liverpoole	0	5	10
spent in goeinge to ormiskirk to fetch / the same	0	1	0
paid to John Syre for 5 fox heades	0	5	0
paid to William Holme for 4 / fox whelpes	0	2	0

$$8 = 15 = 5$$

[f.119r]

paid to Joseph Holdinge for one fox head	0	1	0
paid to Thomas Rose for the Carpen- / ters dyett when they hang'd the bells	0	1	4
paid For ingrosseinge these Accountes / and a Coppie for the Justices	0	3	0

$$0 = 5 = 4$$

The totall of Receiptes are	30	= 4	= 8	
Disbursmentes	31	= 13	= 5	
more disburst then Received	001	= 8	= 9	

---

171 Unclear abbreviation, possibly *decl.* Formby was Mayor of Liverpool and this entry refers to the dispute over payment of leys.

paid more to a Councellor for manageinge / the busines against Liverpoole and for the / horse Charges	1	8	8
more paid Thomas Wiggan for / mendinge the Churchyard wall	0	0	6

Soe the totall of disbursmentes are	$32^{172} = 02$	$= 7$
there is more disburst then received	1	$= 19^{173} = \ldots$

oweinge by the Maior and Baylives of / Liverpoole towardes these 3 leyes six poundes ...
more spent at ...

[f.119v]

Aprill the 16th 1658

These Accountes were Read and Allow'd on, And / Thomas Boulton of Kirkdall >Elected< Churchwarden / and Lawrence Turner of Fazakerley / sydeman, and a £12 Ley thought fitt / to bee Collected towardes the repaire of the / Church by us

Robert Eaton	Richard X Worsley
Henry Finch	Thomas X Wharton
John Whitfield	William X Mercer
John Rose	William X Whitle
John Mercer	Nicholas Valentine
John Johnson	
Richard Blackmoore	
William Robertson	
William Johnson	
Henry X Halsall	
John X Much	
Thomas X Rose	
Roger Hey[174]	

[f.120r]

Delivered by James Standish unto / [*line space*][175] / Churchwarden and scoole Reeve for the / yeare 1658 for the use of the scoole in / bondes and money as followeth videlicet

Edward Aspinwall and William Caddicke	20	00	0
Thomas Story with others for	13	00	0
William Rose of Walton	10	00	0

172 Corrected from or to *31*.
173 Corrected figure, the original being unclear. The total appears in the following account as *£1 19s 11d*.
174 Marks are *R* (Thomas Rose and Richard Worsley), *T* (Thomas Wharton), *M* or inverted *W* (William Whitle) and as previously noted.
175 The name of the elected Thomas Boulton is not filled in: in fact James Standish appears to have served a second year himself.

John Tyrer of Darbye	3	00	0
Raph Hill of Walton	5	00	0
<John Tyrer of Alkar> Thomas Hughson of Westderbie[176]	4	00	0
Hugh Rose of Clubmore	6	00	0
Thomas Watmough of the same	3	00	0
Thomas Tyrer of Litherland	10	00	0
more another bond	6	00	0
Nicholas Copple of the same	5	00	0
William Aspinwall of Walton	6	00	0
<Robert> Mary Wright of the Low hill	7	00	0
Master Roger Bryers	17	00	0
Ann Turner of Walton	3	00	0
Richard Stones of the same	1	00	0
Hamlett Boulton of Bootle	4	00	0
one old bill of Master Alexander Mollineux	42	00	0
one desperatt bond of William Higginsons	6	4	9¾
delivered in money of the scoole stocke	0	4	3

1658–1659

[f.120v]

[*Page has doodles in the left margin including the word* Accounts.]

The Accomptes of James Stan- / dishe of Westdarbye Churchwarden /
of Walton for the yeare 1658

Receiptes

Received from the Baylives of Liverpoole / for 2 Church leyes and parte of theire Arrears	£11	10s	0d
Received from Henry Halsall	1	5[177]	10
Received from the Cunstable of / Walton	1	00	0
Received from the Justices of peace / >which was allowd to mee uppon the last Account< / for the parish use	12	16[178]	7
Received from the Cunstable of <Walton / with> Fazakerley	00	19	1
Received from the Cunstable of Kirkdall	00	15	0
<Received from the Cunstable of Darbye	03	4	0>
Received for a Ley stall for John Whitfeild	00	2	4
	28	= 8[179]=10	

---

176 Amended name, added in a different hand.
177 Corrected to or from *4*.
178 Corrected from *14*.
179 Corrected to or from *7*.

whereof there is received from the / parish this yeare but[180]	15 = 11 =	3	
received more for a leystall for Mistress / Fazakerley	00	2	4

28 3s 7d

[f.121r]

Disbursmentes for the yeare 1658

Moneyes due uppon the last yeares Accountes	1	19	11
paid to William Ryelance for a poore Child in Kirkby	0	10[181]	0
Paid to Eight witnesses at the last Assizes / at Lancaster by order			
from the Judge / they were John Boulton, Nicholas Cowper /			
Thomas Watmough, Thomas Smith / Edmund Webster,			
William Mercer, Richard / Everard and Nicholas Valentyne	08	0	0
more for my selfe and horse	01	00	0
paid to three Councellors	04	00	0
paid Master Andrewes as appeares by / his bill	01	15	0
spent extrordinaryly in Attendinge / the Councell and the			
Cause that weeke	00	2	6
paid to John Walls of Prescott for the / silver Can againe[182]	02	5	0
paid to William Simkin for executinge a warrant at Liverpoole	0	2	6
paid the overseers of the poore of / Kirkby	01	17	6
paid the Clarke for his wages	01	0	...
	22 = 14 =	11	

[f.121v]

Paid to Jonathom[183] Hunter for 18 / fox heades	00	18	0
Paid to George Webster for glase / inge the Church windowes	00	15	0
paid For wyre and oyle	00	1	0
paid Master Chandler for wine for / the Sacrament	00	5	10
paid to Edward Formebye >for another time< for wine	<00	3	8>
	00	5	10
paid for bread for both	00	1	0
paid for layinge even the flagges / in the Church	00	1	0
paid for the glasiers dyett	00	2	3
paid for a bushell of lime	00	00	10
paid for hayre	00	00	4
paid for nayles	00	00	6

180 That is, the parish's contribution disregarding the money from the JPs (which does not seem to feature elsewhere in the accounts), allowing for a mistake in the arithmetic.
181 Or possibly *12*.
182 Distrained from the Mayor of Liverpool.
183 Or *Jonathone*.

paid for 3 poore travellors with / a passe for a Collection	00	1	6
paid to 7 travellors uppon the / same Account	00	2	0

2 = 15 = 1

[f.122r]

spent in goeinge to Prescott to make my / Account to the Justices	00	1	0
spent in goeinge to ormiskirke for / the subpenas for the Assizes	00	1	6
spent in goeinge another time to / bespeake them	00	1	6
paid the Attorney for them	00	5	0
spent at Liverpoole severall times / in goeinge to receive theire money	00	2	6
spent when I mett the Justices at / the swan	00	00	10
given to the Ringers November the 5	00	6	0
given to a poore welchman	00	00	6
paid to John Syre for 2 fox heades	00	2	0
paid Edmund Webster for a spade / for the Church	00	2	4
paid to Mathew Gleave for a fox head	00	1	0
paid Edward Formeby for 4 quartes of wine	00	4	0
paid for bread for <the s...> 2 severall Sacramentes	00	0	...

1 = 8 = 8

[f.122v]

[Page has doodles in the left margin.]

Paid to John Webster overseer of / the poore in Kirkbye	00	12	6
paid to Thomas Rose for Leadinge slates / to the Church	00	1	6
paid for slates	00	3	4
paid Robert Bushell for layinge them on	00	5	6
spent on him then	00	00	6
paid For 2 new bellropes	00	7	0
paid to Thomas Strange for worke / don to the bells	00	1	6
paid to Richard Boulton for Lime	00	1	6
paid to Richard Williams for wine for / 2 severall Sacramentes	0	11	8
paid to Thomas Boulton for worke don / to the bells	0	1	0
paid to Thomas Wigan for mendinge / the Church yard wall	0	3	8
paid to Henry Howard for mendinge / the bell Wheeles	0	2	4
paid F[or][184] a poore womans dyett that Came / by warrant from Manchester	0	0	8
For my horse and selfe goeinge to ormiskirke / to pay the Attorney	0	2	0

2 = 14 = 8

184 Double *ff* abbreviation used by scribe.

[f.123r]

paid F[or] writeinge 8 preceptes for a Church ley / and sendinge them away	0	1	8
paid F[or] writeinge a letter and Certificatt / to London for the bread money	0	0	6
paid to Master Mercer for receiveinge / the money these 2 yeares	0	2	0
paid for ingrossinge these Accountes and Coppie / for the Justices	0	3	0

	0 = 7 = 2
in all	30 = 00 = 6
received from the parish this yeare	15 = 13 = 7
soe there is more disburst / then received	14 = 9 = 11[185]

More spent at the makinge and delivery of these accountes / and at the Ellection of the new churchwarden[186]	0	3	0

[f.123v]

[*A jotted calculation at bottom right of the page has not been transcribed.*]

Aprill the 4th 1659

These Accomptes were read and Allowd on / And Thomas Boulton of Kirkdall Church / warden and John Hey of Everton sydeman / then Elected

Robert Eaton	Nicholas X Mercer
Henry Finch	Thomas X Martin
James Standish	Richard X Boulton
John Boulton	Nicholas Cowper
George Glover	Thomas X Hughson
Richard Blackmoore	Thomas X Haward
Nicholas Cowper	Henry X Halsall
Richard X Fazakerley	Richard Croppe
Roger X Hey	Thomas Henshaw
John X Much	Henry X Haward
Thomas X Barnes	Nicholas Valentine[187]

1659–1660

[f.124r]

[*In this account £ s d symbols usually head the columns, and colons are used as separators, except on this page, where there are no column headings and points are used.*]

185 Calculation excludes the JPs' contribution itemised on f.120v, p. 118.
186 Entered in a different hand.
187 Marks are *R* (Richard Fazakerley and Richard Boulton), *TB* (Thomas Barnes), reverse *N* (Nicholas Mercer), *T* (Thomas Martin), *H* (Thomas and Henry Haward) and as previously noted.

13 day of June 1659

At a generall Meeteinge of the churchwardens and the / parishoners of Walton and upon view of the great / decayes of the said church by sufficient Workemen Wrightes / slayters and Maysons thereunto appoynted It doth / Appeare that the sume of two Hundred <pounds> and fourty / pounds will be Expended upon the Necessary repaire of / the same In regard the roofe is to be wholly taken of and / New builded It is therefore thought fit and agreed upon / by the churchwardens and the inhabitants here assembled / that the sume of an hundred and twenty pounds be forthwith / Layd upon the particular towneships as hereafter / followeth

Walton cum Fazakerley	13	06	08
Westderby	40	00	00
Liverpoole	26	13	04
Kirkby	13	06	08
Formby	13	06	08
Kirkedoll	08	00	00
Bootle cum Linacre	08	00	00
Everton	03	06	08

Edward Moore	Richard Blackmore
Robert Eaton	John Johnson
Henry Finch	John X Much
Thomas Boulton	Henry X Hallsall
James Standish	Thomas X Worton
Nicholas Cowper	John X Heyes
	William X Mercer[188]

[f.124v]

October the 12th 1659

Att a meeteinge of the minister / Churchwarden with severall parishoners / of the parish of Walton for the viewinge / of the present necessitie of the repaire / of the Church, It was then agreed and / thought fitt by them, that a ley of £12 / should bee Collected and gathered through the / said parish, <should bee Collected and gathered> / and paid to Thomas Boulton of Kirkdall / Churchwarden on or before the first / day of November next

Edward Moore	
Robert Eaton	Thomas X Wharton
Henry Finch	Richard X Worsley
Thomas Boulton	John X Bridge
Richard Blackmoore	William X Mercer
John X Hey	Nicholas Valentine
John Boulton	
Hugh Rose[189]	

188 Marks are *IH* (John Heyes), unformed cross mark (William Mercer) and as previously noted.
189 Marks are sideways *V* (William Mercer) and as previously noted.

[f.125r]

	£	s	d
Walton cum Fazakerley	01	06	08
Kirkby	01	06	08
Formby	01	06	08
Westderby	04	00	00
Liverpoole	02	13	04
Bootle cum Linaker	00	10	00
Kirkdale	00	10	00
Everton	00	06	08
Everton[190]			

<at a meeteing>

[f.125v]

The Accompts of Thomas Boulton / of Kirkdale Churchwarden of Walton /
In the yeare of our Lord God 1659

Receipts
Received from

	£	s	d
The Constables of Walton cum / Fazakerley	01	06	08
The Constables of Formby	01	06	08
The Constables of Kirkdale	00	10	00
The Constables of Bootle cum Linaker	00	10	00
The Constables of Everton	00	06	08
The Ley layers of Westderbie	04	00	00
Received by the Appoyntment of / Master Thomas Williamson Maior / of Liverpoole, from Thomas Story and Edmund Lievsey / Bayliffes there	02	13	04
Received for a Leystall for Mistress / Fazakerley	00	02	04

[f.126r]

	£	s	d
Received for a Leystall for / Richard Worsley	00	02	04
The totall Received	10:	18:	00
Oweinge by the Inhabitants / of Kirkby to the Parish of / Walton, beinge their proporcion- / able parte of a £12 ley	01	06	08

[f.126v]

Disbursments	£	s	d
Imprimis Spent at Liverpoole in movinge / for a warrant for Church Leyes	00	01	00

190 First version with abbreviated -er; the two versions bracketed together.

In attendinge at Walton for the / old Churchwardens Accompts	00	00	04
At Receivinge those Accompts and / severall other thinges belonginge / to the Church	00	02	00
Spent on severall of the Parish / and on some Wrightes, slaters and / masons, that came to survey / the decayes of the Church	00	01	04
Paid to the Justices Clerkes for / a Confirmation	00	02	00
Paid to Nicholas Valentine for / Richard Whitfield for receivinge / the bread money	00	01	00
For Lettre and Certificate	00	00	06
Paid to the Ringers on the 5th / day of November	00	06	00
Paid to the Justices Clerkes / for a warrant for Church leyes	00	02	00
	00:	16:	02

[f.127r]

	£	s	d
Spent at Liverpoole when I procured / the said warrant and at severall other / times in goinge about the same	00	02	06
Spent on Thomas Boden and William Fleetwood / when they viewed the Church Roofe / leades, and windowes	00	00	04
Paid to the Clerke for his wages	01	00	00
Paid to William Fleetwood for / new glasse for the Church windowes / and mendinge the old	00	12	03
Paid to him for soderinge the leades	00	13	04
Paid to Thomas Bankes for pointinge / the Church windowes and leades and / for makinge up an end of a / dormon window, and other necessaries	00	02	00
Paid to Thomas Rose for dyet and drinke / for them for 2 dayes	00	03	08
Spent at Liverpoole when I Received / theirs and some other Church leyes	00	00	08
Paid for a bushell and a halfe of / lime, and halfe a bushell of haire	00	01	07
Paid for lats and nailes	00	01	02
Paid to Thomas Rose for fetchinge the / said lime, haire, lats and nailes from Liverpoole	00	00	04
	02:	17:	10

[f.127v]

	£	s	d
Paid to Richard Worsley for two / pieces of timber for the Church / Roofe, and leadinge them	01	00	00
Spent on the said Richard, Thomas / Boden and my selfe at buyinge them	00	00	04

Paid to Thomas Rose for fire to heat / the soderinge Irons	00	00	06
Paid to Jonathan Gleave for / Cleansinge the Clocke	00	02	06
Paid to him for makinge astepp / for the balance wheele, peecinge / the spindle, for a stay and springe / for the hammer, for keyinges, and other worke done to the Clocke	00	05	00
More paid to him for wyre for / the same	00	02	00
Paid to him for mendinge the / lockes of the Church and steeple <doores> / doores	00	01	00
More Paid to him for a key / for the belhouse doore	00	00	06
Paid to Thomas Rose for drinke and / dyet for him, whylst hee did the / said worke	00	02	00
	01:	13:	10

[f.128r]

	£	s	d
Paid to William Seacom for one foxe head	00	01	00
Spent at Liverpoole when I Received Formby / Ley goinge purposely thither about / the same	00	00	08
Spent at the Receivinge Walton Ley	00	00	02
Paid to Edward Formby for Eight / quartes of wine for 2 sacraments	00	07	04
>Paid for bread for the same	00	00	08<
Spent at the Receivinge of Derby / Ley, and in goinge severall times / thither, and twice to Liverpoole / about the same	00	02	02
Paid to Joseph Holden for / one foxe head	00	01	00
Paid to Nicholas Coopper for / a piece of timber for the / Roofe of the Church	00	10	00
Paid to Thomas Boden for leadinge / the same to Walton	00	00	06
Paid to Thomas Strange for / layinge new the shanke of / a bell clapper, and makinge a / new bow for the same	00	03	00
	01:	06:	06

[f.128v]

	£	s	d
Paid to Thomas Carr for a new / belrope, and a new corde for / the Clocke	00	04	00
Paid to Roberte Harvey for / two bottles of oyle for the Clocke	00	01	06
Paid to Jonathan Hunter for / 7 foxe heades	00	07	00
Paid to William Greaves for a new / wine bottle for the sacrament	00	01	00
Paid to Thomas Boden, as by his / bill may appeare / For squaringe and sawinge / Thirteene score and ten foot of / timber	00	06	00

Paid to him for puttinge up / 6 pieces of timber into the / Roofe
of the Church, and doinge / other necessaries, as mendinge /
a bell wheele, the north doore, / and some formes, for
himselfe / and his 2 men five dayes   00   14   02
Paid more to him for helpinge to / load and unload 2 trees
bought of / Richard Worsley, and for carryinge / borrowed
ladders to the Church, / and bringinge the same home agen /
himselfe and his 2 men 1 day   00   01   06

                                                                                    01:   15:   02

[f.129r]

	£	s	d
Paid more to Thomas Boden which hee / laid downe for nayles	00	00	06
Paid to Jonathan Hunter for / 3 foxe heads	00	03	00
Paid to Thomas Rose for mendinge / the Churchyarde wall	00	02	00
Paid for 3 bushels of lime, and one / bushell of haire	00	03	00
Paid to Thomas Rose for fetchinge / the same to Walton	00	00	09
Paid to Thomas Bankes for pointinge / the topp of the steeple	00	03	00
Paid more to him for pointinge the / Church and schoole windowes, and shootinge / over 4 sides of dormon windowes	00	01	00
Spent on him and his partner	00	00	04
Paid to Thomas Boulton for nayles	00	00	02
Paid to William Syer for a piece of / Ashwood to be baldrickes for / the belclappers	00	03	00
Paid to Thomas Boden for a piece of / saplinge to bee pins for the same	00	00	06

                                                                                    00:   17:   03

[f.129v]

	£	s	d
Paid to William Washington for sixe / dayes worke done at the bels	00	07	00
Paid to Thomas Glover for fyve / dayes worke	00	05	10
Paid to Thomas Boden for 2 dayes worke	00	02	04
Spent on William Washington and Thomas / Glover	00	00	04
Paid to Thomas Rose for grease for / the bels	00	00	02
Paid to William Fleetwood for glazinge / the schoole windowes	00	09	06
Paid to William Haddocke for 3 foxe / heads	00	03	00
Paid to Thomas Boulton for worke / done to the bels, and for prids and nailes	00	00	08

                                                                                    01:   08:   10

The Totall disbursed	10:	15:	07
The Totall Received	10:	18:	00

More Received then disbursed / which is Remaininge in my
handes   00:   02:   05

Spent on severall of the Parishoners at the / makinge of these
Accomptes, and a new election   00:   02:   06

[f.130r]

These Accounts were Read and Allowed, <and> / on Tuesday in Easter weeke,
and Thomas / <Knowle> Knowles of Walton elected Church- / warden and
Nicholas Mercer of Walton sideman / and a £12[191] Ley thought fit to bee collected /
before Tuesday in Whitsun weeke by us

Edward Moore

Thomas X Martin	Robert Eaton
Thomas X Warton	John Boulton
John X Much	John Johnson
John X Bankes	Richard Blackmoore
William X Mercer	Henry X Halsall
William X Whittle	Peeter Johnson
Richard X Stones	William X Turner
Thomas X Boulton	Roger X Hey
Nicholas Valentine[192]	

[f.130v]

May 14º 1660

Delivered by Thomas Boulton of Kirkdale to / Thomas Knowles his successor In
Bonds and money / for the use of Walton schoole as followeth, scilicet

	£	s	d
Edward Aspinwall of Biccursteth	10	00	00
Thomas Story of Liverpoole	13	00	00
Anne Turner of Walton	03	00	00
Hamlet Boulton of Bootle	04	00	00
Nicholas Copple of Litherland	05	00	00
Thomas Harrison of the same Junior	06	00	00
Thomas Tyrer of the same	06	00	00
Received in another bond	10	00	00
Master Roger Bryers	17	00	00
Hugh Rose of Clubmore	06	00	00

191 Roman numeral.
192 Marks are *TM* (Thomas Martin), symbol resembling double *H* (John Bankes), inverted *V* (William
   Mercer), *R* (Richard Stones), *M* or inverted *W* (Thomas Boulton), *W* (William Turner) and as
   previously noted.

Thomas Hughson of Westderbie	04	00	00
Thomas Watmough of the same	03	00	00
John Tyrer of the same	03	00	00
Mary Wright of Cureley	07	00	00
Raphe Hill of Westderbie	05	00	00
William Rose of Walton	10	00	00
William Aspinwall of the same	06	00	00

[f.131r]

	£	s	d
Roberte Mercer of the same	04	00	00
Richard Stones of the same	01	00	00
	123:	00:	00
One old bill from Master / Alexander Molyneux	42	00	00
One desperate bonde of William / Higginson of Maghull	06	04	09¾
Delivered alsoe in money of / the schoole stocke	00	04	03

1660–1661

[f.131v]

[In this account dashes are used as separators in the £ s d columns.]

The accompts of Thomas Knowles Church- / warden of Walton for the yeare of /
our lord 1660

Receipts	£	s	d
Received from the Balives of Liverpoole	2	13	4
received from the Constables of Kirkdale	0	10	00
Received from the Churchwardens of / Formby	1	6	8
Received from the Churchwardens of Kirkby	1	6	8
Received from the Constables of Darby	4	0	0
Received from the Constables of Everton	00	06	8
Received from the Constables of Bootle	00	10	0
Received from the Constables of Walton / and Fazakerley	1	6	8
summa inde	12 –	0 –	0
other receipts			
Received for aley stalle for John / Wigan	00	02	04
received for another for Captain Smiths / <wife> Child	00	01	2
received for one for Richard Woods / Child	00	01	02
Received for aley stale for Thomas / Bootles wife of Kirkdale	00	02	4

[f.132r]

	£	s	d
Received for aley stale for Richard Woods	00	2	4
for one for his Child	00	1	2
for another for Mistris Dorothy	00	2	4
received for aley stalle for Mary / Gleave	00	2	4
<in toto	12	15	2>
<Oweinge> Received for for aley stalle for / henry Pembertons wife	00	3	4[193]
<Received for the same	02>		
in toto	£12 –	17 –	6

Other Receipts	£	s	d
Received for the poores ley of / Walton parish	1	10	0

[*The remainder of the page, which appears to be an account of expenditure out of the above poor ley, is written in a different hand using roman numerals.*]

disbursments of the same

Payd to Fields Child of Kirkbys[e]	8s 4d
Payd to Thomas Mercers Children	8s 4d
Payd Edward Harissons lame Childe	5s 10d
Payd to John Mollyneux wife	2s 6d
Payd to Jane Woodes of Derbye	12s[194]
Payd to Margret Gregson	12s
Payd to Widdow Halewoodes Childe	12s
Payd for writinge 8 precepts and sendinge / them away	18d
Spent upon severall of the parish att layinge the poores ley	6d

By mee Thomas Knowles / Churchwarden

[f.132v]

[*Small crosses against some amounts in this account, perhaps relating to addition, have not been transcribed.*]

Disbursements	£	s	d
Imprimis spent upon severall of the / parish and the ould Churchwardens / att receiveing of the bookes from the / ould Churchwardens	00	01	10
Paid to the ringers att the tyme / of his majesties proclamacion for / Ringing	00	05	0
spent att the same tyme to bring the / ringers together and for makeing / the Badrix lesse[195] and mending the / Clapper	0	01	0

193 Mistake for 2s 4d, the correct amount added in to the total.
194 Shillings are clearly shown for this and the next two entries, but only if the amounts should actually be pence can the total of £1 10s be achieved.
195 i.e. shortening the baldricks.

Paid for one Bottle of oyle for / the Clocke	0	0	10
spent in goeing to aprivy sessions / upon my selfe and my horse Master / Rostren then sitting there	0	1	2
paid for acertificate to Nicholas / Valentyne	00	00	6
paid to Master Winstandley for receiveing / the bread money and for acquittance	00	1	9
paid to Master Smith for his paines / when wee demanded possession of / the Barnes[196]	0	3	4

The summe wherof is   0 – 15 – 5

[f.133r]

	£	s	d
Given by Nicholas Mercer to the / ringers att the tyme of his Ma- / jesties Comeing into England	0	5	0
spent upon Master William Aspinwall / for receiveing Master Eatons answere / and for Copieing out the same and / of severall others of the parish att the / same tyme	0	3	3
Paid for alocke for the Church doore	0	5	6
Paid to the smith for nailes to sett / the said lock on for Comeing to take / measure and setting it on the door >3 times<	0	1	7
Paid to Nicholas Valentyne for goeing / with the order Concerning tyth to Master / Fogg and Master Crompton[197] and for writeing / Copies of the same and delivering them	0	1	6
spent upon giveing the like notice / to the minister of Formby	0	0	6
Paid to Master Smith for 2 severall / motions one as Concerning Fields / Chield of Kirkby and another made / upon tuesday for preventing William / Rose sonne being laid on the parish	0	6	8

1 – <...>2 – 0

[f.133v]

	£	s	d
Paid for bread >and wine< for Communion	0	5	6
paid for Carriadge to Walton	0	0	2
paid for writeing of disbursm[en]ts	0	0	4
paid to Nicholas Valentyne for / writeing 8 precepts to give notice / of the poores ley >that they were to meet<	0	1	4
paid to henry Haward and his man / for one day work for repaireing of / the Church formes	0	1	4

196 Probably relates to disputed tithe; see Introduction, p. xii.
197 Incumbents at Liverpool and Toxteth Park, referring to the tithe dispute.

	£	s	d
Paid to John Fazakerley for repaire / of >the< Church Walls	0	6	6
spent when Kirkby Chappell warden / sommoned mee to appeare att prescott / before the justices	0	1	0
spent in goeing to Blaky about re- / paire of the Clock	0	0	6
paid to John Syer for a fox head	0	1	0
spent when severall of the parish / did meet to lay aley for the poore	0	0	6
spent att another privy sessions / att Prescott upon the parish busines / Master Entwistle and Master Norres sitting / there then	0	1	2
The summe wherof is	0 –	19 –	4

[f.134r]

	£	s	d
spent att another privy sessions holden / at Prescott sir Gilbert Ireland sitting / att that tyme	0	1	0
Paid to Anthony Lunt of Darby for / one fox head	0	1	0
paid to William Lewis for a fox head	0	1	0
spent by Nicholas Mercer att apri- / vy sessions at prescott	0	0	6
Paid for William Blakies jo>u<rney to / Walton for his dyet and repaire of / the Clock	0	3	0
Paid for timber for aturne gate for / Iron geere for the same bringing / it to Walton the workemanshipp of / the same the setting of it upp the / makeing of ahead stock for a bell / takeing of the Iron and henging it / levell	3	5	...
Paid to Thomas Nailor for 28 Foote / of new glasse	0	11	8
paid for 5 foote of ould glasse sett / in new lead	0	1	3
paid for repaireing of ould glasse	0	4	[?8]
The summe wherof is	4 –	8	–[?7]

[f.134v]

	£	s	d
spent att measureing of the glasse	0	0	10
spent by Nicholas >Mercer< att receiveing / of Kirkby ley and bringing fields / Childs parte of our ley	0	0	6
Paid to Master Eaton for one bushell / of lyme morter	0	1	0
paid for 2 bell ropes	0	6	6
paid for 4 pounds and ahalfe of soder	0	4	6
paid to Elline Mercer for one / fox head	0	1	0
Paid for repaireing and sodring of / the leads	0	3	2
Paid to Lettice Bolton for >fi...<[198] the / glasiers use and for repaire of the / leads	0	0	10

198 Perhaps *fire*.

	£	s	d
paid to Margret Butler for / nailes to sett up the glasses	0	0	1
Paid for fetching of the ladders / >and bringing of them agayne<	0	0	6
spent att 2 severall tymes attend- / ing att the Church upon the / workmen there	0	0	10

The summe is   0 – 19 – 9

[f.135r]

	£	s	d
Paid for mending of the Church / Flaggon	0	0	4
Paid to Master Eaton for lyme	0	12	0
Paid to Thomas Hollis for / his work	0	12	6
Given to aministers wife towards / releefe of her Children	0	1	0
paid to William Syer for one / fox head	0	1	0
Paid to Captaine Croft for 7 / fox heads	0	7	0
Paid for writeing to Nicholas / Valentyne for writeing 8 pre- / cepts sending them away and for / other writeing for the church ley	0	1	4
spent att receiveing Liverpoole / ley and for acquittance	0	0	5
given to the ringers upon the / 5th of November	0	6	0
Paid for agenerall Warrant	0	2	0
And for a Confirmacion Warrant	0	2	0
	2 –	5 –	7

[f.135v]

	£	s	d
...ent upon the Churchwardens of / ...ormby and for acquittance att re- / ceiveing of the Church ley	0	0	6
spent att receiveing Kirkby / Church ley and for aquittance	0	0	4
spent about the same occasion / att receiveing Darby Church ley / and for acquittance	0	0	5
spent on Henry Haward when / hee Came to give directions / what to buy for repaire of / the Church formes	0	0	4
Paid to William Johnson for one / fox head	0	1	0
Paid to Thomas Rose for / his wages	01	0	0
Paid to Master Entwistle for his / opinion Concerning the suite / betwixt Liverpoole and this parish / and about everyones poore rent[199] in / their respective quarters	0	10	0
Paid for aho>r<se for Robert Mercer / to ryde to Ormischurch to certify / to Master Entwistle how long every / quarter have kept theire poore	0	1	0
	1 –	03 –	7

---

199 Word uncertain due to overwriting.

[f.136r]

	£	s	d
spent upon our selves and our horses / att the same tyme	0	1	9
spent upon Richard Whitfield / waiteing for his master Comeing / from the earle of Darby	0	0	6
Paid to Peter Walker for one / fox head	0	1	0
spent upon severall of the parish / att ameeteing Concerning keepeing / of every quarters poore	0	1	6
paid to William Tarletonne <Nicholas Valentyne>[200] for / writeing sommons to give di- / rections for the parish to meete / Concerning theire poore att the / same tyme when Kirkby denyed / to keepe theire poore	0	0	8
given to 7 in Company with passes	0	1	0
spent att the Bargaine made / with William Poltney and when hee / Came to take measure of the yates	0	1	0
spent at severall meeteings about / renueing of the Schoole bonds att / Walton Ormischurch and Liverpoole	0	1	6
The summe wherof is	0 –	8 –	11

[f.136v]

	£	s	d
Paid to John Darbyshire for nailes / for repaire of the Church Formes	0	1	0
spent when I went to the quarter / sessions of my selfe and my horse 2 / daies and 2 nights <...>[201]	0	3	10
paid to Richard Mercer for 2 / stone of haire and Fetching of it	0	2	0
paid for apeece of timber to Roberte / Gibbons	0	1	0
Paid more to Thomas Hollis	0	1	0
Paid to Thomas Alker and Thomas / Tatlock for 5 fox heads	0	5	0
Paid <to Thomas> to Thomas / Bolton for Iron work for prids for Iron for the bells / and for his owne work	0	1	0
The summe is	0 –	14 –	10

		<...>	
		s	d
The totall disbursed	12[202]	18 –	0
The totall received	12 –	17 –	06
more disbursed than received	00 –	00 –	06

200 One name written over the other, but unclear which is correct.
201 Two lines deleted.
202 Corrected from or to *13*.

[f.137r]

[*Written in one or more different hands from the foregoing.*]

	£	s	d
Payd unto William Tarlton for writinge / and castinge up of theise Acounts	0	3	0
more disburced then received in the totall	0 –	3 –	6
more spent at the election and / the readinge of theise accounts	0	1	0

Theise Accounts were read / and allowed on tuesday in the / Easter weeke: and Master John / Bennet of tuebrooke elected / Churchwarden and Matthew gleave / of the lowe hill sideman and A / £24 ley thought fitte to bee / Collected before tuesday in Whitson / weeke by Us

Edward Moore	John Heywood[203]
Richard Henshaw	Henry Finch
John Mercer	Joshua Ambrose
John Smarley[204]	Ro[bert] Mercer
Thomas X Martin[205]	James Standish
Richard Croppe[r]	John Boulton
	William Ellisonne
	John Rose

[f.137v]

Nicholas Cowper	<...>
William Johnson	John John[son]
John X Boulton	William X Robertson
Richard X Bridge	Peter Hurdis
John X Higginson	
William X Syer	
John Swift	
John X Much	
John X Burgeas	
William X Whittle	
Robert X Henshawe	
Lawrence X Wetherbie	
Thomas X Harper	
Roger X Heye[206]	

203 Now Rector.
204 Or *Smorley*.
205 Marks *T*.
206 Marks are *I* with bar (John Boulton and John Burgess), *R* (Richard Bridge and Robert Henshaw), *H* (John Higginson and Thomas Harper), *W* (William Syer), plus sign (William Robertson) and as previously noted.

1661–1662

[f.138r]

[Amounts in the accounts from here to 1665–66 inclusive, except for the supplementary account in 1664–65, are usually separated by the = sign, occasionally by colons. Columns have £ s d headings only where shown. The handwriting appears to be largely the same as the 1658–59 account.]

<The>   The Accomptes of John Bennett / Churchwarden of Walton for the / yeare 1661

Receiptes

Received from the Cunstables of Darbye for / there proporcion of the Church ley	8	00	0
received from the Chappewarden of Formebye	2	13	4
received from the Baylives of Liverpoole	5	6	8
received from the Chappelwarden of Kirkbye	2	13	4
From the Cunstables of Walton / Cum Fazakerley	2	13	4
From the Cunstables of Bootle / Cum Linaker	1	00	0
From the Cunstables of Kirkdall	1	00	0
From the Cunstables of Everton	0	13	4
	24 =	00 =	0

[f.138v]

Received from Maior Fox	2	10	0
received for a Ley stall for Richard / Worsleys daughter	0	2	4
received for a ley stall for John Henshaw	0	2	4
received For a Ley stall for John Roses / daughter of Prescott lane	0	2	4
received of Peeter Johnson for the little yate / and one stoope, at the Churchyard	0	1	2
	2 =	18 =	02
The totall is	26 =	18 =	02

[f.139r]

Disbursmentes

	£	s	d
Imprimis >paid< to Raph Hall for a booke of / Comon prayer	0	9	0
spent >and paid< in Charges to Master Russell for / my selfe and partner and our horses, when / wee tooke our oathes for our office	0	3	6

	£	s	d
paid for a Coppie of the Articles	0	0	6
spent in goeinge to a privie sessions / to Prescott	0	1	0
paid for a Confirmacion warrant	0	2	0
spent on severall of the parishoners / when I received the bookes, they beinge more in number then was usuall	0	3	0
paid more at Thomas Roses the / same day for severall of the parish	0	2	8
paid for bread and wine on Whit- / sunday for the Sacrament	0	5	0
paid to Peeter Walker for a fox head	0	1	0
paid to Master Moores man for 3 fox heades	0	3	0
	1 =	10 =	8

[f.139v]

	£	s	d
paid the Ringers for Coronation day / and the 29 of May	0	11	0
paid to William Poultney for Timber / for a Turne gate for Iron geare / for the same and bringeinge it to / Walton, for workemanshippe and set- / tinge it uppe	3	7	6
paid to William Turner the elder for / takeinge downe the wall and lay- / inge the groundworke for the / gate	0	3	6
spent uppon the workemen two / severall times at the settinge upp / of the same	0	1	0
spent on Master Withins and his man / when hee preacht at Walton June / the last	0	0	6
paid the Clarke for his wages	1	00	0
paid to Nicholas Valentine for a / Certificatt for the bread money	0	00	6
	5 =	4 =	00

[f.140r]

	£	s	d
paid for the receiveinge it at London	0	1	6
paid the old Churchwarden which hee / was in Arreare as appeares by bill	0	19	7
Given to Benjam[i]n Austin, who had / a petticion beinge in much necessitie	0	3	0
spent on my selfe and horse at a privie / sessions at Prescott	0	1	0
paid to <Benjamine> Jeremie of Warington for / another Comon prayer booke	0	6	0
paid for oyle for the Clocke and bels	0	1	0
paid Thomas Boulton for 2 keyes for / the Church Chest, 3 lockes, and hange- / inge the pulpitt doore	0	1	0

	£	s	d
paid for bread and wine for a Sacrament[207]	0	4	0
paid to the Clarke for Carrijnge the same / from Liverpoole 2 severall times	0	0	4
spent at a meeteinge of the overseers / of the poore and severall Chappelwardens / about the poore	0	0	6
	1 = 17 = 11		

[f.140v]

	£	s	d
spent at another privie sessions at / Prescott on my selfe and horse	0	1	0
paid to Jonathom[208] Gleave for Clensinge / and dressinge the Clocke	0	3	6
paid Mathew Gleaves man for a fox head	0	1	0
paid the Ringers November the 5th	0	6	0
paid for 2 bosses for the Church use / and for bringeinge them	0	2	0
paid to Nicholas Valentine for 8 pre- / ceptes for the Church ley and sendinge / them away	0	1	6
more for 6 Coppies of a warrant from / the Chancellor at Chester, for the sever / all Chappels and the vickaridge	0	3	0
For deliveringe them to the severall / Chappelwardens, or mi[ni]sters	0	2	0
paid for bread and wine for a Commu- / nion on Chrismas day	0	4	6
	1 = 4 = 6		

[f.141r]

	£	s	d[209]
spent in goeinge to the privie sessions / to pay moneys Collected by breife / for Rippon, to Master Rigbye	0	1	0
paid for an acquittance to his Clarke	0	0	4
paid for another acquittance for Master / Harrisons breife	0	0	4
paid for a locke and key for the scoole doore	0	1	6
paid for a grave spade	0	1	8
paid Henry Haward for a stancheon / for the Church window and fastininge / the formes in the Church	0	0	8
paid to Thomas Boulton for a filbow / haspe and hinge for the Church yard yate	0	0	8
paid to Captain Lathom for a fox head	0	1	0
paid to William Fleetwood for 19 foot of / new glasse, for mendinge the old and for / nailes and wyre for the same	0	11	4

207 Entry annotated *october 13* in left margin.
208 Or *Jonathone*.
209 Headings inserted twice.

paid Master Finch for a bushell of lime / for pointinge the same	00	00	10
paid to Robert Bushell for pointeinge the / glasse and			
sweepeinge the Leades	00	00	10
	1	= 00 =	...

[f.141v]

	£	s	d
paid William Turner the elder for 2 bushell / of stone lime for			
the Church yard wall / and brininge it from Liverpoole	0	2	0
paid more to him for gettinge and leadinge / stones for the same			
wall	0	17	6
paid to William Turner the younger / for 3 dayes worke for him			
selfe, and 12 / dayes for his men	0	13	6
paid to him more for worke don at the / Church yard wall	00	11	8
paid more to William Turner the elder / for gettinge Stones and			
leadinge them	0	8	4
paid to William Hey for leadinge 24 load / of Stones	0	10	0
paid to William Aspinwall for leadinge / stones to thafforesaid			
wall	0	11	0
paid to William Turner the elder for get- / tinge more stones			
>for< the said wall	0	16	0
	4	= 10 =	0

[f.142r]

	£	s	d
paid to William Turner the younger for / wallinge the new wall			
and dressinge / the Crispe stones	1	2	0
spent of the Masons, leaders of / the stones, and others at two			
severall times	0	1	0
paid to Henry Woodes overseer of the / poore in Kirkbye,			
towardes the puttinge / forth of a poore Child Apprentice by /			
order from the sessions	2	0	0
paid more towardes the maintenance / of Lettice Gleast[210]			
beinge blind and / impotent by order from the sessions	0	10	0
For my Attendantes on the worke / men about the Church yard			
yate, the / wall, slateinge, glaseing and point- / inge about			
the Church beinge / Fifteene dayes	00	10	0
paid Thomas Higginson for 3 hundred / of slates	00	7	6
paid to William Aspinwall for leadinge them	0	9	0
	04	= 19 =	6

---

210 Or possibly *Glease*.

[f.142v]

	£	s	d
Paid to Master Finch for eight bushell and a / halfe of Lime	0	7	0
Paid to Edward Stockley for <...> Five bushell / of haire and bringeinge it to the Church	0	2	6
Paid to Robert Robinson for halfe a hun- / dred of Saplinge Lathes	0	2	6
Paid to Robert Bushell for him selfe and two / men for slateinge, and for slate pins for / the Church	0	11	0
Paid for three hundred of Lath nailes / and 9 penieworth of single and dooble spikes	0	1	6
paid to Richard Wyke Henry Wyke and Richard >Atherton< for five / Fox heades	0	5	0
paid For ingrosseinge these Accountes and for / a Coppie of them	0	3	0
	1 = 12 =		6

The totall received is	26 = 18 = 02		
The Totall disbursed is	21 = 19 = 3		
there remaines due to the Account	04 = 18 = 11		

[f.143r]

These Accomptes were Read Aprill the / first 1662: in the parish Church, and Allowed / And William Syre of Kirkdall and / Lawrence Wetherbie Sydeman / for the yeare ensueinge

by us
John Heywood Rector

Henry X Aspinwall	Henry Finch vicar
William X Turner	John Boulton
William X Whittle	Nicholas Cowper
Richard Blackmoor	Robert Mercer
David X Ruson	John X Boulton
Hugh X Rose	William X Mercer
John Johnson	Nicholas X Mercer
Hugh Rose	John X Much
John X Watmough	Peter Johnson
Nicholas Valentine	John X Banke[211]

[f.143v]

Memorandum It is thought fitt by us / That a Ley of Twenty Fowre poundes / should bee Laid and Collected within the / parish for and towardes the repaire of

211 Marks are *H* (Henry Aspinwall), *R* (David Ruson), sideways *H* (Hugh Rose), *I* with bar (John Watmough), *M* (Nicholas Mercer) and as previously noted.

the / said Church, and to bee paid unto William / Syre Churchwarden on or before / Tuesday in Whitsunweeke / next

	John Heywood Rector
Richard Blackmor	Henry Finch Vicar
John Boulton	Nicholas Cowper
John Bennett	John X Banke
Matthew Gleave	Peter Johnson
John Johnson	John X Boulton
William X Whittle	David X Ruson
William X Mercer	John X Much
	Nicholas Valentine[212]

[f.144r]

A List of Scoole bondes belong- / inge to the Free scoole at Walton / delivered to William Syre of Kirkdall / Churchwarden for this present / yeare 1662

	stocke with ½ yeares interest[213]		
Imprimis Master Roger Bryers	17	10	2
Master Nicholas Fazakerley	8	4	9
Hugh Rose	6	3	7
Thomas Tyrer	10	6	0
The same	6	3	7
Thomas Hughson	4	2	4
Hamlett Boulton	4	2	4
Henry Aspinwall	6	3	7
Robert Mercer	4	2	4
Henry Trustram	3	1	9
Thomas Story	13	7	9
Ann Turner	03	1	9
Richard Stones	01	0	7
James Plumpton	07	4	2
Thomas Harrison	06	3	7
Nicholas Copple	5	3	0
Edward Aspinwall	5	3	0

17   108 – 3 – 4 – 5[214]

[f.144v]

William Rose	10	6	0
Raph Hill	5	3	0
one desperate bond of William Higginsons of / Maghull with sureties	6	4	0

212 Marks as previously noted.
213 Represents 3% per half year.
214 Represents a calculation arriving at £108 from the pounds column + £3 from the shillings (i.e. £111) 4s 5d, the pence being incorrect.

Another desparatt bill of Master Alexander / Mollineux £42. As alsoe a Coppie of / James Berries will, another of Thomas / Harrisons Legacy for the scoole, a note for / the disposeinge of the bread money and / delivered the same time in ready Cash	0	4	3

Moneyes disburst by the old Church warden after / the Ellection of the new

spent on severall of the parishoners at that time / at Thomas Roses and Lettice Boultons	0	2	6
paid Thomas Rose for Carrijnge <100> halfe / a hundred of Lathes from Bootle	0	0	4
paid to Robert Bushell for himselfe and two / men for a day and halfe slateinge at the Church		3	8
spent on my selfe and horse at the privie / sessions at Prescott	0	1	0
paid the Justices Clerkes for signeinge / the Accomptes	0	2	0
	0 =	9 =	6
soe there remaines due / to the Accompt	4 =	9 =	5

1662–1663

[f.145r]

The Account of William Syre / of Kirkdall Church warden of Walton /
Walton for the yeare 1662 – videlicet

Receiptes	£	s	d
Received from the old Churchwarden beinge / due uppon his Account	4	9	5
Received from the Cunstables of Darbye	8	0	0
received from the Cunstables of Walton cum Fazakerley	2	13	4
received from the Chappelwarden of Formbie	2	13	4
received from the Chapelwarden of Kirkbie	2	13	4
received from the Cunstables of Kirkdall	1	0	0
received from the Cunstables of Bootle cum Linaker	1	0	0
received from the Cunstables of Everton	0	13	4
received from the Baylives of Liverpoole	5	6	8
received for a Ley stall for William Rydeinge	0	2	4
received for a Ley stall for Edward Strange	0	2	4
received for a Ley stall for Master Mercer	0	2	4
received for a Ley stall for Mistress Boulton	0	2	4
received for a ley stall for Ann Wiggan	0	2	4
received for a Ley stall for John Mercer	0	2	4
	29 =	3 =	5

[f.145v is blank]

[f.146r]

Disburs[men]tes

spent at a privie sessions at / prescott on my selfe and horse	0	1	0
paid the Justices Clarkes for a Confirmacion warrant	0	2	0
spent on severall of the parishoners at the re- / ceiveinge of the bookes Aprill 16th	0	2	2
given to the Ringers on <Coronation day Aprill 23rd> the Kings returne January 30th	0	5	0
paid for a Certificatt for the bread money	0	0	6
paid for rec[eiving] it at London and returneinge it	0	1	6
paid for 8 preceptes for the Church ley and sendinge / them to the severall Chappelries	0	1	8
given the Ringers on Coranation day	0	4	0
paid for Carrijnge a Collection to the high Cunstable	0	0	2
paid for mendinge the pulpitt Cloth	0	0	6
paid to Henry Guy for 2 fox heades	0	2	0
paid Henry Atherton for one fox head	0	1	0
paid for bread and wine for the sacrment on Whitsunday	0	3	8
given the Ringers May the 29th beinge the Kinges birthday	0	5	0
paid for oyle for the Clocke and bels	0	0	10
paid the Clarke in parte of his wages	0	10	0
paid for 2 new belropes	0	7	6
spent at a meeteinge with th'old Church war- / den to make presentmentes to Chester	0	1	0
	2 =	9 =	6

[f.146v]

paid for writeinge the presentmentes and / a Coppie thereof	0	1	0
paid the Register for my oath and my partners	0	1	10
spent at Chester that time beinge 3 dayes / on Master Benett, my selfe and partner and our horses	0	12	0
paid to William Blackey for dressinge the Clocke	0	3	6
spent uppon the Plummer when hee / Came to view the Church leades	0	1	10
paid him for 2 dayes takeinge downe the / old Lead	0	2	0
paid Robert Bushell and his man for helpinge / the Plummer to Lay the new Lead	0	2	0
spent on 4 men goeinge to Wiggan / to Carry the old Lead	0	1	10
spent on the plummers when the Cast / the Lead	0	1	0
paid for 7 horses a night and day at Wiggan	0	3	6

paid to two Cartes for Carrijnge the old Lead / thither and bringeinge the new lead backe	0	18	0
paid for Leadinge sand to Levell with and / spent on the plummers at the Clarkes	0	2	8
paid for 6lb of Sawder	0	6	0
paid for mendinge the Lead on the north syde / the Church with that sawder	0	1	0
	2 =	18 =	2

[f.147r]

paid for Castinge 1200 of old Lead at 5s per 100[215]	3	0	0
paid for 300 and ½ of new sheet lead at 22s 6d[216] per 100	3	18	0
For my Attendance on the worke 4 dayes	0	2	8
spent at 2 severall privie sessions at / Prescott and Childwall	0	1	4
paid for bread and wine for the sacrament october 12	0	2	4
paid for the booke of Articles	0	2	0
paid for 2 bookes of Common prayer	0	17	0
spent at the makeinge presentmentes / to Chester October the 21	0	0	6
paid for writeinge those presentmentes	0	1	0
paid the Clarke in full of his wages	0	10	0
spent on my selfe and horse 2 dayes at Chester / in makeinge presentmentes october 21	0	4	0
paid there for a surples for the Parson	03	0	0
>paid the Register and th'officers there 6 – 6 and<[217]/			
spent at Warrington in makeinge presentmentes /			
>other 6 – 6 beinge in all<			
at the Archbishopps visitacion, beinge 2 dayes / on my selfe and partner and our horses	0	13	0
Given the Ringers November the 5th	0	5	0
	12 =	16 =	10

[f.147v]

paid for Changinge the Comunion flagon[218]	0	1	8
paid for 2 bread plates for the Table	0	2	4

215 Written *C*, perhaps for hundredweight.
216 Roman numerals.
217 Two lines have been inserted either side of the first line of the entry beginning *spent at Warrington*. The four lines beginning *paid the Register* should therefore be read alternately to make sense. There is only one total for the combined entry, viz. 13s (i.e. 2 × 6s 6d), written as a correction to 12s 6d.
218 Entry annotated *november 11th* in left margin.

paid for a napkin for the same	0	1	4
paid for washinge the surples	0	1	0
paid for wood, nailes and worke to mend / the formes in the Church	0	1	8
For my Attendance that day	0	0	8
paid John Runckorne for dawbinge a dormer / window in the Church	0	0	6
paid for bread and wine for the Sacrament / on Chrismas day	0	3	8
paid for wyre and oyle for the Clocke	0	1	0
paid for two pullies for the same	0	1	0
paid for a surples for the Vickar	1	16	4
paid Thomas Strange for worke don about / the Clocke and his expences	0	1	0
paid for the West gate for the Churchyard	3	10	0
paid for Carrijnge it from Liverpoole	0	2	0
spent on the workmen at the setting upp	0	1	0
For my Attendance that day	0	0	8
paid Nicholas Mercer for takeinge uppe / the flagges and layinge them againe	0	3	0
paid for a new belrope	0	3	0
	6 =	11 =	10

[f.148r]

paid for Washinge the Vickars su>r<ples	0	1	0
paid For the Vickars hood	1	2	4
paid to Henry Guy for 4 fox heades	0	4	0
paid for the Parsons hood	1	0	0
paid for a stoope for the Churchyard yate	0	2	8
paid for Leadinge stones and Clay to the wall	0	1	8
paid Thomas Boulton for Iron worke for the yate	0	0	8
paid Henry Howard for his worke	0	0	6
paid Nicholas Mercer for makeinge the new / wall at the scoole end, and makeinge upp the / breaches in the old wall, and for 2 bars in the yate	0	18	0
For my Attendance on the worke 2 dayes	0	1	4
paid William Turner for gettinge the / stones for the Battlementes of the new wall	0	6	0
paid Jonathan Gleave for dressinge the clocke		2	6
spent uppon him the same time	0	0	4
paid for writeinge Coppies of my / Accountes for the whole yeare	0	2	0
paid Richard Athertons son for 2 fox heades	0	2	0
paid for ingrossinge these Accountes and a / Coppie thereof	0	3	0
	4 =	8 =	0

[f.148v]

Re[c]eiptes[219] this yeare is	29	= 3	=	5
Disbursmentes is	29	= 4	=	4
soe there remaines due to the / Churchwarden uppon this Account is	0	= 0	=	11

These Accomptes were Read in the parish / Church Aprill the 21st 1663 and Allow'd / on by us

John Heywood Rector
John Walton Vicar[220]
Richard Blackmoore
John Boulton
Thomas Latham
John Bennett
Richard Henshaw
James Smoult
Thomas ...

[f.149r]

Hugh Rose
Nicholas Cowper
Thomas Martin
Roger Hey
Nicholas X Mercer[221]

At the same time was Ellected by / the said generall Consent for / Church warden for the yeare ensueinge / Richard Fazakerley of Fazakerley / Church warden and John Eaton of the / same Sydeman: And lykewyse it is / Thought fitt that a Ley of Thirtie six / Poundes should bee Collected and gathered / through the said parish, for and towardes the / repaireinge and bewtifyinge of the said / Church and to bee paid to the said Church / warden at or before Whitsuntyde next.

[f.149v]

A List of Bondes belonge to the Freescoole / at Walton, and delivered to Richard Fa- / zakerley Churchwarden for the yeare / 1663

Imprimis / Master Roger Bryers	17	10	2
Master Nicholas Fazakerley	8	4	9
Hugh Rose	6	3	7
Thomas Tyrer	10	6	0

219 Possibly written *Reseiptes*.
220 Replacing the expelled Henry Finch.
221 Marks as previously noted.

The same	6	3	7
Thomas Hughson	4	2	4
Hamlett Boulton	4	2	4
Henry Aspinwall	6	3	7
Robert Mercer	4	2	4
Henry Trustram	3	1	9
Thomas Story	13	7	9
Ann Turner	3	1	9
Richard Stones	1	0	7
John Edwardson	7	4	2
Thomas Harrison	6	3	7
Nicholas Copple	2>10s<01[222]		6
Richard Boulton	2>10s<01		6
Edward Aspinwall	5	3	0
Henry Mercer	10	6	0
Raph Hill	5	3	0

$$122 = 3 = 13 = 3^{223}$$

[f.150r]

[More than half the lower portion of this folio has been torn away.]

more one desperatt bond of William Higginsons / of Maghull with sureties	5	4	0
another desperatt bill of Master Alexander Mollineux / of £42 as alsoe a Coppie of James Berries / will, another of Thomas Harrisons Legacie / for the Free scoole, and delivered at the same / time in ready money	0	4	3

[f.150v is blank except for a few figures]

1663–1664

[f.151r]
[The receipts for this account have been written after the disbursements]

The Accountes of Richard Fazakerley / Churchwarden of Walton Anno 1663

Disbursmentes
Imprimis spent at the receivinge of th'old Churchwardens /
Accomptes	0	1	0

222 Has been corrected in this and the next entry from *11* to *01* as if deducting the *10s* subsequently inserted with a caret mark.
223 Represents a calculation arriving at £122 from the pounds column + £3 from the shillings (i.e. £125) 13s 3d.

Item spent and given the Ringers May 29	0	5	6
Item spent on Henry Webster when hee / Came to make the style and the Comunion / table Rales	0	1	0
Item paid the deanes Register for our oathes at a / Visitacion at ormiskirke	0	1	10
spent on our selves and horses that day	0	1	2
Item paid for bread and wine for the sacrament on / Whitsunday	0	3	6
spent at makeinge presentmentes to Chester	0	0	6
paid for writeinge them	0	1	0
paid for sendinge them to Chester	0	1	0
paid for writeinge 8 preceptes and sendinge them	0	1	8
paid for writeinge a Certificat for bread >money<	0	0	6
paid for receiveinge it at London	0	1	6
spent uppon the slater when hee Came / to view the Church	0	0	2
paid for haire for the lime	0	4	4
For Carrijnge it from Prescott with / two horses and my expences	0	1	8
	1 = 6 = 4	<1 = 5 = 10>	

[f.151v]

paid Captain Lathome for 30 bushells of lime / at 9d per bushell	1	2	6
paid to 4 slaters for a weekes worke	1	1	0
For my Attendance 2 dayes measureinge the lime	0	1	4
paid For Lath nailes	0	0	6
paid Margrett Johnson for Carryinge the lime / into the Church	0	0	8
spent on the worke men that weeke	0	0	6
For my attendance on the worke 5 dayes	0	3	4
For Leadinge 4 load of Lime from Liverpoole	0	6	8
For 20 Bushells of Lime at 9d per bushell	0	15	0
For Leadinge the same	0	3	4
paid 4 workemen for the 2[n]d weekes worke	1	1	0
paid Margrett Johnson for Carryinge in the lime	0	0	4
paid for a Load of slates and Leadinge them from the parke[224]		5	6
For my Attendance 2 dayes	0	1	4
spent uppon the slaters for takeinge 4 owles	0	1	2
paid more for 8 bushells of lime at 9d per bushell	0	6	0

224 Refers to the delph in Toxteth Park.

For Leadinge it to the Church	0	1	8
For my Attendance that day	0	0	8
spent at a meeteinge on Saint James day	0	0	8
paid to 4 slaters for that weekes worke	0	19	6
spent on them when they tooke the old owle	0	1	0
	6 =	13 =	8

[f.152r]

paid for leadinge a loade of sand to the Church	0	0	...
spent on the plummer when hee viewd the leades	0	0	8
For my attendance 2 dayes this weeke	0	1	4
spent at Receiveinge of Darbye Ley	0	0	4
paid to James Standish beinge >due< to him uppon Account	14	12	11
paid the slaters for another weekes worke	1	0	0
paid them for takeinge of the slates and pointinge the / steeple	0	1	8
paid Henry Webster for the Eastgate	3	0	0
paid him for 32 foote of planke for the gutters / betweene the Chancells at 4d per foote	0	10	8
paid for Layinge the plankes and for nailes	0	2	0
paid William Watmough for Iron worke for the gate	0	11	11
paid for Carryinge the same from Liverpoole to Knowsley	0	0	8
paid for flagges for the same gate	0	1	0
paid the Mason and laborer for takinge uppe the flaggs / and layinge them againe	0	3	6
paid for bringeinge the yate and the plankes from / Knowsley and for 10 flaggs	0	4	0
spent at severall times on the Carpenters, plummers / and masons at the finishinge of the worke	0	3	0
For my Attendance 2 dayes	0	1	4
For oyle For the Clocke	0	0	4
paid Margrett Johnson for Carryinge a load of lime	0	0	3
paid F[or] 2 belropes and a line for the font Cover	0	6	0
paid for 100 of slates and leadinge them to the Church	0	5	6
paid to 4 slaters for a weekes worke at the Church and scoole	1	1	4
	22 =	8 =	11

[f.152v]

paid to James Massam for a fox head	0	1	0

paid for a sacke of haire and Carrijnge it from Prescott	0	1	8
paid F[or] 10 bushells of lime at 9d per bushell	0	7	6
paid For fetching it	0	1	8
For my Attendance 2 dayes on the worke	0	1	4
paid Margrett Johnson for Carrijnge in the lime	0	0	3
spent on the worke men that weeke	0	0	6
paid Robert Gibbon for 2 load of Clay for the scoole	0	1	0
For Rydeinge to the Parke to provide slates	0	0	8
paid to Henry Guy for 3 fox heads	0	3	0
paid 4 slaters for 2 dayes worke at the scoole	0	6	10
paid William Fleetwood for glasse worke / don at Church and scoole as appeares by his bill	1	1	7½
paid for a spade for the Church use	0	2	0
given the Ringers the 5 of November	0	4	0
paid 2 slaters for pointeinge the windowes in the / Church and scoole beinge 2 dayes and ½	0	5	0
paid the Clarke his yeares wages	1	0	0
spent 2 severall dayes on the glasier and slaters / when they finished there worke	0	1	0
paid the deanes Register at a visitacion at ormiskirke	0	2	6
spent on my selfe and partner there	0	1	2
	4 =	2 =	8½

[f.153r]

paid William Syre and his partner[225] for there expences <...> / beinge scyted before the Chancellor at his visitacion / at Warrington	0	9	0
paid him more beinge due uppon his last yeares account	0	1	0
paid the Plummer for takeinge uppe the old lead / and layinge the new betweene the Chancells	1	8	0
paid the halfe Charge of Leadinge the Lead to / Wiggan and backe againe	0	4	6
spent at Castinge the Lead for the whole	0	0	8
more by the way at Holland	0	0	4
more at Walton at the layinge the Lead	0	0	8
paid to a messenger that Came from the plummer / to fetch mee to him, and spent when I paid him	0	0	9
For my attendance 2 dayes on the worke	0	1	4
paid the Ringers for another day Ringeinge	0	5	0
paid for bread and wine for the Sacrament on / Chrismas day	0	3	6

225 The previous year's churchwarden and sidesman.

paid Henry Haward for makeinge a ladder for the / steeple, mendinge the Coffer, the beare, and fittinge / the font Cover, for Iron and nailes, and spent then / on the worke men	0	1	4
For my Attendance that day	0	0	8
	2 =	15 =	9

[f.153v]

paid to Daniel the Huntsman for a fox head	0	1	0
paid for writeinge presentmentes to ormiskirke February 18	0	1	0
spent at makeinge them	0	0	4
spent at ormiskirke then on my selfe and partner	0	1	2
paid John Fradsome for a fox head	0	1	0
given to a Captain and 10 other Travellers hee have- / inge beene in his majesties service beyond seas and robd / homeward bownd	0	3	0
paid For >a< breadth of holland and puttinge it into the vickars / surples beeinge eaten with myse in the Church Chest		4	0
paid Alexander Mollineux per fo[x] head	0	1	0
paid for mendinge the Churchyard wall	0	0	8
paid Henry Webster For the rales about the / Comunion Table, and a table for the scoole	4	0	0
paid to Bibbie for bandes for the Rales	0	1	8
paid for a boult for the Rales	0	0	6
paid for Leadinge the Rales and table from Know / sley	0	3	0
spent on the workemen when they sett / uppe the rales	0	1	0
for my Attendance that day	0	0	8
For oyle for the Clocke	0	0	4
	5 =	0 =	4

[f.154r]

paid for a locke for the font	0	0	10
paid Jonathan Gleave for Clensinge the clocke	0	2	6
paid for writeinge Coppies of my / Accountes for the whole yeare	0	3	0
paid for ingrossinge these Accountes	0	3	0
	0 =	9 =	4

Communion Rails[226]

The totall received is	45 =	17 =	4
The totall disburst is	42 =	17 =	0½
soe there rest due to the parish	03 =	00 =	3½

---

226 Note added in a different hand.

[*f.154v is blank*]

[f.155r]

Richard Fazakerleyes Receiptes 1663

Received From the Cunstables of Darbie	16	0	0
Received from the Baylives of Liverpoole	10	13	4
Received from the Cunstables of Walton / Cum Fazakerley	03	6	8
Received from the Chappelwarden of Kirkby	5	6	8
Received from the Chappelwarden of Formebye	5	6	8
Received from the Cunstables of Bootle cum Linaker	2	0	0
Received from the Cunstables of Kirkdall	1	5	0
Received from the Cunstables of Everton	1	6	8

45 = 5 = 0

Received for a Ley stall for Mistress Johnson	2	4
Received for a Ley stall for Roger Hey	2	4
Received for a Ley stall for William Bootle	2	4
Received for a Ley stall for Master Lawrence Bryers	2	4
Received for a Child of John Johnsons	1	2
Received of Richard Blackmore for a peece of lead	1	4
Received of William Mercer for a peece of wood	0	6

0 = 12 = 4

Summa totalis   45 = 17 = 4

[f.155v]

These Accomptes were Read in the / Church Aprill the 12th 1664 and Allowd / on by us whose names are subscribed
At the same time was Ellected Churchwar- / den Richard Henshaw of the greene lane / and Thomas Whitfeild of Darbie sydeman / to serve for this yeare ensueinge
And a Ley of £12 to bee paid to the said / Churchwarden before Whitsuntyde next

John Heywood Rector
John Walton Vicar
Ro[bert] Mercer
James Standish
John Mercer
John Bennett
John Rose

[f.156r]

Richard Blackmoore
William X Syre

Thomas X Barnes
Robert Mosse
Thomas X Martin
Nicholas Cowper[227]

1664–1665

[f.156v]

[*Memorandum in different handwriting from the rest of the account.*]

Nov[ember] 1 1664

Wee whose names are Subscribed / doe thinke fitt that a Church-ley / of £12 bee layd and Speedily gather- / ed for the use of the Parish-Church / of Walton.

	John Heywood Rector
Nicholas X Marcer / his marke	John Walton Vicar
William X Mercer / his marke	Nicholas Cowper
William X [?Tornar] / his marke	Thomas X Warton / h[is] marke
Robert Mercer	John Heaton
	John X Brige / his marke
	Richard Blackmore[228]

[f.157r]

[*The style of this account follows the description given under 1661, except that most page totals are only roughly noted, being added in different ink and without separating characters.*]

The Accompt[s] of Richard Henshaw / Churchwarden of Walton for the yeare / 1664 as Followeth

Receiptes

Received from the old Churchwarden	1	14	0
Received from the Cunstables of Darbie / the first Church ley	4	0	0
received from the Baylives of Liverpoole	2	13	4
received from Formebye	1	6	8
received from Walton Cum Fazakerley	1	6	8
received from Kirkbie	1	6	8
received from Kirkdall	0	10	0
received from Bootle Cum Linaker	0	10	0

227 Marks are procumbent *V* (William Syre) and as previously noted.
228 Marks are inverted *V* (William Mercer), *W* (William ?Tornar), *T* (Thomas Warton), *IB* (John Brige) and as previously noted.

received from Everton	0	6	8
the 2d[229] / Ley received from the Cunstable of Darby	4	0	0
From the Baylives of Liverpoole	2	13	4
From Formebye	1	6	8
From Walton Cum Fazakerley	1	6	8
From Kirkbie	01	6	8
from Kirkdall	00	10	0
from Bootle Cum Linaker	00	10	0
from Everton	00	6	8

[f.157v]

received for a Leystall for Master Richard Lathom	0	2	4
received for ley stall for Captain Lathoms wyfe	0	2	4
received of Mistress Heywood for old seeleinge[230] / in the Church	0	15	0
received for a leystall for Rowland Johnson	0	2	4
the totall receiptes are	26 =	16 =	0

[f.158r]

Disbursmentes

spent at the receiveinge the bookes / from the old Churchwarden	0	1	0
paid the deanes register May the 13	0	1	10
spent that day uppon our selves and horses	0	3	6
paid for bread and wine for whitsunday	0	5	6
spent on the Clarke and my selfe at / the buyinge of it	0	0	4
paid for Cordinge for the Clocke	0	1	0
paid Master Walton for money <hee>[231] laid out / in the yeare 1663 Concerneinge fishinge[232]	0	1	6
spent on >James Webster[233]< my selfe and horse in goeinge >to Ormiskirke to him< /<James Webster> about beutifyinge the / Church	0	2	0
given the Ringers May the 29 beinge / the Kinges birth day	0	5	0
For writeinge 8 preceptes for the first / Church <ley and sendinge them away>	0	1	8
For writeinge a Certifate for bread money		0	6

229 Written in the left margin, indicating that all subsequent entries refer to the second ley.
230 Second letter uncertain, see also f.162v, p. 158 and glossary, p. 173.
231 May be blotted rather than deleted.
232 Probable though not certain transcription. No reference found to explain it (Master Walton is the vicar).
233 Surname either deleted or written over an underline of the date above.

For receiveinge the same at London		1	6
spent in gettinge the >8< preceptes to the / severall Townes	0	1	0

1 5 10

[f.158v]

paid John Everitt for a Fox head	0	1	0
spent on the glasier and slater when / they Came to view the worke	0	1	0
given the slater in earnest	0	0	4
paid John Syre for a Fox head	0	1	0
spent on James Webster and other of his / workemen, my selfe and severall others / of the parishoners when hee tooke the / worke	0	2	4
given him in earnest	0	0	6
paid the scoole master for writeinge / Articles of our bargaine[234]	0	0	6
For 2 severall times goeinge to toxsteth / parke to provide slates and pay for them		0	8
spent in receiveinge the Church ley / from the severall townes,[235] beinge forct / to goe severall times to Liverpoole for Formebye Ley	0	2	0
paid for 300 of slates	0	7	6
paid Robert Gibbon for leadinge them	0	7	0

1 = 03 = 10[236]

[f.159r]

[The bottom third to a half of the folio has been torn away except for a narrow strip on the binding side. Letters and figures surviving on the latter indicate that written matter extended to the bottom of both pages.]

spent uppon the same Robert	0	0	6
paid William Fleetwood for glasse >inge< at the / Church as appeares by his bill	0	18	9[237]
spent uppon him dureinge the / time of his worke and at the finishinge	0	0	10
For my Attendance on the worke / 4 dayes	0	2	8
paid for 100 of Lathes	0	2	4

234 Entry annotated with pencil cross in left margin.
235 This word obviously intended, though several letters carelessly formed.
236 Total corrected by overwriting in different ink.
237 Or *0*.

spent on Thomas Whitfeild when hee / Came to take off 5 lockes, and the broken / Hinges off the doore betweene the Chancells	0	6
paid the same Thomas for make ...		

s...
C...

[f.159v]

paid to Henry Haward for mendinge the / Boadrickes and hanginge the said Clappers	0	4
paid Thomas Rose for Carrijnge the said / Clappers to Darbie and back againe	0	1	0
spent on Thomas Whitfeild and Thomas Rose / whilst the worke was in hand	0	0	6
paid for 7 measures of lime for the slates / of the porch, and the dormar windowes and to point the windowes about the Church	0	4	10
paid for putinge abourd into the south gate	0	0	2
paid for 14 foote of rale, to bee an evepole / ... Church porch		1	8
	...	2	3
	...	2	6
	...	5	4
	...	1	2

[f.160r]

paid Thomas Rose for old spokes to bee / pinwood for the said slates		0	4
paid to Robert Bushell for his worke / at the porch	0	16	0
spent on him and his men, dureinge the / worke and when I paid them	0	2	4
for my Attendance 4 dayes	0	2	8
paid Thomas Rose for fetchinge a load of / sand to mix with lime, and for digginge / and loadinge 3 load of Clay, for the / repaire of the dormar windowes and / beame fillinge in severall places	0	4	4
paid John Webster and his man for 2 dayes / and ½ worke at the dormar windowes / in Clampstaffinge, windeinge / dawbinge and plasteringe	0	3	8
spent on them those dayes	0	0	6
For my Attendance 2 dayes	0	1	4

paid Thomas Rose for eveninge at the / entrie of the porch, gutteringe at the / north doore, layinge on step there and / Levellinge flaggs in the north / Chancell	0	1	0

... 13   ...[238]

[f.160v]

paid Thomas and John Webster for one dayes / worke mendinge at the Church / in mendinge the formes	0	2	0
paid for there diners that day	0	0	6
spent on them that day	0	0	6
for my attendance	0	0	8
paid Thomas Rose for Clensinge the leades / on the Church and Chancell	0	0	4
paid James Webster for the whole / worke of bewtifyeinge the Church / hee findinge all materialls	4	4	0
spent on him and his men dureinge the / whole worke	0	6	10
For my Attendance on the plasterrers and pensall man twelve dayes	0	8	0
paid Thomas Rose June the 25th <Clenseinge> for Tendinge / the Clocke, sweepeinge the Church / and ringe>inge< Corfey	1	0	0
paid Master Walton, which hee gave to Robert / Rigbie who desyred a Collection under / the handes of the Earle of Darbie all his / deputie Lieutenantes and Justices of the / ... in this County		2	6

| | 6 | 5 | 4 |

[f.161r]

spent in goeinge to the deanes Court / July the 27 <of July>	0	2	0
paid for a pint of oyle for the Clocke	0	0	10
paid for a lb of wire for the Clocke	0	1	8
paid Jonathan Gleave for mendinge / and Clensinge the Clocke	0	3	6
spent at the buyinge of the oyle and wire / and on the said Jonathan 2 Jorneyes to / Liverpoole to procure him to doe the worke	0	1	0
paid for bread and wine for a sacrament / October the 2d	0	4	0
spent at buyinge the same	0	0	4
paid Thomas Rose for Carrijnge Rubbish / from the Church doore after slateinge	0	0	6

238 Has been corrected, but tearing obscures the full entry.

given to 10 poore people who had / his Majesties lycence for particular / Collections, viewed by Master Walton / October the 9th	0	2	6
spent at the generall meeteinge of the / parishoners for the layinge the 2d Church ley November the 1º	0	2	0
	...	18	4

[f.161v]

given the Ringers November the 5th	0	5	6
spent at makeinge presentmentes November 7th	0	1	0
paid for writeinge the same presentmentes	0	1	6
spent in goeinge to the deanes Court / November the 8	0	2	0
paid the deanes register that time when / wee delivered presentmentes and returnd / the scitacions[239]	0	1	0
paid to the parater	0	0	4
paid for 2 new belropes	0	7	6
spent at buyinge them	0	0	2
paid for writeinge 8 preceptes for the / 2d Church ley	0	1	8
spent in sendinge to the severall townes	0	1	0
paid for washinge the vickars surples / 4 severall times	0	4	0
spent at the recieveinge of Liverpoole ley	0	0	4
more at receiveinge of Darbie ley	0	0	4
spent at the receiveinge of the said / ley from the rest of the Townes	0	0	8
	1	7	0[240]

[f.162r]

paid for bread and wine for the Comunion / on Chrismas day	0	5	6
spent at buyinge of it	0	0	4
paid for Carrijnge it \<from\> to Walton	0	0	3
paid John Higginson for a Fox head	0	1	0
paid Thomas Boulton for makeinge a / latch for the Churchgate	0	0	8
given to 8 travellors January the 8 which / had passes under 2 Justices handes	0	1	0
spent on Thomas Webster and my selfe / goeinge to Hyton to view that reed- / inge seat, Churchwardens and Clarks / seat for a patterne to sett ours by	0	1	4
spent in goeinge to the deanes Court / January the 21	0	2	0
For my Charges goeinge 2 severall times / to Knowsley to Thomas Webster about the / said worke	0	0	8

239 Or *soitacions*.
240 Replaces thickly struck through total.

spent on Thomas Webster January 26th when / I set him the worke	0	0	6
given him in earnest	0	0	4[241]
			...[242]

[f.162v]

paid Master Waltons boy for Carrijnge a letter / to Alkar for the procureinge a scoolmaster	0	1	0
paid for a pint of oyle for the Clocke / January the 4th	0	0	10
paid for fetchinge the seelinge from / Knowsley to Walton	0	3	0
paid for 4 paire of hinges for the / reedinge deske and Churchwardens seate	0	2	0
spent uppon the Joyners and Carter	0	1	0
paid for staples, Clapes and nailes for / settinge uppe the said worke	0	1	0
paid Nicholas Mercer for a load of Ashlers / from Liverpoole hill, for fetchinge and / dressinge them and others about the Church / and for 4 dayes and ½ worke in layinge the / ground worke and flagginge under and / about the said reading deske, Church- / warden and Clarkes seate		10	9
spent uppon him those dayes when / I paid him	0	1	0
paid Thomas Webster for the said read- / inge deske Churwardens and Clerkseat[243]			

[f.163r]

and 5 dayes worke of two workemen / in settinge uppe the same and mend- / inge the pulpitt	4	15	0
spent uppon them those 5 dayes	0	3	4
For my Attendance on the mason / and Joyners 4 dayes	0	2	8
spent in goeinge to Prescott beinge / [?warnd][244] as scoolereeve Concerninge / hearth money[245]	0	1	0
paid for a Coard for the font Cover	0	0	3
paid to Richard Ball for 5 Fox heades	0	5	0
paid for washeinge the Parsons / surples 4 severall times	0	4	0
paid for writeinge presentmentes to the / deanes Court May the 13th	0	1	6

---

241 Or *9*.
242 Total thickly struck through, then bottom edge of page lost.
243 No amount, since the entry continues on the next page. A total for the rest of the page, *1:0:7*, is written in the left margin.
244 Corrected word, not clearly decipherable.
245 The hearth tax, levied from 1662 on.

paid for writeinge Coppies of / my Accountes for the whole
yeare	0	3	0
For ingrossinge these Accountes	0	3	0

5	<...>[246]

[f.163v]

The totall Receiptes is	26	=	16	=	0
The totall disbursmentes is	24	=	12	=	9
more received then disburst	02	=	3	=	3

These Accomptes were Read march the 28th / 1665 and Allowd by us – lykewyse was / Elected the same day
Churchwarden – William Halsall
Sydeman –   Thomas Hollis } of Bootle
And three Church leyes to bee Collected / and gathered for the repaire of the said /
Church   £18

                    John Heywood Rector
                    John Walton vicar
        Thomas Boulton
        Richard Blackmoor

[f.164r]

        James Standish
        John Bennett
        William X Syre
        John Rose
        Robert Mercer
        Peter Johnson
        Richard Fazakerley
        William X Whittle
        John X Rose / of Everton
        John Johnson
        Nicholas Cowper[247]

[f.164v, originally blank, has been filled with some verse apparently added later, and transcribed with the notes on annotations, p. 176.]

[f.165r]

[This supplementary account appears to relate to the year 1663–64, and to have been submitted late by the churchwarden for that year, Richard Fazakerley. It is in

---

246 Thickly struck through.
247 Marks are *IR* (John Rose) and as previously noted. The page also has some erased lettering.

a different hand from the accounts before and after it. Pounds, shillings and pence are separated by dashes on the first page and by = on the second. The top and one side of the folio are torn, matter being lost from the first lines and from parts of the entries. The scribe writes a, e, and o in very similar form, so the precise transcription is uncertain in some instances.]

...
for the parish by Richard F... / for the yeare 1664 After N... / hee was Discharged from his office and the N...[248]

	£	...	
Imprimis Spent at the Election of the New / Church warden	0	...	
Item paid for washing the Communion Table / Cloth and Napkins Twyce	0	...	
Item paid for A hack for the Church	0	...	
Item paid[249] for Mendinge the Scolle doore Keye	0	0	...
Item paid for Copying the Regestar	0	1	...
Item paid for Ingroseing the Regestar	0	1	...
Item spent at Makeing presentmentes After Estar	0	2	...
Item paid for writeing those presentmentes	0	1	...
Item paid for An Inke horne to be in the / Church, for the Regestering of Marreges / Birthes and Buryales	0	0	...
Item paid to the hed parator at the delivaring of / our presentmentes as Foloweth			
for Aperence Fee Att Mighalmus and Estar	0	3	...
for A booke of Common prayor for the Fast	0	1	...
for Retorneing the Regestar	0	0	...
Aparatores Fee	0	0	...
Item spent in Goeing to the vissitation the tyme / Afore said upon our Selves and our horses	0	...	

[f.165v]

...od Fryday	0	3	...
...nt at the bying of it	0	0	4
... for the Caridge of it to Walton	0	0	2
paid for Bread and Wyne for Acommunion / upon Ester Day	0	3	9
spent att the Bying of it	0	0	4
paid for the Caridge of it to Walton	0	0	2
	0	= 7	= 9

---

248 Both the queried *N...* words could be either *Nov* or *New*, though both appear to have marks of contraction.

249 Scribe's contraction (which has been expanded) appears to be *pe* rather than *pd* for the rest of this page.

thes adicionold account / hath beene perused received into the booke and allowed by
  John Heywood Rector
  Ro[bert] Mercer
  Nicholas Valentine
  William X Halsall / his marke[250]

1665–1666

[f.166r]

The Accomptes of William Halsall / Churchwarden of Walton for the year / 1665
as Followeth

Receiptes

Received From the Cunstables of Darbie	6	0	0
Received From the Baylives of Liverpoole	4	0	...
Received From the Cunstables of Walton / Cum Fazakerley	2	0	0
Received from the \<Cunstables\> Chaplewarden of Kirkby	2	0	0
Received from the Chappelwarden of Formebie	2	0	0
Received from the Cunstables of Kirkdall	0	15	0
Received from the Cunstables of Bootle Cum / Linaker	0	15	...
Received from the Cunstables of Everton	0	10	0
Received for a ley stall for Alis fare	0	2	...
Received for a ley stall for John Rose of everton	0	2	...
	18 =	4 =	...

[f.166v]

Disbursementes By William Halsall 1665

	£	s	d
Imprimis paid for writeinge 8 preceptes for a Church ley / and sendinge them away	0	1	8
April 14th[251] / paid the deanes Register for our oathes	0	1	2
spent on ourselves and horses that visitacion	0	1	6
For writeinge a Certificatt for bread money	0	0	6
\<For\>			
May 1° / spent at Receiveinge the Bookes from the / old Churchwarden	0	1	6
paid for 2 Timber trees in Simonswood[252]	3	4	0

---

250 Marks with a loop or *8* shape.
251 Dates on this and the next two pages are actually written in the left margin in line with the entries to which they refer.
252 *9* in left margin, perhaps for *May 9*.

spent on Thomas Boden and my selfe at / the Buyinge of them	0	0	8
paid John Bridge and John Burges for lead- / inge the Timber beinge 4 Loades	0	12	0
spent on them	0	0	8
spent on Thomas Boden when hee viewd / the Bellwheeles and the Formes to mend them	0	0	4
spent at receiveinge of Liverpoole Ley / goeinge Twyse for it	0	0	4
paid for bread and wine for the Sacrament on / Whitsunday	0	4	6
paid for Carrijnge it to Walton	0	0	2
given the Ringers May the 29th beinge / the Kinges birthday	0	5	0
	4 =	14 =	0

[f.167r]

[*Fading makes the distinction between* 0 *and* 6 *in the r.h. column difficult on this page. Some figures are also lost by tearing.*]

paid Thomas Boulton for 2 bandes for the belwheel.	0	0	3
paid Thomas Boden for mendinge the Belwheele / the Beere and the formes in the Church	0	1	[?0]
paid for a board for the Wheele	0	1	[?6]
For nailes for the worke	0	0	6
paid for fellinge the trees in simonswood	0	0	10
paid Thomas Boden for his dayes worke when / wee bought the Timber	0	0	6
paid For Cuttinge, squareinge and makeinge / them Loadable	0	2	[?6]
paid him for gettinge them into the Church	0	1	...
June 10th / spent on my selfe and horse at the visitacion at / ormiskirke	0	1	2
spent in goeinge to Prescott about the scoole / Chimney[253]	0	1	...
paid Henry Mercer for a fox head	0	1	...
paid for a pint of oyle for the Clocke	0	0	...
paid the Clarke his wages	1	0	...
For wire for the Clocke	0	0	...
paid Henry Haward for settinge uppe the Belfrie / particion and puttinge 2 baordes in the Churchyard yate	0	...	...
paid Richard Everard for a fox head	0	1	0
paid Jonathan Gleave for Clenseinge the Clocke	0	3	6
spent on him at severall times	0	0	8
paid for a booke of Articles for the Bishopps / visitacion	0	0	6
	1 =	19 =	1

253 Perhaps a hearth tax query.

[f.167v]

spent on the pariter and given him that time	0	0	8
paid Thomas Alkar and Henry Leadbeater for 5 fox heades		5	0
paid Thomas Hollis for pointinge the Leades / Clenseinge the gutters and for lime and haire for the worke	0	2	0
For writeinge presentmentes to the Bishops / visitacion at Wiggan August the first	0	1	6
spent 2 severall times meeteinge about them	0	0	6
For a booke of paper to write strange ministers / names in that shall preach here	0	0	3
paid the Chancellor for our oathes that time	0	4	0
For Charges of my partner and horse >thither<	0	1	2
...gust / ...d paid for a booke for publicke humiliacion	0	1	0
paid the pariter for bringinge it	0	0	6
paid for bread and wine for the Sacrament / October the 15th	0	4	0
spent on my selfe and horse goeinge to the / deanes visitacion at ormiskirke october 23rd	0	1	2
paid For a key for the scoole doore and mend- / inge the Church yate Latch	0	0	6
	1 =	2 =	3

[f.168r]

given the Ringers November the 5th	0	5	[?0]
paid for oyle for the Clocke	0	0	9
paid for mendinge the Churchyard wall	0	0	6
paid for a Clape of Iron for the south yate	0	0	3
paid the Register at the Bishops Corrections / at Wiggan december the 11th	0	3	...
spent on myselfe and horse that Jorney	0	1	...
paid For bread and wine for Chrismas day / for the Sacrament	0	4	...
>paid Thomas Boulton for a ...hoote[254] for the scoole locke and other worke		0	...<
paid the Carpenters for mendinge the Church / yard gates and the seates within the Church	0	1	8
paid Thomas Rose for a board for the same worke	0	0	...
paid the smith for nailes, for mendinge the snecke / and the Latch	0	...	3
For my Attendance that day	0	0	...
paid Henry Leadbeater for a fox head	0	1	0
paid For a booke of Canons	0	1	8

254 Unclear interlineation: probably *shoote* or perhaps *sheete*.

paid the glasier for mendinge the / Church windowes	0	5	6
paid Henry Gibbon for mendinge the / Church yard wall	0	0	2
	1 =	7 =	1

[f.168v]

For my Attendance uppon the glasier 1 day	0	0	8
For 6 yardes and ½ of kersey for a Carpett for the / Comunion Table >at 3s 4d per yard<	1	1	8
For silke to make the same	0	0	6
spent on 3 at the buyinge of it	0	1	4
paid <the> Thomas Whitfeild for wedginge the / Gudgeons at the great bell	0	2	0
spent uppon eight men to raise the bell forth / of the steppe >at that time<			...²⁵⁵
paid for a booke of homilies at London	0	10	0
paid for Carrijnge it downe	0	1	0
spent in goeinge to the deanes Court / march the 22th	0	1	2
paid for bread and wine for the Sacrament / on Palme sunday and Easter day	0	9	10
paid for 18 ow018s and ½ of silke fringe for the / Comunion Table Cloth	2	7	0
paid for makeinge the same Cloth and settinge / on the fringe	0	2	6
paid Henry Guy for 5 fox heades	0	5	0
paid for washinge the Parsons surples and / the vickars the whole yeare	0	8	0
paid for keepeinge Coppies of these Accountes	0	3	0
For engrosseinge them	0	3	0
	5 =	18 =	2

[f.169r]

The totall Receipts this yeare is	18 =	4 =	8
The totall disbursmentes is	15 =	0 =	6
more received then disburst is	3 =	4 =	2

Theis Accountes were Read Aprill the 17th 166... / and Allowd on by us whose names are subscr...

At the same Time was Ellected for / Churchwarden Robert Hitchin of / Toxteth Parke and John Bridge of Walton / sydeman to serve for the yeare ensueinge

And a ley of £12 to bee forthwith paid to / the said Churchwarden or sydeman

Edward Moore   Richard Henshaw

John Heywood Rector   Thomas Knowles

---

255 Folios from here to 172 are damaged by a worm hole.

Thomas Marsden vicar[256]	William Johnson
Richard Blackmoore	Richard Syre
William X Syre[257]	William Mercer
John Bennett	

[f.169v]

Thomas X Martin	William X Mercer
Richard Fazakerley	Thomas Haworth
John Johnson	Nicholas X Mercer[258]

more disburst since			
spent uppon the severall people that we... / at the election	0	2	10
paid For writeinge presentmentes to the / deanes Court May the 28th 66	0	2	0
spent at that time	0	0	6
...pent on our selves and horses at the / ...isitacion at ormiskirke May 28th 66	0	2	8
paid the Register for the oath and paritors fee		4s	
paid F[or] bread and wine at whitsunday for the / Sacrament	0	6	8
more towardes payinge for Richard Fazakerleys		1	00[259]
	0 =	19 =	8

1666–1667

[It appears that Robert Hitchin did not carry out his duties, probably because of his excommunication (see Introduction, p. xv). Presumably due to this breakdown of the system and the need to elect Nicholas Mercer as replacement part way through the year, the entries for 1666 are confused and difficult to place in chronological order. Various hands have contributed.]

[f.170r]

[William Halsall's account for his elected year of office, 1665–66, already contains payment to the ringers for 29 May and for bread and wine for the Christmas sacrament, whereas Nicholas Mercer's account to run from his election in November 1666 lacks a payment for Christmas but does include Easter expenses. So although it might appear that William Halsall continued to carry out churchwarden's duties to cover the vacancy left by Hitchin, the changeover was

---

256 Succeeded John Walton during the year.
257 Marks as previously noted.
258 Marks are *T* or badly-formed cross (William Mercer), *M* (Nicholas Mercer) and as previously noted.
259 Corrected by overwriting.

possibly not clear cut and the September date below may be misleading. This account uses dashes in the £ s d columns as separators.]

May the 27 1666

Received from Richard Henshaw late / Churchwarden his Arreares	0	12	6

September the last 1666

paid F[or] holland and inlainge[260] in Doctors sirples		1	...
paid F[or] mendinge the Church yard yate and stiles		1	6
paid the vickar for expences at ormiskirke at / the visitacion		1	...
paid F[or] bread and wine for a Comunion at >Christmas<[261]		4	...
paid Thomas Rose his wages	1	0	0
paid for a bellrope	0	2	...
F[or] mendinge the great Bell	0	1	...
Charges to ormiskirke twise	0	1	...
F[or] Candles for the ringers	0	...	...
paid the Ringers for the 29th / of May, and for the victorie over / the Hollander	0	10	0
	2	...	...

[f.170v]

memorandum that uppon the 25th of / march 1667 this latter Account of William / Halsall was received wherein wee finde / him in Arreare to the parish   1s   5d
>received more   12 – 6<

Thomas Marsden vicar
Nicholas X Mercer
John X Bridge
Nicholas Valentine[262]

[f.171r]

November the 13 1666

Ellected by Speciall order of the / Consistorie at Chester Nicholas Mercer / of Walton Churchwarden for this said / year. By us –
Thomas Marsden Vicar
Richard Blackmoore
William X Halsall
William X Mercer

260 Uncertain spelling but probably for *inlaying*.
261 Written *Xmas*.
262 Marks as previously noted. The page also has 'practice' writing of the name *Nicholas*.

Robert X Pemberton
Raph X Stones
Robert X Gibbon
William X Boydall[263]

[f.171v]

Disburs[mentes]

The Account of Nicholas Mercer / for march t[h]e 25 1667[264]

paid to Master Marsden which hee had laid downe / to the Ringers for the 5th of November	0	5	0
spent on our selves and horses at Ormiskirke / March the 6 at the visitacion	0	2	0
spent on severall people at receiveinge / the bookes	0	3	4
paid the glasier for worke at the / Church as appears per bill	0	5	0
paid for writeinge 8 precepts for a / Church ley and sendinge them away	0	1	8
paid for a pint oyle for the Clocke	0	1	2
paid Richard Parrs man for settinge the / Clocke agoeinge	0	0	4
paid for a pound of wyre for the Clocke	0	2	0
paid Richard Parr for mendinge the / ...nges, makeinge priddes and other worke / don at the Clocke	0	5	6
spent on him the same time	0	0	6
	1 =	6 =	6

[f.172r]

paid him for a new locke and key for the / steeple doo...	0	4	0
paid Thomas Boulton for 4 new steps / for the Church yard gates and nailes to / mend the same	0	...	1
paid William Poultney for mendinge / them	0	1	2
paid Thomas Rose for mendinge the / Church yard wall	0	0	...
paid for washinge the vickars surples	0	1	[?0]
paid for Bread and wine for the Sa- / crament on palme sunday and gooday	0	7	[?6]
spent at the buyinge of it	0	0	...
paid for Carriage of it to Walton	0	0	...
paid for bread and wine for Easter day	0	7	6
spent at buyinge of it	0	0	2
paid for Carriage of it	0	0	2

263 Marks are inverted *V* (William Mercer and Raph Stones), reversed *N* (Robert Pemberton), *R* (Robert Gibbon), *M* (William Boydall) and as previously noted.

264 To be understood as for the year ending March 1667. His receipts are written after the disbursements.

paid for 3 new Belropes	0	...	7
paid Thomas Knowles for a fox head	0	1	0
paid Henry Atherton for a fox head	0	1	0
	1 =	12 =	4

[f.172v]

spent at the receiveinge of all the leyes	0	1	0
paid For washinge the doctors surples	0	3	0
paid For receiveinge the bread money / at London the last yeare	0	2	0
For <keepe> writeinge Coppies of the Accountes	0	3	0
For Ingrossinge the Accountes	0	3	0
The totall of disbursmentes is	3 =	10 =	10
<The totall of receiptes is	7 =	11 =	7>
<more received then disburst	4 =	0 =	9>

Edward Stockley[265]

[f.173r]

Nicholas Mercers Receiptes for the y... /
1666

Received from the old Churchwarden	...	...	...
Received from the Chappelwarden of Formbie	1	6	8
Received from the Chappelwarden of Kirkbie	1	6	8
Received from the Baylives of Liverpoole	2	...	...
Received from the Cunstable of Everton	0	...	...
Received from the Cunstables of Kirkdall	0	...	...
<spent at the receiveinge of all these	0>		
received from the Cunstable of Walton	0	13	...
from the Cunstable of Fazakerley	0	...	...
from the Cunstables of Darbie	4	...	...
from the Cunstable of Bootle	0	1	...

[f.173v]

These Accountes were Read the ninth day / of Aprill 1667 and Allowd on By us / and the same time was Ellected for / Churchwarden for this yeare / Nicholas Mercer of Walton / and Edward Turner of Fazakerley / sydeman

Item a Lay of £12 forthwith to bee paid to / ... Churchwardens[266]

Thomas Marsden Vicar

---

265 Apparently a signature.
266 Lines added in the same handwriting as Thomas Marsden's signature.

William X Halsall

... Johnson

William X Boydall

... X Mercer

Richard X Fazakerley

John Bennett

Nicholas Fazakerley

Ro[bert] Mercer

James Standish

Richard Henshaw

Mathew Gleave

John Mercer

Richard Blackmoore[267]

267 Marks are as previously noted, the incomplete Mercer mark being that of William.

APPENDIX 1

GLOSSARY OF TERMS, UNFAMILIAR SPELLINGS AND DIALECT WORDS

In addition to use of the Oxford English Dictionary, Joseph Wright's English Dialect Dictionary (1898) and J.S. Purvis's Dictionary of Ecclesiastical Terms (1962), advice has been received from the Vernacular Architecture Group and R.J. Griffiths, Curator of Prescot Museum (clock terms).

acquittance, receipt.

apparitor, official messenger of the Archdeacon's court, bringing citations to appear at visitations, etc.

assign (v.), here often used in the sense of *sign*.

assyted, scytacion (etc) = cited, citation (i.e. summons to appear at the visitation).

baldrick, boadricke etc, thong for attaching a bell clapper to the crown staple; normally leather but f.129r has 'a piece of Ashwood to be baldrickes for the belclappers'.

bande, usually a long hinge, but used in connection with a bell wheel on f.167r.

barr[i]age, workman's allowance for beer.

baylive = bailiff.

beam filling, action of using daub infill in timber wall construction.

bear(e) = bier or sometimes beer.

blecke (n.), may translate as *bleach* rather than *black* (ink, soot or black grease) on f.44v.

bosse, hassock made from a bundle of rushes or straw.

bow, use of this word in connection with bells seems to refer to part of the clapper rather than the soundbow (e.g. f.128r).

cale (f.59r), no meaning other than *call* found for this.

carpet = table cloth (covering the altar).

cast (v. and n.), reckoning (of accounts), here sometimes used for the audit itself (f.29v).

certiorari (Latin, used as noun), writ for removal of a cause to a superior court.

chanclor, chanseler, etc = chancellor (official acting as private secretary to the bishop).

chist = chest.

clam(p)staff/stave (v. and n.), method of wall construction with staves/wattles and daub infill.

clape = clip or clasp, used in various contexts concerning ironwork.

clockhouse, case around the clock movement to keep off dust.

colles = coals.

coram (Latin), in the presence of (e.g. *coram Nevill Kaye vicario et ministro ibidem*, in the presence of NK, vicar and minister of that place, f.77r).

171

corfey, **corfie**, **curfuer** = curfew.

correction, churchwarden's appearance to answer the visitation Articles.

crispe stones, probably stone masonry dressed in some way: perhaps the 'battlements' on f.148r.

dellfe (delph), quarry or diggings.

dobe, **dawb** (v. and n.), plaster/clay daub and the action of applying it (see also clamstave).

dormon = dormer.

dress (v.), to clean, trim, sweep etc.

dyall = sundial.

earnest (n.), payment to seal a bargain.

eve pole (f.81v and 159v, in connection with the church porch), uncertain – fascia boards would not be normal on eaves at that date, and the cost is too low to indicate replacement wall plates.

fil(l)bow, the part of a hinge driven into a gate.

firste (n.), possibly a beam for the roof ridge (f.58v).

gudgeon, metal pivot, e.g. that on which a bell swings, one being set at each end of the headstock.

gyfe = gyve (f.70r), i.e. shackle for a clock weight, *see also* **hucke.**

hack (n.), mattock or similar implement.

halme, **hame**, haft or handle.

hayr, **heare**, **heauer**, **hewer**, **heyre** = (horse) hair used for tempering plaster etc to improve adhesion.

headstock, structure supporting a bell and attaching it to the wheel.

hengling (f.68) prob. = hanging.

holland, **hollandes**, coarse linen fabric for covering furniture etc.

hucke (f.50v) = hook (for attaching the line of a clock weight, fixed to the stone by insertion in a hollow filled with molten lead, *see also* **gyfe**).

inde (Latin), thereof.

ingrose = engross (write out e.g. the accounts or register).

juratus (Latin), sworn.

kersey, coarse woollen cloth.

keyinges (for the clock, f.127v), possibly small wedges holding the mechanism together, or the moving levers of the striking mechanism.

lat(e) = lath.

lead (v.), to transport materials by cart or wagon.

ley stall, grave in the church.

manet (Latin), there remains.

moss (v.), to pack moss under and between roof slates for weatherproofing.

noverint (Latin), let them know.

parator, *see* **apparitor**.

passenger = traveller.

patches (for sizing etc, f.25r and f.44v), uncertain; the 'white patches' may refer to a substance used for whitening limewash.

peece (v.), to repair by adding or joining pieces.

pelf, refuse, rubbish.

pensall man (f.160v), probably an artist (= *pencil* in the sense of fine brush).

prayser = appraiser (assessor).

prentisse = apprentice.

presentment, report by the churchwarden, usually either for the courts or in answer to a question in the Articles.

prid(d), type of nail, possibly the same as *prig* (for laths) or *brod* (for roofing).

quarrell, small diamond pane of window glass.

quarter, township or administrative subdivision.

quarterage, allowance paid quarterly.

quittance *see* **acquittance**.

replevin, action to recover distrained goods.

rigdgeinge (f.44v) = ridging (apparently for capping the roof ridge).

roode, linear measure of 8 yards.

rowle (f.89r) prob. = roll (strip of wood rounded on the top and fastened on the ridge or lateral joints of a roof to raise the edges of sheet lead).

sallet oyle = salad oil (used as a clock lubricant).

sawder *see* soder.

scilicet (Latin), namely.

sclating, solating = slating.

scytacion *see* **assyted.**

seeleinge (f.157v and f.162v) probably = wood panelling.

shoot (v.), unidentified in the example 'shootinge over 4 sides of dormon windowes' (f.129r), but appears to imply some kind of rendering.

shoote (n., f.129r), unidentified piece of ironwork, perhaps just meaning a general repair (OED has *to shoot* meaning to mend, weld, splice).

shorkene (f.61) prob. = shaking/shaken (i.e. rocking, loose).

sive = sieve (e.g. for sifting lime).

slats (f.50) = slates.

sleck(e) = slake (as in slaking lime).

sneck = snick (latch of door or gate).

soder, sother, sawder = solder.

sodman = side(s)man.

spike, single *and* **double**, types of nail without a head.

starr, marram grass, used like rushes on the floor (e.g. f.105v, to save wear on bellropes).

steel *see* style.

steipe, stipe = steep (part of the process of preparing lime).

step, (a) step for balance wheel of clock (f.127v): possibly a tooth of the escape wheel or the pivot hole in which the bottom of the verge rests; (b) step supporting a bell (f.168v): probably the part of the frame or stock bearing the gudgeons.

stiple = steeple.

stock lock, one enclosed in a wooden case, usually fitted to an outer door.

stone nail, one used for fixing slates etc.

stoope, post, especially for a gate.

style, steel, gate, often a lych gate.

syses = assizes.

taynter = tenter (i.e. frame/hooks – here for holding the pulpit cover taut.

thacktable (f.76r), literally thatch table, probably the cornice below the eaves.

tunnel (for the clock stones) = weight chute.

turne gate, probably the kind fixed to a central post which revolves on a pivot.

uxor (Latin), wife.

vidua (Latin), widow.

watch parte, timekeeping part of clock.

wind (v., as in *windeing*, f.160r), possibly refers to weaving-in the cross pieces of a clamstave wall.

wright(e), maker, often specifically a carpenter or joiner.

yate = gate, recalling medieval usage of the Saxon 'yogh' character.

APPENDIX 2

ANNOTATIONS AND ADDITIONS TO THE FOLIOS

From their style it appears that the following were all added later than the writing of the original accounts, in some cases probably considerably later.

1. Numbering

Some folios have been numbered on the face, usually at top left, in a relatively modern – perhaps nineteenth-century – script. The rationale behind this pattern has not yet been determined. Numbering ceases before the end of the book and folios 158–173 appear to be unnumbered. The correlation with the present numbering system is as follows (two numbers have not been found, perhaps due to tearing or fading):

old number	present folio number	old number	present folio number
1	?	26	84
2	2	27	85
3	4	28	89
4	8	29	90
5	12	30	91
6	?	31	95
7	19	32	99
8	23	33	103
9	27	34	104
10	31	35	105
11	35	36	109
12	39	37	121
13	42	38	137
14	46	39	138
15	47	40	139
16	48	41	140
17	49	42	141
18	53	43	142
19	57	44	143
20	58	45	145
21	59	46	146
22	73	47	147
23	74	48	151
24	75	49	152
25	76	50	157

2. Items relating to the school

Some entries concerning expenditure on the school in the years 1630–36 have been marked with marginal or interpolated crosses in ink, sometimes with notes keyed to them. These may be relatively early in date and have been included in the footnotes. They occur on folios 10v, 41r, 44r, 57r, 86v, 88v and 89r. What appears to be a later pencil cross has been marked against an entry referring to the schoolmaster on f.158v (1664).

3 . Fox heads

Many of the entries concerning the bounty on fox heads have been marked with a pencil cross. The six entries on f.100v have 'Fox heads' written vertically next to them, and there are marks for some though not every one of the entries between f.104r and f.135r (part way through 1660), but for none of those thereafter. Because of their number, these annotations are not separately mentioned in the footnotes.

4. Page marking

Pencilled crosses appear, usually at top left, on folios 96r, 100r, 106r and 119r and are not separately mentioned in footnotes.

5. Verse on f.164v

The following has been written in on a blank page, presumably following a death:

> This for my ever loving frind Mr [?Thomas *or* Shornas]
> From whenc [*or* where] to whom this same doth goe
> the beare full well doth know
> William Smith
> CC [*or* 66]

The handwriting appears to be later than the accounts, but has some seventeenth-century characteristics. The '66' might indicate the date 1666, but there is no relevant burial at Walton itself that year to confirm this.

———

Other occasional markings are dealt with in the notes or ignored (e.g. in the case of casual jottings made in the process of addition).

INDEX OF PEOPLE AND PLACES

Places are in bold font. The names of frequently recurring townships are included only where they appear in the introduction. They are: Bootle-cum-Linacre, Everton, Fazakerley, Formby, Kirkby, Kirkdale, Liverpool, Walton and West Derby. For significant occurrences in particular contexts, refer to the **INDEX OF SELECTED SUBJECTS.**

INDEX OF SELECTED SUBJECTS